Ragnar Lothbrok and a History of the Vikings:

Viking Warriors including Rollo, Norsemen, Norse Mythology, Quests in America, England, France, Scotland, Ireland and Russia [3rd Edition]

Copyright 2017 by Noah Brown - All rights reserved.

This document is geared towards providing exact and reliable information in regards to the topics and issues covered. The publication is sold with the understanding that the publisher is not required to render accounting, officially permitted, or otherwise, qualified services. If advice is necessary, legal or professional, a practiced individual in the profession should be ordered.

- From a Declaration of Principles which was accepted and approved equally by a Committee of the American Bar Association and a Committee of Publishers and Associations.

In no way is it legal to reproduce, duplicate, or transmit any part of this document by either electronic means or in printed format. Recording of this publication is strictly prohibited and any storage of this document is not permitted unless written permission is granted by the publisher. All rights reserved.

The information provided herein is stated to be truthful and consistent, in that any liability, in terms of inattention or otherwise, by any usage or abuse of any policies, processes, or directions contained within is the solitary and utter responsibility of the recipient reader. Under no circumstances will any legal responsibility or blame be held against the publisher for any reparation, damages, or monetary loss due to the information herein, either directly or indirectly.

Respective authors own all copyrights not held by the publisher. Noah Brown is referred to as the author for all legal purposes but he may not have necessarily edited/written every single part of this book.

The information herein is offered for informational purposes solely and is universal as such. The presentation of the information is without contract or any type of assurance guarantee.

The trademarks that are used are without any consent, and the publication of the trademark is without permission or backing by the trademark owner. All trademarks and brands within this book are for clarifying purposes only and are owned by the owners themselves and are not affiliated with this document.

Table of Contents

Chapter One: Vikings in America   9
Additional Reading 28
Chapter Two: Vikings in England   29
Additional Reading 48
Chapter Three: Vikings in France   50
Additional Reading 67
Chapter Four: The Legend of Ragnar Lothbrok   69
Additional Reading 82
Chapter Five: Vikings in Russia   83
Additional Reading 107
Chapter Six: Rollo the Warrior   108
Additional Reading 118
Chapter Seven: Vikings in Ireland   120
Additional Reading 149
Chapter Eight: Vikings in Wales   152
Additional Reading 174
Chapter Nine: Vikings in Scotland   175
Additional Reading 204
Chapter Ten: Vikings in Greenland and Iceland   208
Greenland 208
Iceland 210
Chapter Eleven: Vikings in Galicia, Islamic Iberia, and the Levant   214
Galicia 215

Islamic Iberia and the Levant 219

Chapter Twelve: Viking Weapons, Sports, and Entertainment — 224

Games and Entertainment...224

Weapons and Armor 225

Viking Sports 227

Chapter Thirteen: Viking Art — 230

Oseberg Style of Viking Art..231

Borre Style of Viking Art 233

Jelling Style of Viking Art..235

Mammen Style of Viking Art..236

Ringerike Style of Viking art..238

Chapter Fourteen: Norse Mythology — 240

Norse Gods and Beings 241

Norse Cosmology 252

Norse Concept of Death and Afterlife 257

Norse Concept of Destiny - WYRD/URD...............................260

Norse Concept of Innangard and Utangard 263

Norse Mythology in Modern Literature, Television, and Film . 265

Conclusion 268

Chapter Fifteen: History of Denmark, Norway, and Sweden (14th to 19th century) — 269

Scandinavia during the Middle Ages......................................270

Scandinavian Countries in the 17th Century 274

Scandinavian countries in the 18th century 285

Scandinavian Literature 296

Conclusion — 303

Chapter One: Vikings in America

> *"Greenland belongs entirely to the Western Hemisphere and is accordingly a part of America. The discovery of Greenland was, in fact, the discovery of America, and Erik the Red was the first European who ever boomed real estate on the Western Continent, and he boomed it successfully. He succeeded in founding in Greenland a colony which flourished for several hundred years. The Icelandic Sagas contain elaborate accounts of this colony and give us the names of a number of the bishops who resided there."*
>
> (Source: *The Norse Discovery of America,* by A.M Reeves, N.L. Beamish and R.B. Anderson, 1906)

Christopher Columbus, as stated by a substantial number of historians, was not the first to discover America because at some point before Columbus left Spain and sailed over the Atlantic to the territory referred to as "The New World," Norsemen – or Viking voyagers (Viking refers to those who slipped up streams called "viks" to loot unsuspecting villagers) – had ventured over the sea from Norway to Iceland,

Greenland and eventually to a territory in North America that they named "Vinland" (Wineland). The Vikings explored and settled in North America about five hundred years before Columbus; therefore, it is appropriate to acknowledge and record the Vikings as the first Europeans in history to reach what is now American territory.

The Viking ships were one of a kind because they were made in different sizes; some of them were a hundred and twenty feet long, with a large number of them capable of holding a hundred men or more. They often had a mast for a square sail in their center, but like the Phoenician ships, oars could be used when needed. They had a shallow draft, which allowed them to land in territories where other ships couldn't, and light enough that extra crewmembers or cargo could be carried if necessary. The Viking ships were known as longboats and were made of covered planks that were held together with iron rivets inside of grooves. This method of boat building is known as "clinker" or "lapstrake", the riveted construction enabling them to flex with the movement of the sea. They were built with a high bow and stern and were the standard means of sailing during that time.

The Viking ship cut through the cobalt waters of the Atlantic Ocean, winds pushing the ship forward by way of its enormous single sail. In the wake of crossing new waters the Norsemen on board saw land, moored and went aground, and so it was – a thousand years before Columbus – that the Vikings were much more likely the first Europeans to have ever stepped on North American soil. Voyaging in their longboats the Scandinavians controlled the North Atlantic from the 9th to 12th centuries.

The Vikings were the Norse – a Scandinavian ocean faring people from Norway, Denmark, Finland, and Sweden – and before the end of the eighth century not only had they secured pockets of land in Ireland, but they were also controlling considerable areas in England and France. Before the end of the tenth century they had colonized Greenland, cruised to America several times, wandered down the Volga as far as the Caspian Sea, and were effectively trading in the Mediterranean as Norwegian settlers; essentially, they had moved from island to island across the North Atlantic and followed rivers deep into Europe and beyond.

They first settled in what is now modern day Iceland then Greenland and later in Canada. Archeological evidence demonstrates that at some point around 1000 A.D. sailors from Greenland established a village at what is presently called L'Anse aux Meadows in northern Newfoundland. Late archaeological research has shown that Viking presence in America is dated to around 1,000 AD – about 500 years before Columbus set sail for America. The Scandinavians called the new land "Vinland" – most likely because of the abundant growth of grapes and the Newfoundland climate, which was substantially more moderate than it is today.

The first known account of Norse contact with any lands west of Greenland is a short reference written in 1130 A.D. which can be found in the *Islendiga-bok* (Book of Icelanders). The first account of any length is attributed to Adam of Bremen, written in the 1070s.

Two lengthier works, known as the Sagas of Icelanders or Vinland Sagas, were composed around 1200 and 1300 A.D. based on prose narratives of historical events that mostly took place in the 9th, 10th, and early 11th centuries, during the so-called Saga Age.

The *Groenlandinga Saga* (The Saga of Greenland) does not fully agree with *Eiriks Saga Rauda* (The Saga of Erik the Red) in regards to the events of 980-1030 A.D. Viking researchers have since wrestled with the accuracy and reliability of the Sagas of Iceland. Is it correct to say that they belong to a category of literature, or history, or both? The two opposing stories of *Freydis Eriksdottir*, (Erik the Red's daughter and the stepsister of Leif Eriksson) who went to North America 1,000 years ago, are an example of what causes historians to question the reliability of some sources.

Erik the Red's Saga tells how Freydis, alongside her husband Thorvard – in the company of Thorfinn Karlsefni and Gudrid Thorbjarnardottir – embarked upon a voyage to the lands known as the New World.

Whenever the Natives infiltrated their settlement, the Norsemen would flee and find another place of safety but even when under attack the pregnant Freydis stood strong and encouraged the men; grabbing a sword from a fallen Norseman she uncovered a breast (probably to demonstrate that she was female), confusing the assailants as they fled. When the danger had passed, Thorfinn approached her and commended her courage.

However, the Greenlanders' Saga instead describes Freydis as a murderer. Unlike in Erik the Red's Saga, Freydis and Thorvard did not go with Thorfinn and Gudrid, rather they welcomed an undertaking with two Icelanders named Finnbogi and Helgi. When they returned to their base in Straumfjord – thought by a few researchers to be the site in Newfoundland now known as L'Anse aux Meadows – they fought about who would live in the longhouses abandoned by Leif Erikson. Freydis won this fight, causing the Icelanders to view her with disdain. After a hard and miserable winter Freydis demanded that the Icelanders give them their biggest ship for the voyage home, even as she was urging her husband and followers to kill all of the male Icelanders. When nobody would slaughter the women who were in the Icelanders' camp, she grabbed an axe and killed them herself.

The last datable reference to a Norse settlement on the American continent refers to events that happened in 1161 A.D., but it should be noted that some different reports do make several unusual references to later events. Researchers presume that climate change may have been disastrous for the Vikings' western settlements. Falling temperatures throughout the region – after 1200 A.D. – would have made navigation more difficult and shortened the growing seasons in the Artic regions of the Northern Hemisphere, and so it was that by the 1500s Greenland was empty of any Norse settlers.

The first five documents on the American Journeys website relate to the Norsemen and their North American activities. The English translations of the two Vinland Sagas are available as documents AJ-056, which is the Saga of Eric the Red (Thirty-one pages of content) and AJ-057, which is the Vinland History of the Flat Island Book (Twenty-two pages of content). The two Vinland Sagas were protected in an original copy volume called Flateyjarbok, which translates to Flat Island Book. It is important to note that the sagas had already been passed down orally for generations, likely for more than three hundred years before they were written down around 1387 A.D. and incorporated into the Flat Island Book. The original copy was found in Iceland almost three hundred years later around 1650 A.D. This composite volume, of about 1,700 pages, is now placed in the Royal Library of Copenhagen in Denmark. The book was first published in the 1860s, with photographic copies printed in the 1890s, and it was translated into English in 1906. The translations included on the site are from The Northmen, Columbus, and Cabot (985-1503 A.D.).

Erik the Red's Saga relates to the story concerning the occupation of Greenland, a narration that records how Erik the Red, whose full name was Eirik Rauda Thorvaldsson, settled in Greenland. It details the adventures of the offspring of Erik the Red and also mentions Thorfinn Karlsefni's adventure in North America and shows how Thorfinn built up a North American base at Straumfjord and made voyages toward the north, maybe even to the Labrador coastline. Afterwards he made another trip south and east, possibly towards the eastern side of Newfoundland's northern tip. The Vinland History of the Flat Island Book describes a progression of voyages made at some point after Eric the Red's colonization of Greenland. This saga recounts two other voyages, one led by Thorfinn Karlsefni, and another led by Eric the Red's daughter Freydis.

Standing above other known Vikings to have set foot in America is Leif Eriksson – Leif being the son of the Viking explorer Erik the Red (Leif's surname means "Erik's son") – who landed in around 1000 A.D. this family trait – if you will – of going on expeditions had already been established as a family tradition and was a deeply held passion for their leader Leif Eriksson. His father had established the first European settlement in Greenland following his banishment from Iceland – around 985 A.D. – for killing a companion, it's perhaps also important to note that Erik the Red's father had in turn been exiled from Norway for killing another man.

Leif – thought to have been conceived in Iceland in around 970 A.D. – spent his first years in an isolated Greenland. Leif described his point of entry into America, according to The Saga of the Greenlanders, as an area where "a river flowed out of a lake," and where the streams were abundant with salmon and the land covered in timber for construction. He also spoke of lush pastureland for livestock and a climate so temperate that the grass remained green even throughout the winter.

Interestingly Leif was not the first Viking to have heard about America. Based on the Icelandic Sagas written in the twelfth and thirteenth centuries (Please note that in view of the previous oral traditions they are more likely to originate from around 985 A.D.) a Norse pilgrim named Bjarni Herjolfsson from Greenland was blown off course while trying to get home, whereupon he saw a region west of Greenland but decided not to go ashore.

Bjarni Herjolfsson did however make a voyage with three landfalls; the first of them is thought to have been Newfoundland, the second Labrador, and the third, notably more remote, could have been Baffin Island. The settlement of Greenland was quickly followed by the first European experience of North America, an accomplishment that is attributed to Bjarni Herjolfsson. Based on the Greenlanders' Saga, which – with Erik the Red's Saga – is the fundamental literary source for the Vikings' discovery of America, Bjarni returned home from a voyage to Norway in 986 A.D. On arriving home he found that his father had moved to Greenland with Erik the Red and although he knew nothing about Greenland, except that it was mountainous, devoid of trees and with good pastures, Bjarni went in search of his father but unfortunately soon got lost.

Following several days of terrible weather and poor visibility Bjarni ended up off the shore of a hilly, thickly forested land. This was clearly not Greenland so, without landing, Bjarni voyaged north. Within two days he came across a level, forested region, but again decided not moor; instead sailing northeast for an additional three days where he encountered a mountainous, glacial land that he thought excessively desolate, making it impossible to be Greenland. Bjarni then traveled east and after four days touched base at the Norse settlement in Greenland.

Bjarni's findings created a considerable measure of intrigue and when he chose to give up trading, Erik the Red's son Leif Eriksson purchased his ship and set off on a follow-up expedition. Leif, who had found out about America from Bjarni, started his journey by reversing Bjarni's course. Prior to setting sail for America Leif had converted to Christianity.

Around 1000 A.D. Eriksson had sailed home to Norway where King Olaf I Tryggvason converted him to Christianity and charged him with spreading the word of the religion to the pagans dwelling in Greenland. Eriksson was able to convert his mother – who established a church considered the first Christian church in Greenland – however; he had no such success with his father. As indicated by one of the sagas Leif later made a voyage in which he sailed along the western coast of Greenland, crosswise over to Helluland, then southward to Bjarni's second landing – which he named Markland – and lastly to Bjarni's first landing place where there were many grapes to be found – the fact behind the naming of the region as "Vinland".

Researchers by and large trust that the Helluland referred to in these stories is Baffin Island and that Markland refers to some place on the shoreline of Labrador. The conceivable locations of Leifsbudir, Vinland, Straumsfjord and other different regions named in the writings are still hotly debated, with potential locations as far south as Cape Cod in Massachusetts. Interestingly enough, L'Anse aux Meadows, in spite of its valuable archaeological record, cannot be clearly identified as any of the sites portrayed in the available historical documents. In addition to the excavations in L'Anse-aux-Meadows there is other significant evidence that shows that there was a Norse presence in America.

The Saga of the Greenlanders – considered to be more-or-less factually exact – claims that Leif set sail in 1002 or 1003 to follow Bjarni's course along with thirty-five other explorers. The saga mentions that the initial area he located while sailing northwest was covered with level rocks, so it was that he named it Helluland, which is Norwegian for "Place of the Flat Stones". Historians generally conclude this area to have been Baffin Island. Then he turned south and went to a land that was level and lush with pale sandy shorelines. He named this area Markland (Norwegian for "Forest"), which is what historians recognize as most likely being Labrador. Journeying southwest for a further two days Leif and his group set out from Markland, where, on yet again discovering land, they named it Vinland. They went ashore and established a small outpost at a place later called Leifsbudir ("Leif's booths") where they spent a comfortable winter. With tasty grapes to be picked and a large number of ready available salmon in the waters they found it to be an excellent place for settlement. The climate was mild and there was very little ice, so they decided to spend the winter there and – unlike Greenland – wood was not difficult to find; come the spring Leif and his men cut a large amount of timber and set off for home.

While returning home Leif found and saved a shipwrecked Icelandic individual and the reason as to how he came to be given the moniker Leif the Lucky. Eriksson's visit and the resulting colonization of Labrador are accepted as historical facts with the archeological investigations of L'Anse-aux-Meadows unquestionably indicating that a Norse settlement existed there in around 1,000 A.D.

In contrast to the Icelandic Sagas the "Saga of the Greenlanders" tells how Eriksson's journey to North America was not by mere chance but rather that the Viking explorer had heard about a peculiar land in the west from the Icelandic merchant named Bjarni Herjolfsson who – even though he did not make a landing – had passed Greenland over ten years earlier and sailed by the coast of North America, whereupon – as mentioned above – Eriksson purchased Bjarni's ship, assembled a group of thirty-five explorers and followed Bjarni's route backward.

After crossing the Atlantic Ocean the Norse came across a rough, infertile land – that sits within modern-day Canada's borders – that Eriksson named Helluland because of the exhausting environment. The Norsemen now traveled south toward a tree-rich area they referred to as Markland, most likely a northern part of Newfoundland. The Norse wintered there and benefited from the warmer climate since it was an advantage not afforded them in Scandinavia. During this time they searched the surrounding region, found streams overflowing with salmon, and thought the land was so appropriate for growing grapes for wine that Eriksson decided to name the area Vinland.

After wintering in Vinland Eriksson's men traveled home to desolate Greenland with the required timber and abundant sacks of grapes, but after this voyage Eriksson would never return, because, having succeeded his father Erik the Red as the chief of the Greenland settlement, he decided to take command of affairs there until his death. And even though other Vikings continued to journey westward to Vinland for about a decade, to take advantage of North America's abundant resources, the Viking travelers stayed in windswept Greenland. This may have been due to the fierce battles that occurred between them and the Indigenous People of North America and the resulting death of Thorwald, Eriksson's brother.

The first encounter between the Norse and First Nation Peoples of North America did not go well for either side. Three years after the discovery of Vinland, Leif's brother Thorvald was preparing for the second summer of a subsequent expedition. He and his men were roaming an area at the mouth of a fjord when they noticed three humps on a sandy beach, upon further examination the humps turned out to be canoes under which nine men hid. The Norsemen caught and slaughtered eight of them but the ninth got away and raised the alarm among his people.

Later that day Thorvald and his men saw a swarm of canoes coming down the fjord towards them. Outnumbered, they took refugee on their ship and with the advantage of iron weapons defeated the attackers. Nonetheless, Thorvald was hit with an arrow in the armpit during the battle and died in a matter of seconds. On the headland – as he had asked – Thorvald's men gave him a Christian burial, using crosses to mark his grave at both ends. Leif is recorded to have been the first European to set foot on American soil; Thorvald was the first to be buried there.

Considering the following history of the Americas its discovery by the Norse turned out to be an exceptional phenomenon and is among the most studied aspects of the Viking Age (800–1100); a period that saw Scandinavian pillagers, traders and settlers play active roles across a large swathe of Europe, as well as some parts of Africa's Mediterranean coast and even as far east as Baghdad. All in all Viking Age Scandinavians arguably managed to see a greater portion of the world than any other previous Europeans.

The Norse route to America is occasionally portrayed as "the stepping stone route," starting with one island, then a drive onto the next, with relatively short crossings between them. The initial step came about 200 years before Leif's discovery of Vinland with the conquest and colonization of Scotland's Northern Isles not long after 800 A.D., this was then followed twenty-five years later by the settlement of the Faroe Islands, after which came Iceland in 870 A.D. The next stage was the establishment of the Norse Greenland settlement by Erik the Red in the 980s A.D. As Greenland is geographically part of the North American continent, this should be viewed as the first European settlement in the Americas.

Leif avoided contact with the locals – with his first experience of the First Nation Peoples having been an unfriendly one, yet Thorvald's death at the hands of the Native Peoples was still not enough to prevent no less than two more attempts by the Norse to settle in Vinland. The first of these occurred around two years after Thorvald's demise, it was commanded by Thorfinn Karlsefni, an Icelandic trader, who brought his wife Gudrid, sixty-five men, five women, and an assortment of animals. He took three ships and a crew of Norsemen to travel to a newly found territory that supposedly guaranteed considerable wealth. Following the course that Leif Eriksson had spearheaded seven years before, Thorfinn sailed up Greenland's coast and crossed the Davis Strait before turning south around Baffin Island until he reached Newfoundland. There Thorfinn and his crew discovered the wealth they'd been guaranteed, which included timber, fish, pasture, and game. The gathering spent an uneventful winter at Leifsbudir, during which time Gudrid brought forth a child, Snorri, recognised as the first European to be conceived in America.

In the spring the gathering experienced its first contact with Indigenous Peoples, who appeared at Leifsbudir to exchange hides. The Norse called them "Skraeings," possibly meaning, "screamers." Originating from a Stone Age culture the Skraeings were won over by the Norsemen's iron weapons and devices, but Karlsefni ordered his men not to make any exchanges with them.

There was another encounter between the Europeans and the Indigenous Peoples later that summer. A man from Karlesefni's group murdered a Skraeing who was said to have attempted to steal some of their belongings, the Skraeing's efforts to avenge the death of was resisted by the Norse, but as a result – and after staying for one more winter at Leifsbudir – Karlsefni decided to leave for Greenland. Needless to say the dealings with the First Nation Peoples went downhill from that point onwards. Thorfinn and his family, along with his remaining group, deserted the North American settlement, maybe because of the barrage of arrows that were being shot at them, importantly noting that archaeologists have discovered arrowheads buried beside the remains of Norsemen. After traveling to Greenland and Norway, Thorfinn eventually created a settlement in Iceland.

The exact location of where Thorfinn's family finally settled is currently unknown, even with the numerous attempts by archaeologists and historians to break through the mystery's opaque sheen. John Steinberg, an archeologist at the University of California in Los Angeles, reported in September of 2002 that he had found the remaining parts of a field manor in Iceland. He suggested that this was the place where Thorfinn and his family spent the remainder of their lives, and was supported in his claim by other researchers. The area surrounding Thorfinn's home in Iceland seems to have amazingly wide implications, for instance, it could reveal new insights into early Viking involvement in North America, which was first proven by an explorer named Helge Ingstad and his archaeologist wife, Anne Stine Ingstad. In 1960 both of them found the remains of a Norse settlement in Newfoundland, which had likely been in existence from around the year 1000.

Yet, these findings aside, the main records of the Norse journey to the New World can be found in the Icelandic Sagas. These are centuries old stories that have caused researchers to try and isolate facts from Norse legends and John Steinberg's findings, if proven, could solidify the current understanding of Viking history.

Only a single further journey into Vinland is documented. Erik Gnupsson, the bishop of Greenland, sailed for Vinland in 1121, but the fate of his attempt is unknown.

According to scholars the Saga of Erik the Red and the Saga of the Greenlanders provide a great deal of the knowledge about Norse voyages to North America. Thor Hjaltalin, an Icelandic researcher who regulates archaeological activity in northwestern Iceland, states that these sagas were, presumably, first recorded between 1200 and 1300 A.D. He adds that they were likely composed either from the oral tales of people in that period or from some other missing documents. Although the two Viking stories provide comparable records of Thorfinn's travels to the New World they diverge on some noteworthy points regarding his arrival in Iceland. Based on Erik the Red's Saga, Thorfinn returned to his hometown in Reynisnes, but based on the Greenlanders' Saga, Thorfinn stayed in Glaumbaer because his mother was less than friendly to his wife.

The Vikings' voyage out of Scandinavia seems to have occurred due to either discomfort or rebellion. During this time – as they ventured away from Scandinavia – Harald Finehair, a Norse king, was accumulating power in Norway. The Viking leaders who left were either uncomfortable following the requests of Harald, or they did not want to pay him tribute. In 874 A.D. the Vikings traveled to Iceland, which is portrayed as one of the world's last, substantial, habitable islands to have been colonized by a human population. In 1930 Vilhemmer Stefansson, a Norwegian anthropologist, shed more light on Viking migration out of Scandinavia, as he considered the Viking migration to be a grand relocation and one in which the nobles traveled and the lower classes remained behind.

In Iceland itself the migrated Vikings seem to have discovered a manageable, habitable haven. Here they found thick, virgin forests with good timber that they could make good use of. Gradually, over a period of sixty years, the population on this initially uninhabited terrain grew to over 70,000 people. In 930 A.D. the need for effective administrative control of the area led to the formation of what is known as the world's first parliament, referred to as the Althing. Members of the parliament – mainly the clan chiefs – gathered to discuss the region's issues, as well as to resolve any conflicts that arose among the people.

Nevertheless, life in this area was not perfect, because even after creating settlements that appeared to be organized and settled, they continued to look for fights to prove their might. If a Norse felt insulted he would become bent on vengeance, the Norse therefore had a tendency to retaliate and fight others, aside from the tendency to war in order to expand their territory. The subsequent grisly fights echoed across Iceland. According to Stefansson, 1930, "The eventual discovery of North America hangs upon a fashionable practice of the day, that of man-killing, which – like cocktail shaking in Probation America – was punished but was indulged by the best people." With this statement, Stefansson seems to be making reference to a die-hard fighter, such as Erik the Red. Erik the Red continually pushed the Norse ability to tolerate disputes. Thus, his fellow leaders had him frequently exiled. At first Erik was forced to move to Iceland's west coast; however, he was eventually ousted from the territory completely.

Based on the Icelandic Sagas Erik's homestead was situated on the west side of Greenland. The muddled name for this barren, cold island, covered by an immense ice sheet, originates from the pariah's attempt to bait different travelers. Erik had heard stories of interesting regions to the west from a Norse mariner, who was traveling to Greenland but was blown off course. Leif, Thorvald, and Thorfinn are renowned for their voyages and as such are given a special place in Viking history.

Thorfinn is said to come from the same ancestry as a king of Ireland named Ugarval and a queen from the British Isles named Aud the Deep-Minded. His childhood started on a farmstead not far from Glaumbaer in Iceland. Thorfinn, who was a rich trader famous for his astuteness, was also a respectable leader. It was on a journey to trade in Greenland that he came across Gudrid Thorbjarnardottir, the charming widow of Thorvald, who he later married. At Brattahlid (Erik's dwelling in Greenland's eastern state) Thorfinn participated in board games while he arranged his outing to Vinland, estimated to be around the winter of 1005. Erik the Red's Saga presents this preparation as rowdy, and random to some degree, taking note of the different Norse chieftains who chose to engage in the expedition.

Despite the fact that the Viking settlement in North America was short-lived, as a result of the threatening tendency of the locals there, the Viking states of Iceland and Greenland were by and large effective. Tax records in Iceland of 1095 show that 72,000 Scandinavians were living there at that time and archaeologists say that around 5,000 Vikings were living in Greenland by around 1150.

Archeologists have uncovered evidence that provides backing for the stories of the Norse voyages to America from the Sagas. In 1960 the Norwegian pioneer Helge Ingstad scoured the shores of Labrador and Newfoundland for indications of a settlement, and he discovered it on the northernmost tip of Newfoundland at L'Anse aux Meadows. A worldwide group of archaeologists – that included Ingstad's wife Anne, mentioned earlier – uncovered Viking relics, which can be traced back to around 1000 A.D. Interestingly, the remains of the Norse settlement are currently part of a UNESCO World Heritage site.

The terrain around L'Anse aux Meadows has some similarity to the saga portrayals of Vinland. There, winters were harsh and wild grapes unavailable, so it is most likely not Leifsbudir. Rather it is thought to be L'Anse aux Meadows.

As of yet there are a few signs that the Vikings made it to either Central or South America. However, a French anthropologist by the name of Jacques de Mahieu claims that he has uncovered the remains of a Norse town containing a divider etched with Norwegian engravings. Mahieu believes that the Norse tenants governed over a territory of Bolivia and Peru for a long period of time, sometime around 800 years ago. Furthermore, the presence of a now extinct tribe in South America has come to light; they are thought to have lived in the far Western ranges of the Amazon River. They are referred to as the Chachapoyas, or "cloud warriors." The physical appearance of these individuals is known because they preserved their dead so well. They were tall, fair-haired and light-skinned. A few scientists suggest that they most likely originated from Northern Europe, as in they seem to be of Scandinavian origin.

There is sufficient evidence of a Viking presence in America going as far back as three millennia. At Peterborough, Canada, which is eighty-six miles east of Toronto, there is a vast limestone boulder that has a number of antiquated engravings inscribed on it. One engraving is titled "Slave of Woden" from Norway, which states that someone had come searching for "amazing copper." The engraving is dated to around 1,500 B.C., which means that it was inscribed nearly 3,000 years before Columbus arrived. This engraving may reveal insight into the 5,000 archaic copper mines that were found near the northern side of Lake Superior.

While Columbus is honored with a federal holiday, the man thought to have led the first European voyage to North America has not been completely overlooked. In 1964 President Lyndon Johnson made an announcement that proclaimed October 9 to be Leif Eriksson Day in order to pay tribute to the Viking adventurer, his crew, and the nation's Nordic-American legacy. The nearness of the days in honor of Eriksson and Columbus is only by chance. October 9th was picked because it is the commemoration of the 1825 entry of a ship in New York that was carrying the first group of Norwegian settlers to the United States.

Additional Reading

Barnes, G. (1995) "Vinland the good: Paradise lost?" *Parergon n.s.* 12:2, 75-96

Barnett, J.H. ed. (2003) "Contact, continuity, and collapse: the Norse colonization of the North Atlantic." *Studies in the Early Middle Ages, 5*

Fitzhugh, William W., and Elisabeth I. Ward. eds. (2000) *Vikings: The North Atlantic Saga*. Washington, D.C.: Smithsonian Institution Press in association with the National Museum of Natural History.

Logan, F. Donald. (1983) *The Vikings in History*. Totowa, N.J.: Barnes & Noble Books.

McGhee, R. (1984) "Contact between native North Americans and the medieval Norse: a review of the evidence." *American Antiquity*, 49, 4-26

Morris C.D. and Rackham D.J. eds. (1992) "Norse and later settlement and subsistence in the North Atlantic." *Occasional paper series 1*

Simpson, Jacqueline. (1980) *The Viking World*. New York, N.Y.: St. Martin's Press.

Chapter Two: Vikings in England

"A furore Normannorum libera nos, Domine"

"Free us from the fury of the Northmen, Lord."

(Verse three of *Be Thou My Vision,* a Celtic Christian song from the Viking period)

(Source: Viking Answer Lady)

At the beginning of the medieval period Britain and Ireland were separated into different groups of people linguistically, religiously, and culturally. The languages spoken by the Celtic Britons and Gaels can be traced to the language of the Celts, which was common during the European Iron Age. In Western Britain, which includes Cornwall, Cumbria, Wales, and Southwest Scotland, Celtic Brythonic was the most spoken language. In Northern Britain – past the Forth and Clyde waterways that constitute a substantial portion of current Scotland – lived the Picts who communicated in their own unique language. Because of the shortage of sacred texts in Pictish, most of which are located in Ogham, researchers still debate the possibility of the Pictish language being similar to the non-Indo-European languages such as Basque, or even being Celtic.

A majority of engravings and place names imply a greater possibility of the Picts actually turning out to be Celtic in both language and values. Most groups in Britain and Ireland had converted to Christianity and a large proportion of southern Britain was thought to be associated with Anglo-Saxon England, where Anglo-Saxon vagrants from mainland Europe had settled during the 15th century CE. They carried with them their own Germanic language (Old English), a different religion (Anglo-Saxon agnosticism) and their own particular, unmistakable social practices. However, at the onset of the Norse attacks, Anglo-Saxon England was for the most part Christian.

The Isle of Man had bolstered agrarian peoples; however, it is broadly accepted that it was the Brythonic language that was commonly used there before Old Irish (later known as Manx) began to spread across the territory. The occurrence of Gaelicisation most likely took place either before the Viking age when the zone was occupied by the Norse-Gaels who honed their own way of life.

In the northern part of Britain, in the land that now belongs to Scotland, there lived three particular ethnic peoples in their own individual kingdoms: the Picts, the Scots, and the Britons. The Picts ruled the greater part of Scotland with a significant population based between the Firth of Forth and the River Dee, as well as in Sutherland, Caithness, and Orkney. The Scottish were a tribal people that had journeyed from Dalriada to Britain near the northern part of Ireland in the late fourth century and although archaeologists were not able to label anything exclusively Scottish, they were able to notice many aspects of similarity between them and the Picts. The Britons were those in the Old North – in areas that have been discovered to be southern Scotland and northern England – which by the 600s had obviously come under the political control of the Anglo-Saxons.

By the mid-9th century Anglo-Saxon England was partitioned into four independent kingdoms including East Anglia, Northumbria, Wessex, and Mercia. Mercia is said to have been

30

the most grounded territory because of its military power. About one million people lived in England around this time and the social hierarchy consisted of the king and his noblemen at the top of the social ladder then, in descending order, were the thegns (i.e. landholders), different agriculturalist workers, manual laborers, and slaves. Most of the population lived on farmland despite the fact that several large towns had arisen, specifically London and York, which were the heartbeat of royal and clerical administration. Additionally, there were various business ports (i.e. Hamwic and Ipswich) where remote trade occurred on a regular basis. The Viking attacks in England created a profound cultural impact on the different regions – in social structure, speech, and individual names.

The Early Medieval period witnessed Norse movement around and within the British Isles. Various Norse groups sailed out to Britain and Ireland to settle, trade, or raid. The Norsemen who went to the British Isles have frequently been alluded to as Vikings; however, they might have included more than just the Vikings. Toward the beginning of the Early Medieval period trade links had been created by the Norse kingdoms of Scandinavia throughout southern Europe and the Mediterranean, and because of this it had access to imported goods such as gold, silver, bronze, and spices. These trade links also extended westward into Ireland and the British Isles.

The archaeologists, James Graham-Campbell and Colleen E. Batey, noticed that there was an absence of verifiable sources on the earliest Viking experiences in the British Isles; which have been presumed to have begun in the northern island gatherings closest to Scandinavia. Nevertheless, the Irish Annals recorded many Norse encounters during the 9th and

10th centuries, also important to note is the fact that the Viking raids that influenced Anglo-Saxon England were archived in the Anglo-Saxon Chronicle, said to have been first written in the late-9th century, most likely in the Kingdom of Wessex during the rule of Alfred the Great.

In England the start of the Viking Age is dated to June 8th, 793 A.D. when Vikings devastated the convent on Lindisfarne, the focal point of learning on an island off the northeast coast of Northumberland. Friars were slaughtered in the convent, tossed into the ocean to drown, or taken as slaves, while treasures were taken from the convent itself.

The major Viking incursion of England, which occurred in 865 A.D., can be traced back to the period following the demise of Ragnar Lothbrok. Ragnar's sons– Ivar the Boneless, Halfdan, and Hubba, drove the invasion. As indicated by the Norse Sagas from 865 A.D., the great Viking leader Ragnar Lothbrok was captured by King Aella of Northumbria and Aella supposedly tossed Ragnar into a snake pit where he later died. Hearing of the death of their father Ragnar's sons became infuriated. It is said that Ragnar's aggravated sons, exploiting the current political insecurity in England at the time, enlisted the Great Heathen Army that arrived in the Kingdom of East Anglia later that year. They attacked and overwhelmed the old kingdoms of East Anglia and Northumbria with the sole purpose of avenging their father's death.

Aside from killing King Aella in 867 A.D. Ivar the Boneless also executed Edmund in 869 A.D.; the King of the East Angles and decimated the stronghold of the British kings of Strathclyde in Dumbarton. The regularly dependable "Archives of Ulster" recorded Ivar's death in Ireland in 873 A.D. and portrayed him as the Lord of the Northmen in

Ireland and Britain. Halfdan, Ivar's brother, led the Viking forces to triumph in Mercia in 874 A.D. and then distributed lands within Northumbria amongst the Vikings in 876 A.D. after which he moved south and forced a large number of the inhabitants in Wessex to surrender to him in 878 A.D.

From 865 A.D. the Norse's mentality towards the British Isles changed as they started to consider the land for potential colonization – as opposed to just simply viewing it as a place to raid and loot. So it was larger armed forces began landing on Britain's shores with the aim of gaining territory and developing settlements. They continued to journey across England into Northumbria and captured York, building up the Viking community of Jorvik, where some settled as agricultural workers and craftsmen. Due to the incursion the vast majority of English kingdoms were in turmoil and could not stand up against the Vikings. In 867 A.D. Northumbria became the Northern Kingdom of the mixed Danelaw, after the triumph of Halfdan Ragnarsson and Ivar the Boneless. The sons of Ragnar introduced an Englishman, known as Ecgberht, who became the puppet king of Danelaw.

In 870 A.D., the "Great Summer Army" arrived in England along with a Viking named Bagsecg and his Five Earls. Supported by the Great Heathen Army (which had overwhelmed much of England from its base in Jorvik), Bagsecg's force and that of Halfdan attacked a large portion of England until 871 A.D. when they invaded Wessex. On the 8th of January 871 A.D. Bagsecg was killed at the Battle of Ashdown alongside his Earls, upon which a large number of Vikings returned to northern England, where Jorvic had turned it into the focal point of the Viking Kingdom. Alfred of Wessex was able to keep the Vikings out of his kingdom for a while but only through desperate means. Alfred and his successors kept driving the Vikings back to the outskirts until they successfully reconquered York. However, another influx of Norwegian Vikings landed in England in 947 A.D. when Eric Bloodaxe captured York for the Vikings yet again.

Prior to the major battle with the Great Heathen Army, there were arbitrary fights in the late eighth century. In the last decade of the 700s the Norsemen raided a progression of Christian convents situated within the British Isles. The Christian convents were frequently located on small islands and other remote, desolate places along the coast, as the clerics wanted to remain isolated in areas where they could worship without the distractions of society. As a by-product, this kept them secluded and unprotected making them an easy and lucrative target.

The historian Peter Hunter Blair commented that the Norse raiders were most likely flabbergasted when they discovered several communities whose dwellers had no weapons yet contained substantial wealth. These raids resulted in the first contact numerous Norsemen had with Christians, but these attacks were not against Christians specifically, rather, the convents were simply "easy plunder" for the marauders. The Viking destruction of Northumbria's Holy Island was a new kind of event, because according to Northumbrian researcher Alcuin of York he describes it as thus: "Never before in Britain has such a terror appeared."

The primary record of Norse raids occurring in Anglo-Saxon England originates from 789 A.D. (in spite of the fact that the Anglo-Saxon Chronicle recorded it as 787 A.D.), when three Viking ships from Hordaland (today's Norway) arrived at Portland Bay in Dorset, near the southern shore of Wessex. All of this occurred during the rule of King Beorhtric of Wessex

(786–802 A.D.). The Vikings were mistaken for merchants and apprehended by the royal officer of Dorchester whose role it was to stop every foreign merchant ship attempting to enter the kingdom. When the invaders were asked to go to the king to pay a commission on their products they murdered the royal officer. It is possible that different attacks (the accounts of which no longer exist) were carried out not long afterward since, in 792 A.D., Mercia's King Offa started to make plans for the protection of Kent from attacks that would come from "the pagan peoples."

The subsequent documented raid on the Anglo-Saxons occurred in 793 A.D. when the abbey that held Saint Cuthbert's relics in Lindisfarne (an island on the eastern side of England) was sacked by a Norse attack on the 8th of June. The raiders murdered the friars and took their possessions. This attack denotes the start of the "Viking Age of Invasion," which was made possible by the Viking's longship. The next year they raided the adjacent Monkwearmouth-Jarrow Abbey. In 795 A.D. they attacked the Iona Abbey near the west coast of Scotland. This abbey would be looted several times in the next decade, first in 802 and then again in 806, when the sixty-eight individuals residing there were executed. Following such decimation the monks at Iona abandoned the abbey and escaped to Kells in Ireland.

During the last decade of the 8th century there were sporadic fights on England's northern and eastern shores. Viking attacks continued at a reduced scale over the coastal areas in England. While the underlying strength of the attacking forces were not strong, it is probable that significant planning took place. Sporadic skirmishes slowly grew into large scale ambushes as war-groups amalgamated. The Norwegians carried out a surprise attack during the winter of 840-841 (most attacks took place during the summer) after wintering on an island off the coast of Ireland. In 850 they spent the winter on the island of Thanet in Kent without many excursions into England and in 854 an armed force settled for a short while at the Isle of Sheppey. Previously, in 835, a major Viking raid had occurred in southern England and was coordinated against the Isle of Sheppey. In 864, they returned to Thanet for the winter.

In 866 A.D., the Norse army took control of York – one of the two noteworthy urban communities in Anglo-Saxon England. In 871 A.D., Aethelred, the King of Wessex, who was the driving force behind the fight against the Vikings, passed on and was succeeded by his younger brother Alfred the Great. This was the turning point since numerous Anglo-Saxon kings started to surrender to the Vikings' requests to give the land over. In 876 A.D., the Northumbrian king Healfdene surrendered his properties to the Vikings, and in the following four years, the Viking incursion increased with the taking of lands in the kingdoms of Mercia and East Anglia. King Alfred continued to clash with the invaders but was driven into Somerset, specifically into the southwest of his kingdom, where he was forced to take asylum in the swamps of Athelney in 878 A.D.

Alfred regrouped his forces and decisively crushed Guthrum and the Norse king of East Anglia at the Battle of Edington. Soon after Guthrum's defeat in 886 A.D. the Treaty of Wedmore was established between the (Norse-controlled) East Anglian and Wessex governments that had set up a boundary between the two kingdoms. The zone toward the north and east of this boundary became known as the Danelaw, on the grounds that it was under the control of Norse political persuasion, while those lands south and west of it stayed under Anglo-Saxon rule. Alfred's government started building a progression of shielded towns (or burhs) and a naval force, sorting out a civilian army framework whereby half of his peasant armed force stayed in active service. Despite the fact that there were constant attacks on Wessex by the Vikings the kingdom's new forces were able to secure victory. In 896 A.D. most of the invaders scattered and settled in East Anglia and Northumbria while others instead sailed to Normandy.

Alfred's strategy of fighting against the Viking raiders and settlers continued under the rule of his daughter Aethelflaed, who married Aethelred, the Ealdorman of Mercia. The strategy further continued under the government of Edward the Elder, who was Alfred's son. In 920 A.D. the Northumbrian and the Scots' governments both submitted to the military might of Wessex and because of this the Battle of Brunanburhled led to the destruction of the Norse forces in northern Britain in 937 A.D. Erik Bloodaxe, the last Norse King of York, was removed from the city in 954 A.D.

To get a better picture of history it is important to see how other sources depict the movements of the Vikings, the Annals of Ulster, for example, provide us with several dates and events. In 794 A.D., for example, there was a fatal strike on Lindisfarne's mother-house of Iona and afterwards, in 795 A.D., there were strikes on the northern shores of Ireland. From their stronghold the Norsemen pillaged Iona again in 802 A.D. causing great havoc among the Celi De Brethren and burning the convent to the ground.

The Kingdom of the Franks – under Charlemagne – was one kingdom notably crushed by the Viking plunderers, because towards the end of Charlemagne's reign (and all through the reigns of his sons and grandsons), a series of Norse attacks began with the Scandinavians continually triumphing over the Franks and finally settling in the locale now known as Normandy.

By the late 9th century the Vikings had invaded a large portion of the Anglo-Saxon kingdoms that constituted England, but be that as it may, Alfred the Great defeated the Vikings at the Battle of Edington in 878 A.D. The resulting shift in power gave the Danes control of northern and eastern England, with Alfred and his successors controlling Wessex. Yet, come the 11th century, the entirety of England, Norway and Denmark was brought under the sole rule of Danish king Cnut.

When Cnut died he was succeeded by the Anglo-Saxon king Edward the Confessor. Edward was able to reign peacefully until his passing in 1066 A.D. upon which the capable Earl of Wessex, Harold Godwinson, succeeded him. Harold's ascension to the throne was not unanimously accepted. Toward the north, the Norwegian king named Harald Hardrada attacked England. In the late summer of 1066 the invaders traveled up the Ouse River before progressing to York. At the Battle of Fulford Edwin the Earl of Mercia – alongside his brother Morcar the Earl of Northumbria – led a northern English army that was defeated on September 20th. On becoming aware of the Earl's defeat, Harold Godwinson marched his southern force north and crushed Hardrada at Stamford Bridge. While Godwinson was occupied in the north, William the Bastard (later to be known as William the Conqueror) had landed his army in Sussex so that he could secure the most sought after area in England.

Unfortunately, Harold Godwinson had been shipwrecked at Ponthieu in 1064 A.D. and abducted by Guy I, the Count of

Ponthieu, who was also known as Wido according to the Bayeux Tapestry. On hearing Harold had been kidnapped William, the Duke of Normandy, sent emissaries requesting Count Guy hand over his prisoner. Once turned over to William, Harold was forced to make a solemn oath of fealty to William supporting his claim to become ruler of England. After taking the oath, it was revealed to him that the box on which he had made his vow contained sacred relics, ensuring that he would never seek to break his vow.

So it was that when Harold took the crown of England William was maddened by Harold's deceit and began assembling an army, gathering his men he reached Pevensey Bay a few months after the summer of 1066 A.D. Harold, having quite recently defeated the Norwegian King Harald Hardrada in the North, led his worn-out army to the South where they met William near Hastings, now located in modern East Sussex, England.

During the fight that took place William's forces endured substantial losses yet still managed to defeat Harold's infantry. Harold and his housecarls (household troops) stood firm, in spite of a downpour of arrows that came from William's bowmen. Not long after Harold died after being struck by an arrow, just as the invading Normans were overpowering his housecarls. William was made the king with the approval of the Archbishop of York in London and once crowned began rebuilding the power structure of the monarchy, also forcing the nobles to accept a feudalistic system of rule.

However, William's control over the kingdom was very weak and the Normans were confronted with various rebellions that occurred mostly in the North of England and East Anglia. An extensive Danish army landed in England in 1069 A.D. and furthered the unrest in the North. During the winter of that year William led his forces from Nottingham to York with the goal of drawing his enemies into a trap. In any case, when William's army acquired York, the opposing army fled. Because the Danish had no place to shelter during the winter, they chose to return to their boats at the mouth of the Humber River. In 1070 they were heartened when a navy from Denmark arrived which then sailed to East Anglia and occupied the territory. William held a meeting with the Danish army and both parties agreed that, provided he made regular payments to them, they would return to Denmark without creating any further problems. Agreeing to this, William then turned his attention to the further uprisings that kept taking place in different parts of the land, the trouble left him with no choice but to ask his earls to manage issues in Dorset, Shrewsbury, and Devon, while he took care of the revolts in the Midlands and Stafford.

The clinker-built longships utilized by the Vikings were built to specifications that allowed them to sail in shallow waters. They helped the Viking raiders to create detailed maps for traders and explorers along the shores and rivers in northwestern Europe. Rurik likewise directed his efforts towards the East and in 859 A.D. he became King through victory in battle, and by invitation from the inhabitants of the city of Novgorod on the Volkhov River. His descendants journeyed even further East until the early East Slavic state of Kievan Rus was established with Kiev as its capital.

Other Norsemen, especially those in the regions that are currently known as Sweden and Norway, proceeded south to the Black Sea before moving down to Constantinople. Every time the Viking ships ran aground, the Vikings would simply flip them sideways, drag them over the shallows, and sail once in deeper waters.

In 884 A.D. a Frisian army – led by Archbishop Rimbert of Bremen-Hamburg – defeated a multitude of Danish Vikings at the Battle of Norditi (also known as the Battle of Hilgenried Bay), which took place on the Germanic North Seacoast. This defeat led to the Vikings pulling out of East Frisia allowing the region to experience some peace.

In 911 A.D., King Charles the Simple, a French King, came to an arrangement with the Norse war-leader Rollo. Charles made Rollo a duke and gave him, and those with him, the lands of Normandy. Accordingly, Rollo gave his oath to Charles, accepted Christianity, and agreed to protect the northern region of France. A few centuries later, the children of the Viking explorers began to recognize themselves as Norman. They brought the Norman language (a language with Germanic influence) and culture with them when they arrived in England in 1066 A.D. The Norman Conquest turned them into the ruling class of the Anglo-Saxons.

Under the rule of King Edgar the Peaceful of Wessex, England became further politically bound together when Edgar became known as the King of England. The Anglo-Saxon and Norse people in England appeared to support his reign. Under the administration of Edgar's son, Edward the Martyr (killed in 978 A.D.) and after Aethelred the Unready, the government's hold on England's politics weakened significantly. In 980 A.D. Scandinavian raiders began to once again attack England. The rulers decided that the main way to fight against these assailants was to offer them tribute; thus in 991, they offered them £10,000. This amount was insufficient and throughout the following years, England was forced to pay the

Scandinavian aggressors progressively more and more money. When the situation became unbearable, numerous English people asked for a more aggressive approach to be used against the Scandinavians. Thus on St Brice's Day in 1002 A.D. King Aethelred announced the execution of all Danes in England, an event that would become known as the St. Brice's Day massacre.

King Sweyn Forkbeard in Denmark soon received the news of the slaughter. It is thought that Gunhilde, Sweyn's sister, was likely to have been among the casualties, which incited Sweyn to invade England the following year. His attack led to Exeter being burnt to the ground and Wiltshire, Hampshire, Salisbury, and Wilton were also casualties of the Scandinavian vengeance, but Swyen was not yet finished. His army plundered East Anglia, pillaged Thetford, and invaded Norwich before he eventually went back to Denmark in 1004. From 1006 to 1007, as well as 1009 to 1012, further raids were carried out with the sole purpose of gathering plunder. In fact, Thorkell the Tall himself was in charge of an invasion of England.

Sweyn Forkbeard returned to attack England with a massive force in 1013 A.D., so Aethelred ran away to Normandy, causing Sweyn to assume control of the English kingdom. Sweyn died that year and Aethelred chose that opportunity to return and regain control of his kingdom. However, another Norse force attacked in 1016, this time led by the Danish King Cnut, the son of Sweyn Forkbeard. After crushing the Anglo-Saxon forces at the Battle of Assandun Cnut became the ruler of England and controlled both the English and Danish territories. Following Cnut's demise in 1035, the English and Danish kingdoms were yet again declared to be independent states. They were separated for a brief period from 1040–

1042, until Cnut's son, Harthacnut, was able to establish a stronger foothold in England.

A large number of fortunes were hidden in England during the Scandinavian attacks. Some of these riches may have been secreted away by Anglo-Saxons – who were trying to conceal them from Vikings – while the Vikings may have hidden others in order to secure their plundered fortune.

In 1862 one of these fortunes was discovered in Croydon (historically a part of Surrey, now a part of Greater London) and it contained two hundred and fifty coins, 3.25 silver ingots and four bits of hack silver in a cloth pack. Archeologists believe that these valuables were most likely hidden by one of the Vikings. By dating the items, archeologists determined this store had likely been buried in 872 A.D. when the army wintered in London. The coins themselves originated from a variety of kingdoms: Wessex, Mercian, and East Anglian cases were found with imported products from Carolingian-line Francia and the Arab world. Not all such Viking fortunes found in England contained coins. For instance, nineteen silver ingots were uncovered at Bowes Moor in Durham, while a silver neck-ring and penannular brooch were found at Orton Scar in Cumbria.

Historian Peter Hunter Blair argued that the effectiveness of the Viking raids, and the ineptness of Britain to fend off such attacks, were the major cause of ensuing Norse invasions and their expansive colonization of the British Isles.

Many have speculated the reason for the Viking attacks, with the desire to explore being a likely contributor of note. At the time England, Wales, and Ireland had separated into a wide range of warring kingdoms that were in constant internal dispute, so they were powerless against the well-coordinated Viking intrusions. The Franks, however, were very much safeguarded as they had a powerful army and a large number of guards around their lands. The utilization of iron or a deficiency of women – resulting from female child murder – also likely had an effect. Another notable factor is the pressure of Frankish expansion toward the south of Scandinavia and their ensuing onslaught upon the Vikings. Harald, I of Norway ("Harald Fairhair") had come to Norway around this time and dislodged many people. Consequently, these warriors sought new bases where they could follow up with counter-attacks against Harald. The Vikings cultivated plants after winter and went raiding when the ocean ice softened; they would then return home with their plunder to reap the fruits of agriculture.

Researchers continue to debate why the Scandinavians specifically expanded from the 8th through 11th centuries. Different models have risen from this ongoing discussion: The Demographic Model, Economic Model, Ideological Model, Political Model, and Technological Model.

The Demographic model posits that Scandinavia encountered a population explosion just before the Viking Age began. Because agricultural production was insufficient for the expanding population many Scandinavians were left without property and status so, in response, these landless men took to robbery to acquire their riches. The population continued to grow and pirates were forced to look further as they moved past the confines of the Baltic and eventually across all of Europe.

The Economic Model argues that the Viking Age was the consequence of developing urbanism and trade throughout

Europe. As the Islamic world developed, so too did its trade routes, and the riches that moved along them were pushed further north. In Western Europe the towns of Anglo-Saxon England began booming in the "Long Eighth Century", a very prosperous time in England's history. Scandinavians, like other Europeans, were attracted to these wealthier "urban" centers, which soon became the target for Viking attacks. The relationship of the Scandinavians to larger and wealthier trade systems drew the Vikings into Western Europe at first, then to the rest of Europe, and finally to parts of the Middle East. In England, masses of Viking silver including the Cuerdale Hoard and the Vale of York Hoard illustrate this phenomenon.

The Ideological Model notes that the Viking Age coincided with the Medieval Warm Period (800–1300 A.D.) and ceased with the beginning of the Little Ice Age (around 1250–1850). The beginning of the Viking Age, which began with the sacking of Lindisfarne, also coincided with Charlemagne's Saxon Wars and the Christian wars against agnostics in Saxony. Historians Rudolf Simek and Bruno Dumezil speculated that the Viking raids might have resulted from the spread of Christianity among agnostic groups. Professor Rudolf Simek believes the concurrence of early Viking action during the rule of Charlemagne is not by chance. When Christianity entered Scandinavia, genuine clashes partitioned Norway for about a century.

The Political Model consists of two fundamental parts. The first part, the "Pull" factor, proposes that the powerless political groups of Britain and Western Europe were alluring targets for the Viking raiders. The factors behind these shortcomings continue to shift yet – for the most part – they can be rearranged into decentralized countries or religious locations. The Viking raiders sacked these regions with ease and afterward withdrew; they followed this pattern of attack and abandon as often as possible. The second part of the Political Model is the inward "Push" factor. The Push factor aligns with a period immediately before the Viking Age in which Scandinavia experienced a mass centralization of power in the current nations of Denmark, Sweden, and especially Norway. This centralization of power forced many chieftains from their properties, which were gradually consumed by kings and new generals. As a result, many of these chieftains sought shelter elsewhere and began harrying the British Isles and Western Europe.

The Mechanical Model proposes that the Viking Age occurred because of mechanical developments that enabled the Vikings to raid extensively. Raiding in the Baltic most likely predates the Viking Age; however, innovations in seamanship, and the technology of the ships themselves, allowed them to venture further and to raid faraway lands. These improvements included the deployment of larger sails, superior attachment practices, and round the clock sailing.

All of these models have made great attempts to pinpoint the cause of the Viking Age. There is little doubt that this age was the consequence of several factors considered by these models. One thing to note is that they are generally depicted by their foes as utterly vicious and destructive. In the medieval English annals they are portrayed as "wolves among sheep". Leading work on insightful research on the Viking Age previously achieved little readership in Britain, while the field of linguistics continued to portray an outdated view of the Viking. However, new works translated from the Old Norse language saw more Victorians read the Icelandic Sagas.

In Scandinavia, the 17th-century Danish researchers Thomas Bartholin and Ole Worm along with the Swedish researcher Olaus Rudbeck were the first to use runic engravings and Icelandic Sagas as authentic sources of history. Later, historians such as Danish-Norwegian Ludvig Holbergand and Icelandic-Norwegian Thormodus Torfaeus developed a more "logical" way to deal with the historical scholarship of the Enlightenment and Nordic Renaissance.

In the latter half of the 18th century, even as the Icelandic Sagas were used as important verifiable sources, the Viking Age had come to be viewed as a savage and uncouth period in the history of the Nordic nations. Not until the 1890s did researchers outside of Scandinavia widely reassess the accomplishments of the Vikings by recognizing their ingenuity, innovative abilities, and seamanship.

Not so long ago the historical framework of the Viking Age had been constructed from sources such as the Icelandic Sagas including Saxon Grammaticus' *History of the Danes*, the Kievan Rus' *Primary Chronicle* and *The War of the Irish with the Foreigners*. Today, most researchers take these writings as non-literal sources and instead depend more heavily on concrete archeological discoveries, numismatics, and other direct logical methods and techniques.

Additional Reading

Blair, Peter Hunter (2003). *An Introduction to Anglo-Saxon England*. Cambridge: Cambridge University Press.

Brink, S. and Price, N. (eds) (2008). The Viking World. Routledge: London and New York

Carey, Brian Todd. (2003) "Technical marvels, Viking longships sailed seas and rivers, or served as floating battlefields." *Military History* 19, no. 6, 70–72.

Crawford, Barbara E. (1987). *Scandinavian Scotland*. New Jersey: Leicester University Press.

DeVries, Kelly (2003). *The Norwegian Invasion of England in 1066*. Woodbridge: Boydell Press.

Downham, Clare. (2007) *Viking Kings of Britain and Ireland: The Dynasty of Ivarr to A.D. 1014*. Edinburgh: Dunedin Academic Press.

Forte, Angelo; Oram, Richard, and Pedersen, Frederik (2005). *Viking Empires*. Cambridge University Press.

Graham-Campbell, James. (1980). *Viking Artefacts: A Select Catalogue*. London: British Museum Publications.

Graham-Campbell, James & Batey, Colleen E. (1998). *Vikings in Scotland: An Archaeological Survey*. Edinburgh: Edinburgh University Press

Hall, Richard (2010). *Viking Age archaeology*. Shire Publications.

Hudson, Benjamin. (2005) *Viking Pirates and Christian Princes: Dynasty, Religion, and Empire in North America.* Oxford: Oxford University Press.

Jones, Gwyn (1968). *A History of the Vikings.* Oxford University Press.

Keynes, Simon (1999). "Vikings". *The Blackwell Encyclopedia of Anglo-Saxon England* (Eds: Michael Lapidge, John Blair, Simon Keynes and Donald Scragg). Oxford: Blackwell. pp. 460–461.

Logan, F. Donald. (1983) *The Vikings in History.* Totowa, N.J.: Barnes & Noble Books.

Maier, Bernhard. (2003) *The Celts: A history from earliest times to the present.* Notre Dame, Indiana: University of Notre Dame Press.

Richards, Julian D. (1991). *Viking Age England.* London: B.T. Batsford and English Heritage.

Williams, G.; Pentz, P. and Wemhoff, M. eds. (2014) *Vikings: Life and Legend.* London: British Museum Press.

Chapter Three: Vikings in France

"Be Thou my breastplate, my sword for the fight,

Be Thou my whole armor, be Thou my true might,

Be Thou my soul's shelter, be Thou my strong tower,

O raise Thou me heavenward, great power of my power."

(Verse three of *Be Thou My Vision*, a Celtic Christian song from the Viking period)

(Source: *1635: The Tangled Web* By Virginia DeMarce)

The French locale of Normandy takes its name from the Viking raiders who, from 790-930 A.D. and from 980-1030 A.D., terrified a wide swath of Europe. Medieval Latin archives alluded to them as Nortmanni, meaning, "Men of the North". This name gives the etymological premise to the cutting-edge words "Norman" and "Normandy", with " – ia" (Normandia, as Neustria, Francia, and so on.). After 911 this name supplanted the term Neustria, which had for some time had been utilized to portray the area that included Normandy, other fragments of Neustria became known as France, Champagne, and Anjou. The degree to which the Norse colonized the region currently known as France is quite evident in the Norman toponymy and in the progression of prominent family names. Even today Nordmann (pronounced as Norman) is used to refer to a Norwegian person in the Norwegian language.

Ragnar Lothbrok, the famous Viking, is still a mysterious historical figure, hidden in myths and links to a few chieftains. He was the father of legendary figures such as Ivar the Boneless, Halfdan Ragnarsson, Bjorn Ironside, Sigurd Snake-in-the-Eye, and Ubba. However, history is very certain of a particular thing about the great Viking named Ragnar. In all the attacks that were coordinated by Ragnar, the Vikings' invasion of Paris in 845 A.D. was one of the most famous feats to be accomplished in history. The courageous Danish Viking, after a progression of horrendous attacks over the district of what used to be called Frankia and what is currently known as France, figured out how to capture the city of Paris. His methods were to be copied by other extraordinary Viking chieftains – including Rolf the Ganger (Rollo) and Earl Siegfried. Around that time, Paris – a small walled city on the island of the Seine – was the dwelling place of the Frankish lord Charles the Bald. After the initial sacking of Paris, the Frankish continued to encounter the Vikings until they were eventually able to stand against another siege in 885 A.D.

Paris, located on the little island of Île de la Cite, was awoken by the tintinnabulation of the local ringer sometime in the year 845. The Vikings, who had been in the local area for as long as 4 years, but had never taken a stab at assuming control over Paris, had finally decided to invade the city. The spring waters of the Seine carried more than 120 rolling boats, which were occupied by 5000 warriors and directed by Ragnar. Prior to their landing, they ransacked Rouen to boost morale and for easy plunder. Ragnar had some issues to resolve with the Frankish king as a result of past dealings. A few years back, in

841, King Charles had offered some lands in Turnholt to Ragnar on which the Vikings were able to begin building their settlement. However, the Danish Leader was later denied provisions from the Frankish king when he asked for further assistance.

King Charles, upon being advised of the Vikings approach to the city of Paris, grew apprehensive of losing the Abbey of Saint-Denis to the Danes (as it was located on the route to Paris) and assembled his soldiers quickly. He gathered his men and separated them into two battalions ordering them to secure both banks of the River Seine. The strategies of the Frankish king were not very effective and the Vikings easily defeated one section of the two armies and took many prisoners. However, the Danes experienced a massive struggle during the siege before they were able to assume control over Paris on the 28th and 29th of March. They took 111 prisoners during their attack, many of whom knew that they were doomed even before they were captured, as it was the custom of the Vikings to use prisoners as sacrifices to Odin, the chief god of the Norsemen.

The Frankish King Charles, being concerned about his people, agreed to pay a tribute to Ragnar. Paris' freedom was agreed upon and bought for 7000 livres of silver and gold, but the king knew he was in trouble because Ragnar needed retribution for Charles' actions concerning their past dealings. After Ragnar pulled back from the city, a few towns along the coastline were also raided. In the process, the Abbey of Saint-Denis was also pillaged, the place which the king had tried so desperately to secure from raiders. That same year the Viking King Horik and his men demolished the archbishopric city of Hamburg. The king of East Frankia sent Cobbo as an ambassador to deal with the issue of the Vikings and made a peace treaty with the Danish king.

When Ragnar returned to King Horik, who was his superior, he described the direct way in which he had entered the city and lost numerous men during the fight at Saint Germain in Paris. King Horik, afraid that their people had been cursed because of their attack on the Abbey, ordered the execution of the surviving raiders and freed the captured Christians.

In 860 A.D. the Norsemen again arrived, but this time they not only raided Paris but also a large number of outlying towns, and when King Charles of West Frankia eventually died in 877 A.D. the city was left in turmoil. Accordingly, a few kings unsuccessfully ruled the land for brief periods but all of them neglected to fortify the city against the Vikings. Finally, in 884 A.D., the King of Germany and Italy – Charles the Fat – came to power in Frankia.

One year later the Norsemen used the River Seine as a strategic point under the leadership of Earl Siegfried the Sinric. This time the Northerners brought with them one of their fiercest warriors named Rollo. The legends say he was so enormous that no stallion could bear him. Hence, the people began to call him Rollo the Walker.

The Franks, having learned from their recent history, had spent time enhancing their defenses so they could withstand and overcome the Vikings. Count Odo, the son of Robert the Strong, was motivated by his father's legacy and volunteered to direct the defense of Paris. Count Odo – the Duchy of France – administered the territory between the Seine and Loire Rivers with the assistance of Joselin, the abbot of St. Germain. Previously Robert the Strong had begun to improve the defense of Paris and he had been successful in keeping the Viking invaders at bay.

Odo constructed the defensive tower, Grand Châtelet, as well as two bridges alongside the river; both bridges were constructed with a guarded tower on either end. During the time that Odo was in control of Paris the city was a safe and secure place. One of the bridges was made of stone and called the Grand Pont, while the other one was made of wood and called the Petit Pont. These bridges took into consideration pedestrian movement into the city; however, they were too low for anyone or anything to go under, thus obstructing passage of anything but the river past the city. By 885 A.D. the city of Paris was organized in such a way as to be ready to confront the Vikings.

The bulk of the Viking attacks began between 790 and 800 A.D. along the coast of western France. The raids were organized in late spring, as the Vikings wintered in Scandinavia. During the reign of Louis the Pious (814 – 840 A.D.), there were a few seaside ranges that were lost to Francia. Nonetheless, the Vikings exploited the conflicts and fights within the monarchy, which started after the demise of Louis the Pious. The Vikings used this as an opportunity to settle their first province in Gascony, which was considered to be the southwest region of Francia. This region was pretty much relinquished by Frankish rulers after they experienced two defeats at Roncevaux at the hands of the Vikings. The attacks in 841 A.D. were extreme in their destruction of Rouen and Jumièges. The Viking assailants first tried to capture the fortunes that were stowed away in religious centers, since they considered the monks to be easy prey and least likely able to defend themselves.

Despite the fact that the Norsemen had invaded some lands in Francia already, they first got to Paris in 845 A.D. but raided the city later. In 845 an expedition of warriors was sent along the Seine to Paris. The Vikings took Paris approximately three more times in the 860s and left when they had gathered enough plunder. Around 864 A.D., the Edict of Pistres requested a passage to be built over the Seine, at Pîtres and in Paris, where two bridges were eventually constructed. There was a bridge on each end of the Île de la Cite, each of which was exploited in the Viking attack of 885. The Duke of Francia (who was also the Count of Paris) was the central king in the district around Paris. He was also in control of the lands between the Loire and the Seine. Initially Robert the Strong – Margrave of Neustria and Missus Dominicus of the Loire Valley – strengthened the capital and battled the Vikings consistently until he was killed in a fight against them at Brissarthe. After that royal power eventually declined, despite his son's efforts to take control and improve the situation. Be that as it may, Paris remained fortified but mainly due to the efforts of the locals as opposed to work from any of the ruling families.

Some Carolingian coins from around 847 A.D. were discovered in 1871 in a store at Mullaghboden, County Limerick. It was observed by archeologists that the coins were not usually stamped nor regularly used as a generally approved means of trade amongst merchants. This discovery presumably represents the bounties following the invasions of 843 to 846.

After 851 A.D., the Vikings began to settle in the lower Seine valley for the winter. In January 852, they attacked and looted the Abbey of Fontenelle. In 858 the friars who were lucky enough to escape ran away to Boulogne-sur-Mer and later to

Chartres in 885. The relics of Sainte Honorine were taken away from Graville to Conflans (later known as Conflans-Sainte-Honorine) within the Paris district, which was considered more secure by virtue of its southeasterly location. The ministers also tried to move their chronicles and religious libraries toward the south, but a few were still destroyed by the Vikings. Twice more in the 860s the Vikings sailed to Paris, only leaving when they had gathered what they deemed to be enough plunder from the Carolingian rulers.

The Carolingian rulers had a tendency to create more issues than they solved, which led to serious consequences for the people. In 867 A.D. Charles the Bald marked the Treaty of Compiegne, by which he consented to yield the Cotentin Peninsula (and likely the Avranchin) to the Breton, King Salomon, on the condition that Salomon would guarantee his loyalty to battle against the Vikings should the need arise. Nonetheless, in 911 A.D., the Viking warrior Rollo forced Charles the Simple to sign the Treaty of Saint-Clair-sur-Epte. The treaty required Charles to give Rouen and the region of present-day Upper Normandy to Rollo, effectively creating the Duchy of Normandy. In return, Rollo swore vassalage to Charles in 940, consented to be sanctified through water baptism, and promised to protect the Seine from any further Viking raids, despite the fact that the opposite was regularly the case. The Duchy of Normandy, likewise, acquired several areas in Northern France increasing the area of land that initially agreed upon.

While numerous villages were raided, consumed, or pulverized by the Viking assaults, clerical sources may have been excessive, as no village was completely destroyed. Then again, several religious communities – and all of the nunneries were raided – through which Rollo and his successors were able to amass plunder.

The Scandinavian colonization was composed primarily of Norwegians and Danes under the leadership of Rollo. There were also a few Swedes among the people but not many. The mingling of the Scandinavians and the local populous eventually led to the establishment of remarkable feudal states in Western Europe.

In the meantime Charles the Fat was trying his best to keep his kingdom under control. The Franks had gained significant ground against the Vikings after Louis III's triumph at the Battle of Saucourt in 881. However, in 885 – a year after Charles became king – the Vikings coordinated their largest attack on Paris yet. One of the major attacks on the Kingdom of the West Franks near the River Seine took place during the Siege of Paris (885–886 A.D.). The attack was the most notable event during the rule of Charles the Fat and became a defining moment in the record of the Carolingian administration as well as in France's history. Additionally, it made the Franks realize that Paris was one of the most important among the large urban communities in France. The attack was also documented through a first-person account that is recorded in the Latin sonnet Bella Parisiacae urbis of Abbo Cernuus.

After raiding the nation's northeastern parts successfully, Danish Vikings in 885 – under the command of Sigfred and Sinric – once again journeyed toward West Francia. They had a considerable army, one that consisted of perhaps a couple of thousand men that were assembled in Rouen after careful planning by Sigfred and Sinric. Recalling the last Viking raid, Rouen surrendered, keeping in mind that the main goal was to remain unharmed. Sigfred requested a tribute from Charles, but his request was rejected; he then quickly assembled 700 ships that traveled up the Seine, moving upwards of perhaps 30,000 to 40,000 men. This number is the largest recorded for a Viking navy in contemporary sources and comes from Abbo Cernuus. Despite the fact that Abbo Cernuus witnessed the events himself, the general assertion among historians is that his numbers are a gross misrepresentation and that he might have exaggerated them. Historian C. W. Previte-Orton has set the number of boats at 300, which is also supported by historian John Norris.

In any event, Odo was low on men; according to Abbo Cernuus, he had only had access to around 200 men-at-arms. However, he led a joint resistance with Gozlin, who was the bishop of Paris and the first bishop in medieval writing to support and even lead a fight. Odo also had the support of two counts and a marquis. Towards the end of November of 885 the Vikings landed outside of Paris with several boats and perhaps a huge number of men. At first they requested tribute from the Franks; however, Odo refused to give them any tribute or bribe. He made this decision despite the fact that he had only a few hundred warriors to protect the city. When the Vikings' request for tribute was denied, they had no choice but to attack.

On November 26th the Danes took the upper east tower with ballistae, mangonels, and slings. In return, they were repelled by a blend of hot wax and pitch. All the Viking attacks that occurred on that day were spurned, and during the night the Parisians built another story onto the tower. On November 27th the Viking strategy included mining, battering rams, and fire, but they did not achieve anything that led to victory. Bishop Gozlin joined the fight with a bow and an ax, after which he planted a cross on the external defenses and warned the general population. Likewise, his brother Ebles took part in the fight. The Vikings pulled back after their failed tactics and constructed a camp on the right side of the riverbank using stone as their primary building material. While recovering their energy, the Vikings began to plan and strategize other means of attack.

They organized a new attack during which they shot a thousand missiles at the city, sent a ship toward one of the bridges, and directed a land infiltration with three different forces. The groups on land surrounded the bridgehead tower, perhaps aiming to bring down the obstruction on the river that denied them easy access to Paris. As they made a noteworthy attempt to set the bridge aflame they also struck the city itself using various techniques.

For two months the Vikings kept up the attack, making trenches and fending for themselves off the land. In January 886 they tried to fill the stream shallows with flotsam and jetsam, plant matter, and masses of the dead in an attempt to get around the tower. They continued with this tactic for about three days. On the third day they set three ships on fire and directed them toward the wooden bridge. However, the burning ships began to sink before they could set the bridge ablaze, nonetheless, this attempt to burn the bridge did yield some results as the structure became greatly weakened.

On February 6th heavy downpours into the flotsam-and-jetsam-filled stream caused a great flood that finally crumbled the wooden bridge. The northeast tower was now isolated, with just twelve guards inside. The tower became an easy access point for the Vikings, who attacked the twelve guards and attempted to force their surrender but because the

Parisian warriors inside the tower declined to surrender the Danes slaughtered them as soon as they breached its defenses. The Viking attack strategies were inferior compared to those of Alexander the Great – like those used against Tire over a thousand years before – demonstrating perhaps how the tactics of battle had declined in their ingenuity during the Early Middle Ages.

Tired of remaining in the same area, the Vikings separated into groups; some proceeded with the attack while others raided the surrounding areas. The Vikings left a group of warriors around Paris so that they could maintain the control they had worked so hard to establish. However, many wandered farther to raid Le Mans, Chartres, Evreux, and the Loire. This allowed Count Odo a chance to ask for assistance and the Vikings who had been holding the captured area were quickly attacked from behind. Odo even managed to slip a few men through the Norse lines who hurried to Italy and begged Charles for help.

Charles listened to the messengers carefully before deciding how to best handle the situation. Finally, he ordered Henry the Count of Saxony (his main ally in Germany) to march with his forces to Paris. Weakened by their winter travel, Henry's troops made a single unsuccessful charge in February before retreating. Nonetheless, the new allies had brought with them supplies and resources. The Vikings' self-esteem was low and Sigfred finally asked for sixty pounds of silver before fleeing the military encampment in April.

In May influenza spread throughout the Parisian population and Gozlin died as a result. At that point Odo himself snuck through the Viking-controlled region to once again ask Charles for help to which he finally agreed. Odo battled his way back into Paris while Charles and Henry of Saxony marched northward. Unfortunately, Henry fell into a Viking trench where he was caught and killed.

The Vikings used an assortment of machinery yet could not get through the city's defenses even after several days siege. The attack was maintained after the initial battles, but it was not successful and as the attack went on a large number of the Vikings left Paris to raid along the river. The Vikings made a last unsuccessful attempt to take the city in spring before Charles the Fat landed with his army in October and scattered the Vikings. Charles strategically surrounded Rollo while his army set up camp at Montmartre.

Charles had no intention of fighting, much to the dismay of the Parisians who had guarded the city and defended tooth and nail against the Vikings. Charles held back before fighting the Viking besiegers. Instead of destroying them completely, he let them sail further up the Seine to attack Burgundy (which was in rebellion) and promised them an installment of 700 livres (roughly 257 kg) of silver, which was paid upon their arrival in 887.

He signed the Treaty of Saint-Clair-sur-Epte with the Viking leader Rollo so that they could maintain some kind of peace in the future. In return Rollo promised vassalage to Charles and consented to sanctification by baptism. Rollo pledged to protect the estuaries of the Seine from any other Viking invasions. Odo, exceptionally shocked by this, did his best to oppose the agreement between Charles and the Vikings. The Parisians and Odo declined to let the Vikings sail down the Seine in peace and the invaders were forced to drag their ships overland to the Marne. The reputation of Charles the Fat was severely undermined by the way he dealt with the Vikings.

When Charles died in January of 888, signaling the end of the Carolingian Empire, the French chose Odo, king of East Francia and West Francia, as the first non-Carolingian ruler of the Franks. Odo's brother was later chosen to be king as well. All through the following century, the Robertians – relatives of Robert the Strong – battled the Carolingians to gain political power in France.

The name France originated from the duchy Francia and while Paris had been a minor city under the Carolingian Empire it became a city of real significance at the center of West Francia. The most important result of the Viking attack was the end of the Carolingian line of rulers and the start of another period led by the Capetians relatives of Count Odo. During this time, the people ceased to be the Franks and became known as the French.

The Vikings sailed back home in the spring of 887 after they had taken their tribute. Rollo returned home with a hostage spouse named Poppa, whose origins are not certain. She was either the daughter of Guy (the Count of Senlis) or Berenger (the Count of Bayeux). Nevertheless, the Vikings sailed to Frankia in 911 with the expectation of sacking the region but instead Charles the Simple – who had met with Rollo – made him a count, and gave to him his daughter Gisela in marriage. He also gave him the city of Rouen. Keeping in mind that the end goal was to marry the princess and become a vassal of the king, Rollo agreed to covert to Christianity in front of Franco, the Archbishop of Rouen. An interesting anecdote is narrated in which he was required to kiss the king's foot to demonstrate his faithfulness. He refused at first and said he would not bend his knee before any man for any reason, neither would he kiss any man's foot, but he agreed in the end. Charles the Simple was on horseback while Rollo remained standing and so he snatched the king's foot and raised it up to his lips, which made the king nearly tumble from his horse to the entertainment of the nearby Norsemen.

Proceeding to Rouen Rollo gave certain sections of his district to his chieftains as vassal states and so in this way he established a feudalistic system as was common during the medieval period. The legend maintains that Rollo was barbarous and cruel in his treatment of Gisela. Her father sent two knights to help her in Normandy but Rollo had the two men caught and decapitated in Place du Vieux Marche in Rouen in front of a group of people. The marriage – or even the presence of Princess Gisela – is absent from any written record. In the event that she did exist, she may well have been the illegitimate daughter of King Charles.

The County of Rouen later became the Duchy of Normandy, sometime around the 11th century, while the dynasty of Rollo continued to rule the lands and acquire more territories. Rollo reigned over the County of Rouen until 927 and died before 933; he was more than eighty years of age at his death. It was a significant accomplishment in the medieval period when most nobles did not survive to see fifty years of age; life expectancy of the common folk was generally below forty.

Even though Rollo ruled Normandy he did not use the title of duke. The first person to use this title was Richard II the Good. The Normans spoke a variation of the Old French dialect with numerous Old Norse words (in the Norman dialect). They extended the dukedom, were successful in their conquest of England and southern Italy, and also took an interest in a number of expeditions. Nevertheless, the King of France Philip II decided to incorporate the Duchy of Normandy into the king's territories in 1204. A war began between England and France from 1202–1214 in which Normandy played a significant role. The Normans performed with excellence in battle and England eventually lost. After the war, England fell into a civil war or the First Baron's War.

The Viking term used to describe a Scandinavian is Northman; this term eventually became Normand in medieval French. Rollo the Northman and his descendants quickly extended their control outside of the original feudal grant and were referred to occasionally as Normans. The resulting dukedom eventually became, and remained, Normandy. Rollo's successors managed the administrative affairs of Normandy for almost two hundred years but ended when Henry I died in 1135. It is important to note that in the end, his lineage became devout Christians.

With a progression of victories the domain of Normandy slowly expanded. The Vikings first acquired Hiemois and Bessin in 924. In 933, King Raoul of France had no choice but to give Cotentin and a piece of Avranchin to William I of Normandy, which included all lands north of the Selune River that the Breton dukes had controlled for about seventy years. In the years of 1009 and 1020, the Normans proceeded with expansion to the west, taking all the lands between the Selune and Couesnon waterways, including Mont Saint-Michel, while completely conquering Avranchin. William the Conqueror finished these crusades in 1050 when he took Passais. The Norman kings (first counts of Rouen and after that the dukes of Normandy) tried to achieve the political unification of the two distinctive Viking settlements of Pays de Caux, which included Seine in the east and Cotentin in the west.

The Frankish land was very dense, making it impossible for the Normans to spread far inside France, yet the insatiable souls of the Vikings did not allow them to lead a simple existence that was based on agriculture alone. They were sailors of the open sea; they could not sit idle. In addition to their excellent fighting abilities on water they also developed fighting strategies on land with the addition of knights and horses. Normandy had little to offer the goal-oriented, youthful child of an honorable family. In any case, the children often grew up with dreams of heroic military achievements through which they could become soldiers of fame and glory.

The Scandinavian colonization was mainly Danish under the Norwegian initiative of Rollo, although there was also a Norwegian component in the Cotentin district. For example, the name Barno was mentioned in two unique reports in 1066 and originally referred to the "frankization" of the Old Scandinavian individual named Barni, a name that was only found in Denmark and in England during the Viking Era. It can be found in numerous Norman place names as well; for example, Barneville-sur-Seine or Banneville in France and Barnby in England. On the other hand, the arrival of the Norwegians left traces in the Cotentin. They left statues and buildings that clearly indicate their Norwegian heritage. Furthermore, a few Swedes may have migrated to Normandy even though their own government did not come into existence until the 12th and 13th centuries.

The Viking colonization was not a sudden surprise. All things considered, the Scandinavians established themselves rather densely, especially in Pays de Caux and in the northern area of the Cotentin. We can regard the Nordic dwellings in Normandy as Anglo-Scandinavian in light of the fact that a large number of the homesteaders most likely came as anglers and agriculturists from the English based Danelaw after 911

A.D. Thus is the subsequent Anglo-Saxon impact obvious in the region. Toponymic and phonetic evidence supports this hypothesis; for example, Denestanville was called Dunestanvilla in 1142 and Venestanville was called Wenestanvillam in the thirteenth century. The Anglo-Saxon Chronicle specifies three plausible times in which the Danes from England settled in Neustria. The first was a Danish force that was positioned in Kent for a long period of time. After the army dispersed, people who possessed boats migrated over the Channel to the reaches of the Seine River. The second mention comes from jarl Thurcytel, who initially settled in the English Midlands and then journeyed to Francia in 920. Lastly, there is mention of a Viking fleet of 1000 people who left England for Normandy around the same time.

Archeological evidence has greatly helped in identifying the presence of the Vikings in France, for example Anglo-Saxon swords have been pulled out of the Seine River that were most likely used by the Danes. In addition, at Saint-Pierre-des-Fleurs, a buried collection of treasure was found. It had nine Anglo-Saxon coins that were dented; most likely due to the blows they received to check their authenticity.

The century between 920 and 1020 was a phase of significant establishment for Normandy with the inundation of various Scandinavian leaders, who had previously had a strong interest in the Kingdom of France. The Scandinavians spread rapidly, intermarrying and embracing the common tongue and later the language of Old French. Guillaume de Jumieges' Gesta Normannorum ducum (composed around the season of the Norman Conquest of England) contains a record of the Viking origin and Norse descriptions of Normandy's leaders.

Additional Reading

Abbo Cernuus (2007). *Viking Attacks on Paris: The Bella Parisiacae Urbis of Abbo of Saint-Germain-des-Pres.* Peeters Publishers.

Bradbury, Jim (1992). *The Medieval Siege.* Boydell & Brewer.

Bradbury, Jim (2004). *The Routledge Companion to Medieval Warfare.* Routledge.

Brooks, Nicholas (2000). *Communities and Warfare: 700-1400.* Hambledon Press.

Davis, Paul K. (2001). *Besieged: 100 Great Sieges from Jericho to Sarajevo.* New York: Oxford University.

Hodgkin, Robert Howard (1959). *A History of the Anglo-Saxons.* New York: Oxford University.

Hooper, Nicholas A & Bennet, Matthew (1996). *The Cambridge Illustrated Atlas of Warfare: The Middle Ages, 768-1487.* Cambridge University.

Kohn, George C (2006). *Dictionary of Wars.* Infobase.

Logan, F. Donald (1991). *The Vikings in History.* Routledge.

MacLean, Simon (2003). *Kingship and Politics in the Late Ninth Century: Charles the Fat and the end of the Carolingian Empire.* Cambridge University.

Norris, John (2007). *Medieval Siege Warfare.* Tempus.

Previte-Orton, C. W. (1955). *The Shorter Cambridge Medieval History*. CUP Archive.

Tucker, Spencer C. (2009). *A Global Chronology of Conflict: From the Ancient World to the Modern Middle East.* ABC-CLIO.

Zupko, Ronald Edward (1990), *Revolution in Measurement: Western European Weights and Measures since the Age of Science.* American Philosophical Society.

Chapter Four: The Legend of Ragnar Lothbrok

"I have fought battles

Fifty and one

Which were famous;

I have wounded many men.

I little thought that snakes

Would cause my death;

Often that happens

Which one least expects."

(Source: *The Viking Age: The Early History, Manners, and Customs, Volume 2*

By Paul Belloni Du Chaillu)

History is a collection of numerous legends. One such legend is that of Ragnar Lothbrok (or Lodbrok), a Norse hero and chieftain to the Norsemen during the Viking Age. Tales of his heroism can be found in several Icelandic Sagas such as "*Pattr af Ragnarssonum*" ("*The Tale of Ragnar's Sons*"), or "*Ragnars Saga Lodbrokar*" ("*The Saga of Ragnar Lothbrok*"), as well as in Old Norse skaldic poems and medieval literature such as the "Anglo-Saxon Chronicle" and *"Gesta Danorum,"* by Saxo Grammaticus.

The 13th-century Icelandic Saga of Ragnar Lodbrok names his father as Sigurd Hring, a Danish king. Ragnar is said to have married the daughter of Sigurd, the Dragon-Slayer, and the Valkyrie Brynhild after Pora, daughter of Sigurd, had died. "Krakumal," a 12th-century Icelandic poem, romanticized Ragnar's death. It further links him to figures from the heroic literature of the ancient Teutons. "Hattalykill," the poem of the Orkney Islands, also recounts the legend of Ragnar and his sons.

The Anglo-Saxon Chronicle narrates how Ragnar Lothbrok had a tremendous impact during the 9th century, it also includes stories about Ragnar's sons and how they continued his legacy across different regions. Ragnar is described to be the father of Ivar the Boneless, Halfdan, and Ubba, who orchestrated a Viking invasion into East Anglia in 865 A.D. to avenge the murder of Ragnar. Ragnar's sons stormed England after his death, as it was at the hands of King Aella of Northumbria that Ragnar was murdered. Based on historical sources, King Aella captured Ragnar and sentenced him to death by casting him into a pit of snakes.

Ragnar's legend is also found in *Gesta Danorum* (c. 1185), written by the Danish historian Saxo Grammaticus. Saxo also recounts how the Anglo-Saxon King, Aella of Northumbria, later captured Ragnar. Book nine of Saxo Grammaticus's *History of the Danes* describes Ragnar as a relative of the 9th-century Dane, Godfred, who became king himself and made heroic conquests across the Viking world.

Ragnar Lothbrok was married three times. His first marriage was to a shieldmaiden named Lagertha, who he later divorced in order to marry the Swedish princess, Thora (Pora) Borgarhjort. This was before he married Princess Aslaug (or Kraka, as she is referred to in some medieval texts).

The story of how Ragnar met Lagertha can be found in Gesta Danorum, which describes how Ragnar met Lagertha while attempting to take Norway back from King Fro of Sweden. Fro murdered King Siward of Norway, Ragnar's grandfather, during an invasion; he then captured the women of King Siward's family as well as some other women who were living in Siward's court. One of the women was Lagertha, who was captured and taken to a brothel to be humiliated. The captured women fought bravely along with Ragnar Lodbrok when he came to rescue them, avenge his grandfather's death, and take back his grandfather's lands from the invaders. It was during this rescue mission that he met Lagertha who is described as "a woman with the courage of a man who fought fearlessly" in *Gesta Danorum.* Lagertha's bravery impressed Ragnar so much that he decided to marry her. However, she was not easy to get as Ragnar had to kill a bear as well as the hound protecting Lagertha's house to successfully woo her and get her to marry him. Lagertha became the mother of Eric, Agnar, Rognvald, and Fridleif Ragnarsson, as well as two unnamed daughters.

Thora Borgarhjort was the daughter of Herrod, the Earl of Gautland. Her father gave her a small grass snake as a present. She kept it in a box that contained a bed of gold. Interestingly, the snake, as well as the gold, grew simultaneously. The snake grew so long that it could no longer fit into the box. Thus, it curled itself in a circle around the house. As it grew, it developed a very bad temper and became so dangerous that no one would dare to approach it, except the man who was tasked to feed it. The snake was so large that it feasted on an ox for each meal. The Earl became so worried about the snake that he promised to give his daughter to any man who was courageous enough to face and kill it. He also promised to offer the gold as a dowry to the lucky man. Nevertheless, no one was bold enough to face and kill the snake.

Except for Ragnar, the tall and handsome son of King Sigurd Hring of Denmark, who decided to take on the task. Sigurd Hring was king of Sweden and Denmark following the reign of Harald Hilditonn. Ragnar is said to have been the largest, strongest man ever seen at that time. He was like his mother and her family in appearance, his mother's lineage (the people of Alfar), according to legend, is said to have been much more handsome than that of other men in the Northern lands. However, in size, Ragnar took after his father and his kinsmen.

Ragnar was distinguished at a very early age for his valor and prowess. When he heard of the Earl's offer regarding the task of killing the giant snake he journeyed with his men to Gautland. Before setting out to attempt the task, he equipped himself with a shaggy cloak and shaggy breeches that had been boiled. In this shaggy attire, he went ashore early one morning and made his way to the Earl's house where he faced the giant snake and thrust his spear through the creature, his shaggy garments preventing him from being killed by the snake's venom. After successfully killing the snake the Earl gave Ragnar his daughter, Thora, as a prized wife. With her, Ragnar had two sons, Erik and Agnar. After her death Ragnar mourned her so deeply that he left his kingdom and wandered about the lands, engaging in several battles.

However, he did not mourn Thora for the rest of his life because one summer found him in Spangereid, Norway, where he decided to lay anchor in the harbor during the night. In the morning he asked his bakers to go ashore to bake bread for him. The bakers found a little farm, where two people, Aki and Grima, lived; these two had killed King Heimir, and had taken into their custody Sigurd Fafnirsbane's daughter, Aslaug (or Kraka, as she was called there). Aslaug was very helpful to the bakers. Later, she decided to bathe outside, something that Grima had forbidden her to do so that no one would be able to discover her beauty. Aslaug loosened her hair, which had grown under the tarred hat she was forced to wear, it was fine as silk and so long that it reached down to the ground when she stood upright.

At the sight of her bathing the bakers – who were to go about their work with her –completely lost their senses, resulting in the loaves of bread being burnt. On finding out what had caused the loaves to be burnt Ragnar learned of the beauty of Aslaug. He commanded his men to summon her into his presence. To test her wit, he requested her to come neither alone nor in the company of another, neither clothed nor naked, and neither hungry nor filled. Aslaug, in accordance with Ragnar's request, took off her clothing and wrapped herself in a net. She then swathed herself in her own hair in the form of a garment. She took a bite from a leek and came along with a dog. Ragnar was so impressed by her beauty and wisdom that he was eager to carry her away and marry her. However, she refused to go with him until he returned from the expedition that he was about to undertake. She only agreed to marry him if he returned without his mind changed.

Ragnar eventually came back in due time and Aslaug then went with him on board the ship. Before she left, she revealed to her stepfather and stepmother that she knew about their malicious deed but she would not seek vengeance upon them. Ragnar and Aslaug entered Ragnar's kingdom and Aslaug bore him the sons Ivar the Boneless, Bjorn Ironside, Whitesark, and Ragnvald. Bjorn Ironside, Whitesark, and Ragnvald were stalwart and heroic. Ivar, having ligaments rather than bones, was not able to walk. He was conveyed about in the company of his brothers. However, he surpassed his brothers in shrewdness causing them to often follow his advice. He was also the only one to think of gaining honor by participating in Viking raids. In fact, he was the one who urged the others to invade Whitby, England, before they seized the town. It was a successful venture but not without loss, because Ragnvald fell during the attack.

Over time, some historians have wrongly ascribed Ragnar to be other historical characters, such as King Reginfrid, King Korik I, Rognvald (otherwise called Ragnall ua Imair), and in particular Reginherus, a Norse warrior during the reign of King Horik. In any case, based on most of the common accounts of the legendary Ragnar, he is known as the tyrant of both France and England. He attacked the territories of West Francia, resulting in the raid of Paris in 845, along with the English territories of Wessex and Northumbria before being killed by an English king.

In March of 845 A.D., Ragnar navigated the River Seine with a fleet of 120 boats and 5,000 men and set out toward Paris. The French King, Charles the Bald, the grandson of Charlemagne, tried to stop this invasion and sent out his armed forces to the banks of the river. The Viking leader Ragnar, with his entire army, butchered the same group of the Frankish force on one bank of the river and, before the eyes of the Franks on the other bank, he hanged the defeated

Frankish men. The remaining French men withdrew and fled in horror. Paris lay before him and the hallelujahs of Easter quickly turned to lamentations as Ragnar looted and pillaged the town. In the wake of looting the city, he received a payment of 7,000 French livres from the French King to pull his army back.

He proceeded with a series of successful attacks against France throughout the mid-9th century and participated in various civil wars in Denmark. Most of the western parts of the Frankish empire faced the Viking attacks during these decades, along the Seine, as well as in the Somme, Gironde, Garonne, Scheldt, Dordogne, and Meuse. The Norsemen also invaded Chartres, Amiens, Bordeaux, Toulouse, Tours, Angers, Orleans, Poitiers, Blois, and Paris. Ragnar became the Legendary Viking hero and was nicknamed Ragnar "Shaggy-Breeches". His moniker came from the trousers he had worn to protect himself during the fight with the giant snake he had killed to marry Thora. The trousers were made from animal skins, or more accurately cowhide boiled in pitch and rolled in sand. He was given the surname Lothbrok, because of the strange coat he wore. Ragnar claimed that he was a descendant of the great Odin, the God of War himself, as indicated by the Völsungasaga. William of Jumieges, the first writer to mention Lothbroc, depicted him to have been an Anglo-Scandinavian king and the father of Bjorn Ironside, who decreed that Bjorn was to become an outcast and to live a life of raiding and plundering.

The legend of Ragnar is intertwined with the feats of his sons who later controlled the Great Heathen Army (an alliance of Norsemen from what is now modern-day Norway, Denmark, and Sweden) that would attack England and turn it into a unified medieval nation from 865 to 878.

In Sweden, there was a king named Eystein, who was very passionate in offering sacrifices. He worshipped a fierce cow called Sibilja, which strolled before his armed forces during battle, filling his adversaries with fear. King Eystein and Ragnar Lodbrok were good friends and visited each other regularly. One day, when Ragnar was feasting at the court of Eystein, Eystein's beautiful daughter filled the beakers for the kings, and Ragnar's retainers encouraged him to make her his wife and put aside Aslaug, who was thought to be a peasant's daughter. King Eystein delightfully supported the union and thus it was agreed that Ragnar was to return later to marry the princess.

Ragnar bade his men say nothing in regards to the arrangement to Aslaug, his wife, but three birds carried the secret to the queen. When Ragnar returned home she scolded him for his plan to set her aside and to marry another. She then revealed to him her true descent and name. She informed him that her true name was Aslaug, not Kraka and that she was the daughter of Sigurd Fafnirsbane and from that moment she was pregnant. She informed Ragnar that it was a child who ought to be set apart with the image of a serpent in his eye; this token would be proof that she was indeed the true daughter of Sigurd Fafnirsbane.

Everything happened in accordance with what she had anticipated and the child was given the name Sigurd Snake-In-The-Eye. King Eystein's anger was set ablaze in light of the fact that Ragnar had broken his vow with his daughter, and from that time on, Eystein became Ragnar's enemy. Ragnar's eldest sons, Erik and Agnar, assembled an armed force to bring the battle within the confines of Sweden. Fortune, however, was against them. Agnar fell, and Erik, who refused to owe his life to Eystein, was impaled after being tossed upon a spear that was fixed into the earth. One of his men brought his ring to Queen Aslaug, who immediately pressured her sons to avenge the dead. With a flotilla of warships they sailed for Sweden and slew King Eystein in battle, after Ivar had succeeded in slaughtering Sibilja.

After completing the incursion against King Eystein they continued to make war throughout the south, gaining fame in every battle. They obliterated the intense fortification of Vivilsborg, caught Luna, and had no thoughts of stopping their adventures until their plan to plunder Rome came to fruition. They asked an old man, who came to them in Luna, if he knew how far Rome was. The old man pointed to a pair of iron boots on his feet and another pair slung over his back; the two pairs, he proclaimed, had been worn away on the journey from Rome to Luna. The sons of Lothbrok then decided not to travel all the way to Rome.

Meanwhile, Ragnar, who had remained quietly at home, soon heard of the prestige and fame his sons were acquiring and decided not to be outdone by them. He gave orders for the construction of two great merchant vessels, so vast that he could transport an entire army abroad to England. Aslaug cautioned him to separate his forces among several smaller ships to make the landing all the more simple. However, Ragnar did not pay attention to her wisdom. Before embarking on the journey to England, he pulled on his shaggy garments so as to protect himself against all manner of wounds. Unfortunately, his ships ran aground on the coasts of England and he was cut off from retreat. At the time that Ragnar chose to raid, Aella was king of England. When the news of Ragnar's invasion reached him, he assembled a vast army and destroyed the invaders through sheer numbers alone.

According to legend, King Aella, who ruled England had heard that Ragnar would be coming his way. He sent men to reveal to him when Ragnar would land, and they soon came with news of Ragnar's arrival. Aella called on every able man within his domain, ordering each man that could hold a shield and ride a horse to help defend against Ragnar's invasion. Aella was able to gather a surprisingly vast number of armed men for the upcoming battle. He is claimed to have said to his men, "If we gain the victory in this battle, and you see Ragnar, you must not attack him with weapons, for he has sons who sooner or later will avenge his death."

Ragnar prepared for the fight to come by garbing himself in his shaggy pieces of clothing and armed himself with the spear that he had used to slay the giant snake that had lain around the home of Thora. He had no other armor aside from a helmet. When the battle began, Ragnar appeared to have fewer men by far. A large portion of Ragnar's men fell within a few hours of the battle. However, wherever Ragnar himself went, his enemies shied away from his attacks. He strolled through their ranks and whenever he charged at them his blows were so heavy that nothing could stand against him. Neither steel nor arrows touched him. He received no injuries and slew a large number of King Aella's men.

At last, when every one of Ragnar's men had fallen, Ragnar was flanked by shields and captured. He was asked to state his identity but he remained silent and gave no answer. Aella is claimed to have said, "That man must be punished if he will not tell us who he is; now throw him into a snake-pit and let him sit there a long time. If he says anything by which we can see that he is Ragnar, he shall be taken away as soon as possible." So Ragnar was thrown into the snake pit where he sat for quite a while and the snakes did not harm him. People began to say, "This is a great man; the weapons did not wound him today, and now the snakes do no harm to him." Aella later instructed his men to remove Ragnar's garment, and when they had done so, the snakes attacked him. In any case, history asserts that Aella did not realize that the man kept hostage was Ragnar until after his death.

Ragnar's sons, who had returned to Denmark, soon heard of their father's death. King Aella sent couriers to inform them of the death of their father, with instructions to note precisely how each of them received the news. The delegates discovered Ivar sitting in the high seat, while Whitesark and Sigurd were playing chess, and Bjorn was occupied shaping a spear shaft. As the envoys were conveying their message, Bjorn shook the shaft until it broke in two, Whitesark crushed a chessman in his grasp so hard that blood sprang from under his nails, while Sigurd, who was paring his nails, sliced his finger deeply without giving the slightest sign of pain. Ivar alone scrutinized the messengers and talked unobtrusively with them; the only hint of shock was the change of his skin color, from flushed cheeks to pallor.

When Aella heard of the various reactions of Ragnar sons he is said to have announced that "It is Ivar we have to fear and none other." Ragnar's sons created a plan to avenge their father; however, Ivar raised his voice against such actions, prompting instead that they acknowledge the wergild from Aella. His brothers, angered at his discourse, marshaled an armed force. In spite of the fact that Ivar followed them to England, he led no army and did not partake in the fight in which the siblings were crushed. He instead sought the presence of Aella himself, in order to request a small forfeit of land for his father. Aella regarded this as a sensible request; yet shrewd Ivar cut a mollified hide in strips, with which he covered a vast plain of lands. There he constructed a house and a fortification and gave the place the name of Lundunaborg (London). Although he had vowed to Aella not to make war against him, he utilized his patrimony to lure the mightiest men of the lands far from Aella. When he judged that everything was suited to his plans, he sent word to his brothers that they should marshal a huge armed force. They did as he asked and journeyed to England.

When King Aella discovered what was happening and how he had been tricked, he tried to put up a defense. However, he found that he was unable to field an adequate force since most of his men had lost confidence in him. In an unequivocal fight during which he was captured he was, at Ivar's request, subjected to the "bloody eagle," an abhorrent Viking technique for torture and execution that can be found in some Nordic saga legends. It was carried out by cutting the ribs of the victim, breaking the ribs so they looked like blood-colored wings, and by hauling the lungs out through the wounds in the victim's back. Salt was then poured into the wounds. With Aella dead Ivar now allowed his brothers to maintain their influence over Ragnar's domain; he took England for himself and reigned there until his death. Whitesark was taken prisoner during a venture to the shores of the Baltic, and chose to die by fire on a pyre of human skulls. Bjorn later ruled in Sweden while Sigurd Snake-In-The-Eye held power in Denmark.

According to Katherine Holman in the *Historical Dictionary of the Vikings*,

> *Although his sons are historical figures, there is no evidence that Ragnar himself*

> *ever lived, and he seems to be an amalgam of several different historical figures and pure literary invention. (2003:241)*

Several of the tales about the legend of Ragnar Lothbrok emerged with the legends of several other Viking heroes, and the authenticity of Ragnar's existence remains a disputed issue among historians. However, Hilda Ellis Davidson, the antiquarian, wrote in 1980, "Certain scholars in recent years have come to accept at least part of Ragnar's story as based on historical fact." Dr. Elizabeth Ashman Rowe, a University of Cambridge Lecturer of Scandinavian History of the Medieval Period and author of *Vikings in the West: The Legend of Ragnarr Lodbrok and His Sons* wrote in her book, "The Viking king Ragnarr Lodbrok and his sons feature in a variety of medieval stories, all of them highly dramatic." She further explains that Ragnar set precise borders for the "Viking" territories while becoming an icon of heroic bravery. Ragnar Lothbrok's legacy continued with his descendants creating an impact in different regions long after he was gone. Two centuries after Ragnar's death, descendants of Ragnar Lothbrok's sons stayed in the western region of France, transforming this region into the "Land of Norsemen;" Normandy, as we know it today. Nevertheless, whether Ragnar Lothbrok existed or not is, and will probably remain, forever a mystery among historians.

Additional Reading

Forte, Angelo, Richard Oram, and Frederik Pedersen (2005). *Viking Empires*. Cambridge University Press.

Logan, F. Donald. (1983) *The Vikings in History*. Totowa, N.J.: Barnes & Noble Books.

McTurk, Rory (1991). *Studies in Ragnars saga lodbrokar and Its Major Scandinavian Analogues*. Medium Aevum Monographs. 15. Oxford.

Schlauch, Margaret (transl.) (1964). *The Saga of the Volsungs: the Saga of Ragnar Lodbrok Together with the Lay of Kraka*. New York: American Scandinavian Foundation.

Simpson, Jacqueline. (1980) *The Viking World*. New York, N.Y.: St. Martin's Press.

Sprague, Martina (2007). *Norse Warfare: the Unconventional Battle Strategies of the Ancient Vikings*. New York: Hippocrene Books.

Strerath-Bolz, Ulrike (1993). "Review of Rory McTurk, Studies in "Ragnars saga lodbrokar" and Its Major Scandinavian Analogues." *Alvissmal* 2: 118–19.

Waggoner, Ben (2009). *The Sagas of Ragnar Lodbrok*. The Troth.

Chapter Five: Vikings in Russia

I have seen the Rus as they came on their merchant journeys and encamped by the Itil. I have never seen more perfect physical specimens, tall as date palms, blond and ruddy; they wear neither tunics nor caftans, but the men wear a garment which covers one side of the body and leaves a hand free. Each man has an axe, a sword, and a knife, and keeps each by him at all times. The swords are broad and grooved, of Frankish sort. Each woman wears on either breast a box of iron, silver, copper, or gold; the value of the box indicates the wealth of the husband. Each box has a ring from which depends a knife. The women wear neck-rings of gold and silver. Their most prized ornaments are green glass beads. They string them as necklaces for their women.

(Source: Gwyn Jones, *A History of the Vikings*)

No matter the way that the Vikings spread out across European lands the impact of their societies on history has to a large extent been overlooked. They moved from Scandinavia to the Mediterranean, and to many places in the East and West including current Eastern Europe, Iceland, Greenland, and present-day America. The start of the Scandinavian-Russian affiliation can be traced back to the 9th century; this is recounted in the Russian Primary Chronicle, a text said to have been written by Orthodox priests.

Based on the Primary Chronicle, the leading East Slavic historical source, the Scandinavian-Russian affiliation began with the Rus. The Rus were a group of Varangians who dwelled alongside different tribes such as the Gutes and Swedes on the opposite side of the Baltic Sea. They may also have been the people who lived in Scandinavia far across from the French and the English lands. The Rus were otherwise called Varangians – a term thought to originate from a Norse word that means "individuals who take part in a pledge" or "individuals who are likely to share their trade". The word was later extended to many other groups including the Norsemen of Russia, the Slavs, and the Anglo-Saxons.

At first the Rus were sent away but were later asked to return where they were welcomed back as the rulers of the contending Finnic and Slavic tribes of Novgorod. Slavs, Chuds, Krivichs, and Merians were the four communities who were later made to pay homage to the Rus. Initially they forced the Rus back across the ocean and refused to pay them any tribute as these tribes wanted to govern themselves without any interference. Since they lacked proper governing laws, they found that each tribe tried to gain an advantage over the other. Disagreement ensued until they began to fight wars between themselves.

From the beginning of the 9th century a group of Swedish Norsemen also called the Rus arrived in the region that is now referred to as Russia. During this period the area was populated by a few groups of scattered Slavic tribes. Various Slavic tribes lived in the North and West of Russia along the Neva and the Volkhov waterways as well as around the lakes Ladoga and Ilmen. The Vikings are said to have overwhelmed Kiev and created the territory of Kievan Rus. They named the region they had conquered after themselves and eventually became the native people of the land.

The vast Russian plain, blessed with forest and meadow, was perfect for hunting, farming, and fishing, additionally, the Russian geographic location allowed massive trade to be carried out between Northern Europe and the Byzantine Empire. This was one reason that led to the building of the town of Novgorod. Novgorod was a capital of Old Northern Russia and a significant centre for commerce.

Soviet researchers believe that there was an existing confederation of Slav tribes three centuries before the arrival of the Vikings. Nonetheless, many Western historians have suggested that the Scandinavians were the first leaders of present-day Russia, Ukraine, and Belarus. Urban areas like Novgorod and Kiev had Viking chiefs as leaders, whose subjects consisted of a predominantly Slavic population. In 862 the Slavic population dwindled due to the continuous tribal wars that occurred amongst them and finally they asked the Rus (a name that originates from the Finns who used it to refer to the Swedes) to come and govern them. According to them, inter-tribal conflicts were beyond their capability to manage and they needed the Rus to ensure stability and peace.

In 860 A.D. a Rus leader named Rurik traveled to the area and established his reign in Novgorod. This occurred around the same time that other leaders were taking control of other parts of the nation. Sineus created a settlement in Beloozerg while Truvor did the same in Izborsk. The newly established domains flourished for about twenty years after which Rurik's heir overcame Kiev, which was situated more than 600 miles south of Novgorod. The initially scattered regions swiftly united until a fully-fledged nation and a massive kingdom had been created.

Two years later Sineus and Truvor both died. After their deaths Rurik was able to solidify his power over the entire nation. He sent two of his lieutenants to Kiev to govern the people with policies that would satisfy the people and prevent any uprisings. Oleg, who succeeded Rurik, also came to Kiev in 882 A.D; and after he had established control over various tribes and towns, Oleg reinforced the new Russian State extensively and became its ruler. The new capital of Kiev slowly but surely became one of the wealthiest towns in Europe. Rurik's successors had created a ruling dynasty in Russia that would last for over 700 years.

Various theories and hypotheses have been put forward to explain the origin of the Rus. According to some of the theories, the Rus were actually a group of Slavic people. However, archaeological evidence has shown that the Rus were not Slavic but were definitely the descendants of a Swedish ancestry. Nevertheless, most historians and researchers are perplexed because by the 11th century the Rus appeared to be very similar to the Slavic people. Within a period of 200 hundred years the Rus who had settled in Slavic regions had let go of their "Swedishness;" and they became noticeably Slavic because of the cultural assimilation that was common among the different territories the Vikings conquered. In any case, the question of Rus origin is not answered, and researchers are still working to establish sufficient evidence that would back up any of the theories that are put forth regarding this matter.

The first western European documents referring to the Rus are the Annals of St. Bertin. These documents recount the time when Emperor Louis the Pious was visited by a Byzantine delegation in his court in 839 A.D. The delegation was sent by Byzantine's ruler and consisted of two men who called themselves Rhos. According to the documentation Louis the Pious inquired about their birth place and they informed him that they were from Sweden. Suspecting that they were Danish spies, Louis the Pious imprisoned them. Latin sources that date to the 10th century mistakenly refer to the Rus as Rugians, who were an East Germanic tribe. For instance, Olga of Kiev is described in one annal as a Rugian queen, and another source from Liutprand of Cremona states that religious governors from Lombard met with the Rus and concluded that they were actually descended from Norsemen.

The intentions of the Vikings in journeying to Russia are surprisingly different from those concerning their ventures into other regions. It is mentioned that they went with the intention of trade as opposed to pillaging. All of this occurred during the 9th century A.D., when their counterparts were creating havoc in other parts of Europe. The waterways of Eastern Europe, streaming north and south, made it very easy for merchandise to be moved between the Baltic and the Black Sea. Close to Lake Ilmen, the headwaters of the Dvina, Volga, and Dnieper waterways were only a short distance away from each other. They would sail the currents into the Baltic, the Black Sea, and the Caspian while carrying products that were essential to basic living. By the mid-9th century the Viking tribes of the Rus had built controlled bases in Novgorod.

These Vikings are said to have sailed across the trading routes from Sweden to reach the border of Russia. While traveling they would come across the Russian waterways such as the Don and the Dnieper. These waterways provided a pathway to the trading centres of Byzantium, Khazaria, Bulgar, and the Caliphate. The Vikings even traveled as far south as Baghdad and also east to the Caspian Sea. They engaged in the trading of slaves, weapons, gold, silver, hides, honey, wax, and silk. They set up the important urban areas of Novgorod, Starja Ladoga, and Kiev. There have been several arguments concerning the roots of their name. The majority believes that "Rus" is the Finnish term for the Vikings in Sweden, yet it appears to have become the standard term for all Russians, regardless of whether they had Slavic or Norse origin. The first reference to the name "Rus" can be found in the Chronicles of St Bertin.

The presence of the Rus in the region during the early 9th century has been proven to be true by historical documents, one such document being the Russian Primary Chronicle. It was composed and collected in Kiev around the beginning of the 12th century. Based on this chronicle, Rurik and his two brothers ruled over the Slavs beginning in 862. Indeed, the Rus appear to have stayed around the districts along the waterways – their relationship with the Slavs was based on tribute and the slave trade. Close to the Rus was the kingdom of the Khazars, which extended around the Black Sea to the Caspian from the Danube. The Khazars were of Turkish origin and are said to have controlled the Rus based on several historical sources.

The Dnieper waterways allowed boats to sail through seven rapids, during which the boats could easily be pulled in to collect their contents. However, in other situations, the shipments would have to be raised above the water and pulled before the waterway would be open for the following ships. Along the Dnieper waterways there was a high risk of raids from hostile groups that would often camp while waiting for the perfect opportunity. One such group recorded in history was called the Turkic Pechenegs.

The Rus would alternate between raiding and conducting business with Byzantium during the 10th and 11th centuries. From around 907 to 1043 A.D. several warships were destroyed around Constantinople by Byzantium's mysterious weapon of Greek fire. There was an incursion in 960, which was quickly put to rest but not before some damage had been done. Kievian Svyatoslav attacked the kingdom of the Khazars and seized the capital called Atil in 965, an event that made the Khazars pull back from the Caspian territory and flee to the Bosphorus shore (now northwestern Turkey), there they settled and tried to begin anew; however, the Rus joined with Byzantium and destroyed the remaining Khazars in 1016.

Around 1016 the Bulgarian King Symeon requested the restoration of a prior tribute that used to be paid by Byzantium to his ancestors. King Nicephoros Phocas declared that he was very offended and so paid the Kievan Russians to invade Bulgaria. With 16,000 men and an Imperial ambassador named Kalokyras under his control Svyatoslav traveled across the Danube in 967 whereupon he attacked and ravaged Bulgaria until he arrived in Thrace. The former ruler of Bulgaria was Nicephoros, who was killed by his wife in partnership with General John Tzimiskes.

Apparently, the Rus had set themselves up in Thrace only for a short duration. Svyatoslav sent impertinent messages to Constantinople stating that the Byzantines would have to leave Europe unless a tremendous tribute was paid. In 977 A.D., Tzimiskes, the leader of a vast and very prepared army, set out on one of the most crucial campaigns of Byzantine military history. In April of the same year he took Great Preslav from the Russians after a heated battle and attacked them in Silesia for three months. The Russians capitulated and vowed to never pillage Bulgaria or Byzantium again in return for freedom and safe passage back to Kiev. In any case, while the Russians were heading home to Kiev, the Pechenegs ambushed and butchered them mercilessly. In fact, the Pechenegs used Svyatoslav's skull as a drinking cup.

As a major part of the treaty, which included marriage to one of the Byzantine princesses and the surrendering of some areas of Byzantium, Kievan Tsar Vladimir consented to become a Christian ruler in 988 A.D. Based on a number of historical documents Vladimir had reviewed the various religious options, rejecting Islam because of its prohibition of liquor, while choosing Orthodox Christianity because of the grandeur of its churches and ceremonies. The Russians committed themselves to become Christians; however, Vladimir conducted the religious ceremonies in Slavic Russian as opposed to Greek, which allowed him to maintain control over Byzantium.

Kievan Tsar Vladimir had led approximately 6000 men, ferried from Sweden to defend and quench a revolt. After the revolt he was burdened with an idle force and did not know what to do with them, but after some thought he sent the men to Byzantium where they became the first group of the Varangian Guards.

Jaroslav the Wise, Vladimir's son, wed a Swedish princess named Ingegerd, and every one of his offspring became linked to various royals. The eldest of his daughters wed the Norwegian King Harald Hardrada, while one daughter became the Queen of Hungary, and another the Queen of France and it was a result of these marriages that numerous churches were built in Russia by subsequent rulers who came from those descendants.

From the 9th to the 12th century a constant movement of the Vikings through Russia has been noted by various historical sources. Interestingly, there was extensive cultural exchange between the Vikings and the Russians. The decrease in trade routes along the territories of Byzantium was one of the major reasons for the reduced significance of the urban areas of Novgorod and Kiev. There were also imperial conflicts and battles between Kievan princes from the 11th to the 13th century. In 1169 Prince Andrei Bogolyubsky captured and gained control over of Kiev and made it the capital of the country. The Rus and the subject Slavs intermarried, causing some political problems since this was against their previous traditions. Although they were yet to be ruled by the relatives of Rurik, they had for all intents and purposes stopped being a different ethnic group from around the 13th century.

Under the leadership of Batu Khan the Mongols secured the Russian regions between 1237 and 1240 A.D. Kiev and other urban areas were conquered, but not before entire populations had been slaughtered; only Novgorod remained standing. The Russians in Kiev only survived in the fiefdom of the Mongols.

In the 13th century the Swedes and the Teutonic Knights of Germany spearheaded numerous attacks. These attacks were repelled by Russian rulers with the outstanding warrior among them being Aleksandr Nevski, who was one of the sons of the Grand Duke of Novgorod. In 1240 Aleksandr Nevski crushed the Swedes on the River Neva. In 1242 he fought alongside the Mongols and dispatched a multitude of Teutonic Knights on the frozen water of Lake Peipus.

The emerging territory of Muscovy (situated in Moscow) crushed a Mongol armed force in 1380; however, Muscovy was once more plundered some time later and again diminished to a vassal. Notwithstanding this, it maintained a persistent resistance and was later able to break free around 1480. Eventually Muscovy became the new focal point of Russian tradition, even though Russia did not have any substantial evidence to demonstrate any significant degree of Viking impact at the time. Fedor, the son of Ivan the Terrible, was the last relative of Rurik who died around 1598 and on whose death the Romanovs took over and established their own policies.

Princes, who were supported by the Duma, ran the administrative affairs of the Rus. The Duma was a consultative body that consisted of nobles referred to as boyars; they were sometimes even more influential than the Tsar. Following them, there was a group of free men called the Veche and any resident using a form of bell called the Veche bell could summon the free men. The people chose and elected a mayor in Novgorod. He was referred to as the Posadnik because he was only elected to rule with the permission of the Veche. His foremost duty was to guard the welfare of the land against the Kievian Prince and as a result Novgorod was autonomous and free from the control of Kiev. Novgorod's special democratic system might be a direct result of its associations with the Vikings and the merchant towns of Western Europe. Despite the fact that the Rus might not really be Slavs, we can say the name Russia came from Rus. Their development of trade, especially along the Dnieper, established the framework for creating a country that would later be called Russia.

Oleg, a Viking chieftain, journeyed to the Dnieper and captured the town of Kiev in 882 A.D and in 911 he arranged a trade agreement with the Byzantine kingdom. Kiev was the first Russian city and so became the focal point of a triangular business relationship between the enlightened Byzantium and other surrounding territories. All kinds of products could be found in Kiev since merchants would gather and amass their merchandise in hopes of finding the best customers. Such products included gold, fruits, wine, garments from the Greeks, stallions and silver from the Hungarians and Czechs, slaves, wax, honey, and hides from the Rus.

The clothing of the early Rus might have been indistinguishable from the ragged garment of the Vikings, but because they were able to disguise themselves as Norsemen, the Rus chose to copy the clothing design of their neighbors. These designs featured hybrid tunics, loose pants, and other eastern or Turkic influenced patterns. Kievan Svyatoslav was documented as shaving his head like the Turkic where he had two long locks that stated his position; also the use of tattoos was common among the Slavs who imitated the Vikings. However, court dresses were highly influenced by the Byzantine styles, because Byzantium silk was the main attire of those within the privileged classes.

The Rus often used their conventional weapons of spear and sword but may have used the Scandinavian two-edged axe at an earlier time. Both in Russia and within the Varangian Guards, there is evidence to show the use of Scandinavian axes later in history. The Rus were later forced to match the weapons and techniques of their neighboring territories. Therefore, in addition to their own mounted forces – that held both spear and sword – the princes in Kiev made use of unpredictable stallion bowmen from the Turkic tribes, as well as curved sabers and helmets that had face masks. In any case, the armies of Kiev had a huge infantry component made up of the elegant druzhina, as well as the modest Voi. The forces had Western-patterned longbows instead of the compound bows that were used in the East. The use of foot soldiers was especially useful due to the forests and swamps found in a large part of Kiev's domain, while a mounted force was needed for the fields.

Kievan strategies developed further due to the danger that arose from horse-arrow based weaponry with the most widely recognized strategy being to place the infantry at the centre with the spearmen, utilizing a shield divider to secure the infantry archers, while rangers held the flanks. Trucks or wagons appear to have been used both for conveying supplies and for making field defenses similar to those among the Pechenegs.

The Radziwill Primary Chronicle has a depiction of mail shirts that reached the elbow and knee; furthermore, there is an impression of Byzantine-style reinforcement that is perhaps lamellar in nature. There were cowhide strips (pteruges) at the shoulder and midriff while a multi-hued tunic secured the shirts of mail. Some of their helmets were framed spangenhelms, while others were made from a single piece of metal or from plates that were bolted to each other in "Incredible Polish". It was their tradition to use a spike that would give a "finishing touch" to everything. The nasals of Russian protective helmets were almost always bent outwards, as this was considered to be their characteristic style. Furthermore, the Radziwill Chronicle shows a Prince wearing a basic bowl-formed helmet.

Both lamellar and mail sections have been found in Russian confinements and a significant number of the Russian mail-rings are very prevalent, about 2 millimeters thick and 15 millimeters in diameter. There appears to be no proof of shields found to date; nevertheless, delineations indicate kite, coffin-shaped, and round shields, in addition to a dented shield that was carried by a Cuman pillager. The Russians seem to have utilized both curved swords in Turkic style (some of them are practically indistinguishable from Seljuk sabers) and the twofold-edged swords that are generally ascribed to the Vikings. There is no confirmation, as far as anyone has found, of a defensive layer that was worn on the leg.

The leaders of Kiev in the 10th century were still Vikings; however, as they settled and became more prosperous, they started to evolve, both socially and culturally, until they became Russians. This theory is especially applicable to Vladimir, who was declared the ruler of Russia in 980 after he captured Kiev from a rival.

Vladimir's younger life was spent fighting, plundering, and gathering women (the annals acknowledge him to have had 800 concubines); however, around 988, he took steps that gave Russia its own unique identity and allowed him to become a "holy" individual among his people. He hired various agents and ambassadors to find out what would be the most suitable religion for his country and after some investigation, they convinced him to choose Greek Orthodox Christianity.

The line of exceptional sovereigns and tsars in Russia appears to be quintessentially Russian, but the progeny of Vladimir governed and ruled in Russia with an unbroken male line for approximately six centuries. The Russian regal administration is therefore as much a piece of Viking history as the Norman success of England or the settlement of inaccessible Iceland and Greenland.

Viking campaigns continued in the west and the east for approximately 300 years, in which there was a decrease in raiding but an increase in trading and settling. Russian history is characterized by a substantial number of archeological discoveries from the east, particularly in Sigtuna and Birka, and by various depictions from runestones. An entire arrangement of tools that were found in a blacksmith's workshop became one of the most popular discoveries from Staraya Ladoga.

The Vikings who came from the east often referenced a region they named Holmgård, said to be Gorodishche (derived from "gorod", which means safeguarded settlement). It is thought to be a trade center that existed at the intersection of the River Volkhov and Lake Ilmen around 800 A.D. Furthermore, many discoveries related to the Scandinavians' garments show that they probably had a settlement in the area. Novgorod was established in the 10th century and situated along the River Volkhov. Iaroslav the Wise, a Russian Prince, journeyed all the way from Gorodishche to Novgorod in the 11th century. He became the husband of Ingegar, a daughter of Olof Skotkonung. Swedish Vikings from the ruling class became a vital part of the country's apparatus fulfilling roles as warriors and merchants.

A large portion of the items that originate from Novgorod show characteristics similar to the possessions of early Russian Christians, with items including adornments, weapons, family articles, tools, toys, and musical instruments. Specifically, there were wooden toys found including a child's horse on wheels. Natural materials such as wood and calfskin were unusually hidden under a smaller layer of muddy topsoil, but which in places could be seven meters thick.

A significant discovery was the workshop of Olisei Gretchen, a famous Greek painter, whose workshop is said to have been in existence since the 12th century. More exceptional discoveries from Novgorod include private letters, letters composed on birch bark, and official records. All of these things suggest a profound understanding of schedules, spirituality in day-to-day life, and the development of the language that was spoken by the Russians.

Around 980 A.D. King Erik Segersall established Sweden's first town and named it Sigtuna. In 995 A.D. his son Olof Skotkonung set plans into motion that saw the first Swedish coins stamped in Sigtuna. In the 11th and 12th centuries, the city of Sigtuna was the main town that encompassed Lake Malar and was also a center for the main body of Christians within the region. A considerable number of runestones and church remains, of about perhaps a thousand years old, are proof of its previous significance.

Some of the Vikings in Russia spent a lot of time enjoying themselves through the various entertainments available at the time. An Arab businessman and historian claimed that the Swedes (who were once colonizers of Russia) would drink so much nabid (possibly beer) that they would be drunk all day.

In some cases, people were said to die while still holding their drinking cups.

The Persian explorer and geographer named Ibn Rustah from the 10th century provides more details, telling how the Rus resided on an isle that took three days to walk round that was protected by dense flora and timberlands. He further mentioned that the Rus harassed the Slavs, utilizing boats to reach them and taking them away as slaves that were later sold. They had no agricultural system of their own, so they survived on what they stole from the Slavs' lands. Also, when a son was conceived, the father would march towards the infant while carrying a sword and toss it down as the child's inheritance.

The Rus lived in wattle-and-smear houses, where they hand-worked iron and bronze to make glass and golden pieces of sculpture. They also used granulating stones, weights, and balances. The principle urban communities had dirt fortifications, offered ship repair and food storerooms, as well as graves with both incinerated and unburnt remains. Among them were craftsmen, blacksmiths, jewel makers, and carvers of bone combs.

Their life revolved around the seasons as they had a schedule to maintain. Starting in November, the Rus lived in small settlements that were built of logs along the waterways and lakes. They would go raiding for tribute, attacking those who declined to pay their due. When the ice melted in April, the Rus would take to the waterways once again, in fleets of ships, but this time they were loaded with their fortunes.

They kept slaves including those from both the Celtic and Russian people. Subsequently, they began to intermarry with Celtic and Russian people, from which numerous

Scandinavians descended to become a part of the Viking family. Even though slavery was a common practice, the Vikings set some slaves free depending upon the circumstances. If a slave did a deed of honor, or saved a Viking from harm, that slave would have a chance to gain his or her freedom.

They had their own form of common assembly during which community and local problems would be resolved, as well as their own version of councils and courts. The assemblies were first introduced in the year 1000 A.D. but were not initially as effective as many thought they would be. Fights continually broke out if things did not go according to the plans of one or more of the parties involved.

Extensive reserves of ancient Viking items have been discovered on Gotland in Sweden in the Baltic Sea, as well as on Lake Ladoga in Russia. Large sums of coins have also been discovered, most likely belongings hidden by those who were being attacked by the Vikings. Out of the 120,000 coins that were discovered in Gotland, 50,000 were linked to an Arabic source while the remaining were either German or English. Objects such as silver Norse-patterned pendants, Slavic-patterned gems, and Arab-patterned bronze decorations – with casing clasps and roundabout shroud latches – were discovered in a Rus graveyard at Gnezdovo, a 10th century residence close to Smolensk. In 1905 a Viking runestone was found on Berzany near the Dnieper at the Black Sea. Similarly in Haghia Sofia in Istanbul various different kinds of runestones have been found.

Byzantium, situated in what was to become Constantinople (currently known as Istanbul), was the wealthiest colony during the time of Norse expansion. It was easier for the

Norsemen to enter into Byzantium via Russian waterways. The Rus made use of two primary trade routes linked to the Baltic Sea. The first trade route swept down the River Dnieper to the Black Sea past Constantinople. The Dnieper path began in Riga on the Baltic Sea. On this route, the merchants would traverse the Western Dvina River down to Vitebsk, where they would travel overland for a while before moving to Smolensk by the Dnieper. However, in the Gulf of Finland, another route was made. Merchants journeyed on the River Neva until they reached Lake Ladoga; from there, they would travel southward on the River Lovat Volkhov to Velikiye Luki before proceeding to Smolensk.

On the Neva River there were usually huge maritime vessels that would journey to Lake Ladoga, which, upon arrival at checkpoints, would have their heavier payloads transferred to smaller vessels so that they could be more easily transported along the smaller interior waterways. To journey from Kiev all the way to the Black Sea, a merchant would spend around a month-and-a-half on the waterways; the Rus took advantage of this time to repair their ships as soon as they reached the Black Sea.

The second trade route was established along Volga to the Caspian Sea. Described as the most traveled course, the Volga pathway began at the Gulf of Finland (situated in the eastern region of Helsinki as an eastern extension of the Baltic); it was here that merchants journeyed across the River Neva to Lake Ladoga, whereupon they would head south on three minor waterways to the two upper extensions of the Volga. En route the Rus merchants had to pay tribute to the Muslim Bulgars and the Jewish Khazars, both of whom controlled the middle passages. Until the 970s – when threatening tribes held it – the Volga route was the main passage for products such as

Arab silver that needed to reach European territories with the Khazar port of Itil and the city of Bulgar the principle trading centers.

On arriving at the Caspian Sea the Rus would sail to the shores that were situated at its southern edge, which is where they would join the Silk Road camel processions, which usually carried merchandise from Persia, Baghdad, and China. Antique coins from Samarkand and China have been discovered in Sweden. This is likely due to the fact that such items were regularly carried along this route.

The Varangians passed on various runestones to the locals that recounted their voyages to modern day Russia, Greece, Ukraine, and Belarus. Large portions of these runestones are still in existence today and do indeed bear witness as physical proof by their very presence. The Varangian runestones recount numerous outstanding Varangian feats and even record the life experiences of several explorers.

In 1748 the Russian Academy of Sciences requested the service of a German historian by the name of Gerhardt Friedrich Müller (1705– 1783). Gerhardt is said to have made the Russians aware of the Western record of the Scandinavians. At the start of an essential discourse in 1749 Gerhardt pronounced that the Scandinavians had conquered all of the Russian territories due to their successful armament. This statement caused outrage among the Russians he was addressing, and earned him great enmity while he was still practicing his profession in Russia. The rest of the discourse focused on a long rundown of Russian losses to the Swedes and the Germans; as a result, Gerhardt was forced to tone down his speech because many people were becoming angry. The strong feedback from Krasheninnikov, Lomonosov, and more Russian historians prompted Gerhardt to pause his discourse on the history of the Russians. Despite the fact that his first publication was destroyed, Gerhardt found a way to put together his findings once again and in 1768 he reproduced it as *Origines Rossicae*.

Despite the turbulence that Gerhardt's dissertation had caused, some Russian historians still acknowledged Gerhardt's view of Russian history; one such historian was Mikhail Pogodin (1800– 75), who followed in the steps of Nikolai Karamzin (1766– 1826). They recognized the narrative of the Primary Chronicle, which claimed that the East Slavs welcomed the Rus and asked them to run their affairs and to restore stability within their chaotic state.

During the 18th century the Normanist hypothesis was initiated by German historian-philologists including August Ludwig von Schlözer (1735 – 1809) and Gottlieb Siegfried Bayer (1694 – 1738), who was from the St. Petersburg Academy of Sciences. Both August and Gottlieb depended on the narrative of The Russian Primary Chronicle, a record composed around the 12th century and one which covered the time from 852 to 1110 A.D. According to this account the Slav requested that the Normans (the Rus) to settle in Novgorod so that they could help in reducing political strife. The Rus agreed to this plan and pushed their administration capabilities to Kiev, which later became their center of defense. During the 19th century German-Russian historian-philologist Ernst Eduard Kunik (1814 – 1899) and the Danish philologist Vilhelm Thomsen (1842 – 1927) promoted this hypothesis. It was noted that past Arabian authors had spoken about the Rus location as, "an island that was secured with the use of swamps and woods". From the 9th and 10th centuries, excavations of tumuli have confirmed the presence of

Scandinavian fighters in places like the region near Lake Ilmen. It is close to the antiquated Novgorod Township and Lake Ladoga, from which the River Neva was said to originate. These Baltic areas have been used to explain the origin of the Rus.

Led by historians such as Lomonosov (1711– 1765), there has been strong criticism from the East Slavic researchers regarding the possibility of Norse invaders. The customary anti-Normanist dogma apparently became irrelevant especially in the beginning of the 20th century; nevertheless, the anti-Normanist contentions were reestablished in Stalinist Russia when it became an official part of Soviet historical studies. Mikhail Artamonov is notable among the individuals who endeavored to bridge both theories. Mikhail argued for the possibility of a nation that was created by the unified efforts of the Southern Rus (from a Slavic origin), the Northern Rus (from a Germanic origin), and the Kievans.

During the post-WWII era Boris Rybakov was a persistent proponent of the anti-Normanist doctrine and he contended that the status of the Scandinavians was not likely to have inspired a welcome from Slavs, who appeared to be significantly more culturally advanced around this time. This argument is also used by Slavicists to refute the narrative of the Primary Chronicle for its claim that the Slavs asked the Rus to rule over them. Boris suggests the possibility that Nestor (the assumed chronicler of the Chronicle) was one-sided in his opposition to the pro-Greek movement led by Vladimir Monomakh. He was instead in favor of the pro-Scandinavian movement that was led by prince Svyatopolk, who was in power at the time. Boris condemned Nestor for being pro-Scandinavian and opposes Nestor's record of

Rurik's welcome with various comparative stories from folk tales around the globe.

Quite a number of non-Normanist dogmas have been mentioned regarding Rus origin, albeit none which have been embraced by the Western scholastic standard. One such theory suggests that there were three initial sovereigns at Caucasus who ruled over the Urartian Empire and – referred to as Russa I, Russa II, and Russa III – they existed from the 8th to 6th century BC and are said to be archived in cuneiform landmarks. In any case, Kiev was established hundreds of years before the Rus came to power. Although the Rus can be said to have been Swedes in 839 A.D, they had become Slavs by 1043 A.D. The Vagarians were acclimatized and when compared to other Vikings in Normandy and in England, they did not leave much of a cultural legacy within Eastern Europe. This near unavailability of recorded cultural influences (besides a few names and maybe the veche-arrangement of Novgorod) is fascinating and as a result the Slavicists referred to the Scandinavians as social chameleons, saying that they came, established themselves rulers and then apparently vanished.

Horace G. Lunt, Omeljan Pritsak and other researchers have provided clarification regarding the basic attempts to infer "ethnicity" on the possible interpretation of scholarly, philological, and archeological signs. According to these researchers the Rus were divergent and had fearsome tribes of enigmatic explorers, including warriors and merchants, who shaped the vast trade networks over the Baltic Seas and the North. The Rus are also said to have been multi-cultural and multilingual and are described as a non-regional group of ocean travelers with trading encampments that contained Vikings as well as Finns, Balts, and Slavs.

In northern Russia there have been discoveries made of various relics of Norse origin. Even so, trade between the south coastlines of the Baltic Sea and the north was fairly common, even from the time of the Iron Age (but limited to coastal regions). Finnic territories and nearby Northern Russia had become a beneficial place for various groups of people; it was the known center for trading animal hides and even though a lot of the merchants were Scandinavians, the dominating traders were the native (Finnic and Baltic) hunters.

The Rus seem to have copied some aspects of the political system of the Khazars, which explains the presence of the Rus chaganus who were present at the Carolingian court in 839 A.D. according to the Royal Frankish Annals. To be a legitimate resident, one was required to be Christian and adopt the culture of the Slavs, a policy that led to the emergence of a group called the Kieven Rus. The tombs of the Kievan Rus appear to have a shallow similarity to the ones that are assumed to be Norse; in fact, it is only the tomb construction that seems comparable, while other things such as the incorporation of weapons, slaves, or horses seem to have no match when compared to the Norsemen. Aside from this, scholars argue whether the Kievan Rus can be said to have emerged from the same tribe as the "Rus", since they supposedly went to the Carolingians in 839 A.D. and pillaged Constantinople in 860 A.D.

Kiev's ascent is baffling. In the 8th century there is little or no information regarding any silver dirham discoveries in Kiev. However, scholars suggested that there should be some evidence for such items due to Kiev's location in the western region of the valuable hide and silver trade links that ran across the Baltic Sea, through the Volga-Kama watersheds, down to the lands of the Muslims. Strongholds and different structures were discovered in the 9th century on a hilltop in Kiev. These structures were made before the legendary presence of the "Rus" near the Dnieper. The marshes around the Kiev region had broad "Slavic" patterned encampments in the 10th century. There is evidence of the trade that was conducted between the Byzantine and Kievan territories, a fact which may have caused a power shift from the north all the way to the Kievan region. Therefore, Kiev seems to have advanced due to the basic trade routes developed by the Norsemen; however, it strategically assumed control over trade since many previous trade centers – operational in the north – had been destroyed, such as the popular Staraya Ladoga.

Additional Reading

Christian, David. (1999) *A History of Russia, Mongolia, and Central Asia*. Blackwell

Danylenko, Andrii. (2004)"The name Rus': In search of a new dimension." *Jahrbueher fuer Geschichte Osteuropas* 52, 1–32.

Dolukhanov, Pavel M. (1996) *The Early Slavs: Eastern Europe from the Initial Settlement to the Kievan Rus*. New York: Longman.

Duczko, Wladyslaw. (2004) *Viking Rus: Studies on the Presence of Scandinavians in Eastern Europe (The Northern World; 12)*. Leiden: Brill Academic Publishers

Franklin, Simon and Shephard, Jonathan. (1996) *The Emergence of Rus: 750–1200*. Longman Publishing Group

Heath, I. (1984) *Byzantine Armies 886-1118*. London: Osprey.

Moscow, H. and Black, C. (1962) *Russia Under The Czars*. London: Cassell.

Pritsak, Omeljan. (1991) *The Origin of Rus'*. Harvard University Press.

Roesdahl, E. (1991) *The Vikings*. London: Guild Publishing.

Stang, Hakon. (1996) *The Naming of Russia*. Oslo: Middelelser.

Chapter Six: Rollo the Warrior

"Many things are better here. Just a few things which were better before."

(Rollo, "Death All 'Round")

There have been many theories regarding the origin of "Rollo". One theory claims that the name came from the Latin roots of the Ancient Norse title "Hrolfr", which is the modern day Icelandic name for Hrolfur and Scandinavian name Rolf. This theory seems to be based on Gesta Danorum, which states that Hrolfr is actually Roluo. Interestingly, another theory states the name might also have been a Latin-origin rendition of an alternative Viking name Hrollaugr. Yet the Normans called him by his mainstream name Rou(f) and sometimes his name was transformed into the Frankish name Rodolf(us), Radulf(us), or the French Raoul, all of which are derived from it.

Rollo (c. 846 – c. 931 A.D.) is for the most part related to one Viking, specifically a person of great status as is stated in the Icelandic Adventures. He is referred to as Gongu-Hrolfr, which is the Ancient Norse title meaning "Hrolfr the Walker". Interestingly, Gongu-Hrolfr is also generally acknowledged as an Ancient Danish variation of Ganger-Hrolf. The "Walker" title was given to him because he was so tall and bulky that he could not be carried by a horse and was thus forced to walk. Some French works do not use "Hrolfr" and only assume Rollo as Gongu-Hrolfr because of the likenesses amongst the attributes and activities given to the two individuals. His name has appeared in different spellings; in Old Norse it is Hrolfr, in Norman it is Rou and in French it is Rollon. The Norman scholar Dudo chronicles that Rollo adopted Robert as a baptismal name. An alternative variant "Roul" is employed as a part of the Norman "Roman de la Rou", which was created by Wace and authorized by King Henry the Second, who was descended from Rollo's ancestry.

Rollo stands out amongst the most powerful Vikings in history and was apparently conceived around the year 860, roughly 20 years after Ragnar Lothbrok's assumed death. His is thought to have died between 928 and 933 A.D.

There are a few speculations regarding the origin of Duke Rollo of Normandy. A reference is made in *Historia Normannorum*, which is the history of Rollo as composed by Dudo of Saint-Quentin. According to this historical document Rollo was the son of a Danish aristocrat and Gurim is said to be the name of Rollo's brother. After the demise of his father, his brother was executed and Rollo was pushed out of Denmark. Dudo presumably had the opportunity to work with relatives and other individuals who actually met Rollo because his work was conveyed by Rollo's grandson, Richard I of Normandy. This may be a reason not to consider Historia Normannorum to be a completely truthful source as it may give a biased account of events.

An 11th-century Benedictine priest and historian, Goffredo Malaterra, proposed that Rollo originated from Norway, from where he traveled to the coastlines of Christian lands with his Norwegian force. William of Malmesbury, an English historian who lived in the 12th century, later promoted this idea. Also a mysterious 12th century Welsh author made reference to Rollo in *The Life of Gruffudd ap Cynan*, and according to this writer Rollo was the brother of a King of Norway who was named Harald Finehair.

Heimskringla and *Orkneyinga*, two popular Icelandic Sagas, recognize Rollo as Hrolf the Walker. As indicated by these adventures, Hrolf was conceived during the 9th century in a western area of Norway, or more precisely in More. The sagas refer to him as the son of Rognvald Eysteinsson (known as "Rognvald the Wise"), the Earl of More and Hildr Hrolfsdottir, an aristocrat. This information may also be misunderstood, as Rollo's relatives came to these conclusions three centuries after his death.

As already stated, Rollo was given the baptismal name of Robert and was a Viking aristocrat of either Danish or Norwegian origin. Historically, he is said to be the first leader of the Scandinavian territory, which soon came to be called Normandy. Rollo's descendants later became the Dukes of Normandy, as well as the Kings of England, after the Normans took over the English territories in 1066. Historical materials have caused considerable debate among researchers as to the origin of Rollo. Dudo of Saint-Quentin recounts a capable Danish aristocrat in disagreement with the Lord of Denmark, who was the father of Rollo and Gurim. After the Lord of Denmark's demise, Rollo was ousted from the region due to political problems.

During the later 900s the Cleric Dudo of Saint-Quentin composed a biography of Rollo and according to him Rollo originally came from Denmark. Rollo's great-grandson was also a scholar like Dudo, and was recognized as Robert the Dane. Even though Dudo probably approached relatives or other individuals with a living memory of Rollo, any predispositions should be ignored as it relays an official life story. As indicated by Dudo, an anonymous ruler from Denmark opposed Rollo's family, which consisted of his father and brother Gurim, and after Rollo's father died Gurim was murdered and Rollo had no choice but to flee Denmark. Dudo seems to be the primary scholar from whose works such details are derived.

In *Gesta Normannorum Ducum,* William of Jumieges also discusses Rollo's early life and tells how Rollo emerged from Fakse, a Danish town. In *Roman de Rou* Wace also touched on the historical background of Rollo, who he referred to as Rou, while Gurim was referred to as Garin. These alternative names can also be found in the Orkneyinga Saga.

Guillaume de Jumieges agrees with the idea that Rollo was of Danish origin. He mentions that the Lord of Denmark murdered Gorm and that Rollo was forced to flee from the region to England, where he met and became friends with Alstem. On the off chance that Alstem was used to refer to Aethelstan – the King of Wessex – the record must been mistaken because of King Aethelstan's succession in 924. Guillaume de Jumieges, according to the historian Freeman, was most likely making reference to "Guthrum-Aethelstan of East-Anglia", in spite of the fact that this does not settle the issue of dates, accepting that the Anglo-Saxon Chronicle is right in recording Guthrum's demise in 890 A.D. Subsequent to recording Rollo's undertakings in Frisia, Guillaume de Jumieges mentions that Rollo arrived at Jumieges while sailing to Seine in 876, which is another speculated date that a historian by the name Houts recommends ought to be rectified to 900. Guillaume de Jumieges says that Rollo defeated "Renaud duc de toute la France", caught "le château de Meulan", crushed and murdered Duke Renaud in another battle, demolished Paris, caught Bayeux, and struck Paris yet again. Meanwhile, his different soldiers crushed Evreux, where they slaughtered "son eveque Sibor". Guillaume de Jumieges records that Rollo attempted to raid Chartres, but pulled back when he was nearly defeated by "Richard duc de Bourgogne" and "Anselme l eveque".

Historians, especially the Icelandic and Norwegian ones, tend to see Rollo as Hrolf the Walker (or Ganger Hrolf). In light of medieval Icelandic and Norwegian tales, Hrolf was one of the sons of Rognvald Eysteinsson, the Earl of More in the Western part of Norway. Orkneyinga Saga referred to Rollo as Hrolf who captured Normandy as son of "Earl Rognwald" and his wife "Ragnhild the daughter of Hrolf Nose". This story confirms that Rollo was so big that no mount could sustain his weight.

Another source comes from Snorre, who confirms what is written in the saga. According to Snorre, "Earl Ragnvald" and his wife Hild had two sons – "Rolf and Thorer". He adds that Rolf was exiled from Norway by King Harald so he journeyed all the way to the Hebrides. He first settled in Orkney before he moved south through Scotland. Eventually, as a commander of a number of Viking warriors, he inevitably conquered Normandy.

The Latin *Historia Norvegiae* is one of the earliest sources of this adaptation of Rollo's prehistory. It was composed in Norway toward the end of the 12th century. Hrolf apparently had a dispute with Harald Fairhair, a Norwegian ruler and after a short battle, he became the Earl of Normandy.

Another of the first known sources to specify Rollo's initial life comes from the French researcher Richer of Reims, who states (in the 900s) that a Norseman named Ketill fathered Rollo. Regarding onomastics, it is intriguing that Richer also mentions a man named Ketill without specifically connecting him to Rollo. He is thought to be the leader of various Norse raids (from 888) that occurred between the Loire and the Seine along the coast of West Francia.

Medieval archives contradict each another when discussing Rollo's family as Danish or Norwegian in ethnicity. It is possible that this dissimilarity arises because of the sharing and swapping of words such as "Norsemen", "Vikings", "Danes", or "Norwegians". In the Medieval Latin writings, Dani vel Nortmanni uses the term "Norsemen" or "Danes" arbitrarily.

In *Chronique des ducs de Normandie*, (1140-1200 A.D.) a writer named Benoit (most likely Benoît de Sainte-More) wrote that Rollo was conceived in a village called "Fasge". This fact was later translated differently as alluding to Fauske in modern day Norway or perhaps as being an ambiguous village that no longer exists today. Benoit additionally revived the assertion that Rollo was oppressed by a nearby ruler and ran away at that point to "Scanza Island", which is actually Scania (or Skane in Swedish). Despite the fact that Fauxe was very near to Scania, the rocky landscape of "Fasge" as portrayed by Benoit suggests a greater similarity to Fauske.

Interestingly, in historical documents such as Hversu Noregr byggdist ("How Norway was settled") and the two stories (Heimskringla and Orkneyinga), there is what researchers call the Yngling ("Fairhair-genealogy") ancestry of Rollo. They appear to point to an ancestry of Rollo, tracing it to Fornjot, a primitive ruler in charge of Kvenland and Finland. This assumed Yngling "Fairhair-genealogy" ancestry of Rollo incorporates Rognvald Eysteinsson, who founded the Earldom of Orkney.

The parentage of Rollo or Rolf is unverifiable and the order of his life is muddled. The subject of Rollo's origins has long provoked heated debate amongst historians, especially the Danish and Norwegian historians of the 19th and 20th centuries, particularly during the buildup to Normandy's millennium commemoration in 1911. Even today, there is still an ongoing argument among historians and researchers regarding Rollo's origin.

Rollo was a leading warrior of the Norse warships that were headed by Sigfred – the fleet that attacked Paris in 885 A.D. According to some historical sources, the French ruler sent an ambassador to the Scandinavian force to find out who their leader was, so that he could meet with him to avoid an attack. When the ambassador requested that they tell him who their leader was, the Norsemen answered him that every one of them was rightfully a leader on his own.

Sigfred withdrew in 886 after an agreement was made in which he would receive some tribute in return. Nevertheless, Rollo did not leave until the French king came and offered him some form of tribute, as well as his daughter, where upon Rollo went on to raid Burgundy. Later on, he and his followers (referred to as the Norsemen or the Danes) returned to the Seine.

Rollo's warriors went on to invade Paris and Chartres in 911. Entreaties for help from Joseaume, the Bishop of Chartres, were answered by Robert, the Marquis of Neustria and Richard, the Duke of Burgundy and Manasses and Count of Dijon. On July 20th of 911, at the Battle of Chartres, they crushed Rollo in spite of the fact that the French King Charles the Simple failed to show.

In accordance with the Treaty of Saint-Clair-sur-Epte, made with King Charles, Rollo promised his loyalty to the lord, changed his name to the Frankish form, and converted to

Christianity, presumably with the baptismal name Robert. Consequently King Charles conceded land to Rollo between the Epte and the ocean and also parts of Brittany. In addition, as indicated by Dudo of St. Quentin, the hand of the king's daughter Gisela was given to Rollo in marriage. Nevertheless, as of yet, this marriage – and Gisela herself – remain absent from Frankish sources.

Rollo was likewise the main leader of Normandy, situated in the city of Rouen. There exists some contention among historians on the matter of whether Rollo was a "duke" (dux) or whether his position was equal to that of another rank under Charlemagne. After 911 Rollo remained consistent with his pledge of safeguarding the banks of the Seine in accordance with the Treaty of Saint-Clair-sur-Epte. Nonetheless, he continued to act like a typical Viking leader as he led raids on several regions including Flanders.

After Charles was dismissed by Robert I, Rollo considered his promise to the King of France to be over, which saw him set out westward to capture many regions. After the arrangements with the French aristocrats came to an end, Rollo was granted Bayeux and Le Mans then, in 924, he attacked and captured Bessin. The next year saw the Normans attack Picardy. Rollo went on to share the land between the Epte and Risle waterways among his chieftains and settled with a considerable amount of wealth in Rouen. As time passed, Rollo's men intermarried with the local women and created the Norman Family.

It is said that Rollo had two main wives. There is Poppa, who, according to Dudo of Saint-Quentin, was apparently the daughter of Count Berenger and was taken captive during an attack at Bayeux. She was his courtesan or wife and they had children together including William Longsword (Guillaume), Gerloc, and maybe Kadlin. William Longsword was conceived overseas and became Rollo's successor. Gerloc became the wife of William III, the Duke of Aquitaine. Dudo fails to mention details regarding her mother, even though this information is found within another historian's work. Ari the Historian states that Kadlin was the daughter of Ganger Hrolf, who was related to Rollo. She wedded a Scottish King by the name of Beollan and bore him a girl who was named Midbjorg, who was later captured by an Icelandic Norseman named Helgi Ottarsson, who married her. Midbjorg gave birth to the poet Einarr Helgason and eventually had a grandson named Gudrun Osvifrsdottir, who is the hero of the Laxdoea Saga.

According to some Icelandic sources, and a medieval Irish record called Banshenchas, Rollo married again in Scotland and a daughter, Kadlin, was born. Subsequently, Kadlin married Beollan mac Ciarmaic, the King of South Brega. Rollo and Poppa's marriage is confirmed by Dudo, who notes that – when Bayeux was taken by force – that Rollo took away the Count of Rennes' beautiful daughter, Poppa. Together they had a son named William Longsword who later succeeded Rollo. According to some sources, Poppa was his wife in danico, which is a free marriage in the Old Norse convention.

It is indicated that his other wife was the daughter of Charles III of France, Gisela of France (d. 919). Her father gave her to Rollo as a part of the Treaty of Saint-Clair-sur-Epte that was signed with Rollo during the siege of Paris; her father also became the Duke of Normandy through this treaty. Legends say that Rollo treated Gisela in a cruel and barbarous manner. As a consequence of this treatment, she went to Normandy accompanied by two of her father's knights; however, Rollo captured these knights and later executed them in the Place du Vieux Marche in Rouen in front of many people. As Rollo was very displeased with Gisela, he divorced her and married his previous wife Poppa again in 919. However, historians argue that neither the existence of Princess Gisela, nor the marriage, can be confirmed by historical records. According to some theories Gisela was an illegitimate daughter of King Charles. If not, it means that she was only five years old when she married Rollo, taking into account that King Charles was wed in 907. The customs at the time allowed men to have more than one wife and even though Poppa was the pagan wife of Rollo he was still allowed to marry another woman. Interestingly, a priest joined him in marriage to Gisela de France, the daughter of the French King Charles the Simple in a Christian ceremony. It appears that Rollo left Gisela later on. Afterwards Rollo remarried and legitimized his son Guillaume and daughter Gerloc. Rollo and Poppa had to send Guillaume to be groomed by clerics to ensure his right to succeed his father as Duke of Normandy. Guillaume was later called William Longsword.

Rollo is considered to be the great-great-great-grandfather of William the Conqueror. Through William he is a progenitor of the modern day British Royal family, and in addition, a precursor of all present European rulers and a large number of claimants of dissolved European thrones. A genetic examination of the remaining parts of Rollo's grandson, Richard I, and great-grandson Richard II, has been done, with the aim of determining the beginnings of the renowned Viking warrior.

Additional Reading

Abbo of Saint-Germain-des-Pres. (2007) *Viking Attacks on Paris: The Bella parisiacae urbis of Abbo of Saint-Germain-des-Pres.* Edited and translated by Nirmal Dass. Peeters.

Bates, David. (1982) *Normandy before 1066.* Longman.

Bates, David. (1993) "Rouen from 900-1204: from Scandinavian settlement to Angevin "Capital"" in *Medieval Art, Architecture and Archaeology at Rouen.* Edited by Jenny Stratford. Maney, 1–11.

Christiansen, Eric (2002). *The Norsemen in the Viking Age.* Blackwell Publishers Ltd.

Crouch, David (2002). *The Normans: the History of a Dynasty.* London: Hambledon and London.

Crouch, David, and Kathleen Thompson, eds. (2011) Normandy and its Neighbors, 900-1250. Brepols.

Dudo of St. Quentin (1998) *History of the Normans.* ed. and trans. Eric Christiansen. Woodbridge, Suffolk: The Boydell Press.

Ferguson, Robert (2009). *The Hammer and the Cross: A New History of the Vikings.* London. Allen Lane, an imprint of Penguin Group.

Fitzhugh, William W. and Ward, Elizabeth (2000). *Vikings: The North Atlantic Saga.* Smithsonian Institution Press.

Flodoard of Reims. (2011) *The Annals of Flodoard of Reims, 919-966*. Translated and edited by Bernard S. Bachrach and Steven Fanning. University of Toronto.

Haywood, John. (1995) *The Penguin Historical Atlas of the Vikings*. Penguin.

Jesch, Judith. (2004) "Vikings on the European Continent in the Late Viking Age." *Scandinavia and Europe 800-1350*. Edited by Jonathan Adams and Katherine Holman. Brepols, 255-268.

Konstam, Agnus (2002). *Historical Atlas of the Viking World*. Checkmark Books

Urbanski, Charity. (2013) *Writing History for the King: Henry II and the Politics of Vernacular Historiography*. Cornell UP.

Wace. (2004) *The History of the Norman Peoples: Wace's Roman de Rou*. Translated by Glyn S. Burgess from the text of A. J. Holden; notes by Glyn S. Burgess and Elisabeth van Houts. Boydell.

William of Jumièges. (1995) *The Gesta Normannorum Ducum*. Translated and edited by Elisabeth van Houts. Clarendon.

William of Malmesbury. (1904) *Chronicle of the Kings of England*. Translated by Rev. John Sharpe, edited by J. A. Giles. George Bell and Sons.

Chapter Seven: Vikings in Ireland

"The wind is fierce tonight

it tosses the sea's white mane

I do not fear the coursing of a quiet sea

by the fierce warriors of Lothlend"

(Anonymous poem "Is acher in gaith in-nocht...")

(Source: Revolvy)

The historical narrative of Ireland includes the period from the initial Norse raids, to attacks brought by the Normans, with the initial two hundred years of this era known for the Norse attacks and the resulting Viking settlements near the coast. Several Norse ports were set up at Dublin, Waterford, Limerick, Cork, and Wexford, all of which went on to become the first big cities in Ireland. Ireland is comprised of numerous semi-autonomous tuatha, each of which has its own unique characteristics. During this period several different groups tried to increase their political power over the entire territory, with the first two hundred years seeing competition between the High Kings of Ireland, including the divisions to the north and south of the Ui Neill. Out of all of these rivals Brian Boru very nearly became the sole ruler but was not fully successful in the end. Nonetheless, he was the first High King of this time period who was not from the Ui Neill.

The Irish called the Vikings names such as Gaill ("Gentiles" or foreigners), Normanni, and Danes while paying little attention to the fact that they might have had their origins in Scandinavia. At the beginning of Viking interest in Ireland the new intruders were simply referred to as Gaill, but over time the Irish started to recognize two sorts of Vikings which they classified as the white foreigners (Finn-Gaill) and dark foreigners (Dubh-Gaill). In their usage of these two names the Irish intended to recognize two separate sorts of Viking raiders, although it is not clear what the real difference between the groups was. It could not be a physical or racial sort, since the Scandinavian groups of this period had no such divisions among them, due to their origination from similar Germanic regions.

A few researchers have suggested that the Norwegian Vikings were addressed using the term Finn-Gaill, while the Vikings of Danish origin were the ones considered to be Dubh-Gaill; nevertheless, this appears to be far-fetched for the neighboring Welsh writers made no such distinction – the greater part of the Welsh expressions for "Viking" were combined with the expression "dark" in order to portray them as "dark hearted", or insidious. For instance the Vikings were referred to as Black Gentiles (Y Kenedloed Duon) and Black Norsemen (Y Normanyeit Duon).

The early Vikings were individuals whose origin can be traced back to Denmark and Norway. In the 700s pressure from an increase in population in Scandinavia had forced numerous nobles and warriors to look for residence elsewhere. They were mainly the youth, those who had no chance to get anything from their father's bequest and so it was that aristocrats with little to lose assembled gatherings of warriors and sailed down the coast to raid various settlements. The

Vikings were merchants, gifted blacksmiths, and metalworkers. Many settled in places like Russia, Iceland, and Greenland. Numerous Vikings also settled in Ireland and set up towns along the coastline including Dublin (which they began to establish in 841), Wexford, Cork, and Limerick. These new settlements became active centers of trading and business dealings in Ireland and Europe.

The Vikings were very severe in their treatment of their captives and their clear lack of regard for anything besides plunder certainly infused fear into the individuals who experienced and heard stories of the Norsemen's raids. Nonetheless, the impact of these attacks should not be exaggerated. A raid occurred, generally, once every year and the likelihood of being hit in any given year more than once was very low. Life continued as would be expected in Ireland; however, the Irish people did not simply relax and let the Vikings plunder at will. While most Irish retaliations on the Vikings ended in defeat, a small number of them were successful. The Ulaid crushed a band of invaders in 811; another group was defeated in Connaght in 812, and one in Munster around the same time.

When the Vikings first landed in Ireland it appeared to be ruled by the Ard Ri, who considered himself the High King of the Irish. The land seemed to have warring kingdoms that gave reluctant, or at least a two-faced tribute, to the ceremonial overlords of the Ui-Naill. The Ui-Naill family controlled the North of Ireland; the Southern Ui-Naill was in charge of Meath, while Njall-Caille of the northern Ui-Naill ran the affairs of Ulster. When the Vikings began to arrive in Ireland's territory the Ard Ri was only "King of Tara" in name and nothing more. Although he seemed to have ruled, he did so from Derry, which was not even in the kingdom of Meath where Tara was located. The warring kings of Ireland were occupied with internal battles among themselves and were more interested in the control of more territories or the collection of cows as tribute. It was their regular conflicts that allowed the Vikings to achieve such incredible triumphs in Ireland. It would be safe to say that the disorderliness of the relatively small Irish kingdoms, with their numerous competitions and conflicts, eventually caused the destruction of the Celts.

The first Viking plunderers showed up in Irish waters around the end of the 8th century, they were exclusively from Norway. The first recorded Viking attack in Irish history happened in 795 A.D. on Rathlin Island of Lambay, off the coast of Antrim where the church was pillaged. On the west bank potentially similar raiders targeted the religious communities on Inismurray and Inisbofin. The Scottish island of Iona was also attacked around the same time. This was shadowed by a strike on Brega's coast in 798 and Connachtin's coast in 807. These initial Norse battles were, for the most part, short and severe.

The first Viking strikes were carried out during the golden age of Ireland's expansion of Christianity and signaled the beginning of two centuries of discontinuous fighting, with groups of Norse raiders pillaging religious communities and towns all through Ireland. A large number of the first marauders originated from the creeks of Norway's west side. In the beginning, they are said to have traveled to Shetland, after which they went south toward Orkney. The Norse then journeyed along the Atlantic coast of Scotland and ended up in Ireland. During the initial raids they headed out toward Ireland's west coast and then to the Skellig Islands that are situated near County Kerry. The first attacks on Ireland appear to have been an aristocratic free venture, and renowned leaders show up in the Irish records, including Saxolb from 837, Turges from 845, and Agonn from 847.

For the initial four decades, between 795 and 836, the attacks followed a pattern of hit-and-run by frequently independent raiders. Battles occurred on the coast for the most part; no Viking assault drove any more than twenty miles inland. These raids were hard to repel; however, the Vikings were defeated in some cases. In 811, the Ulaid butchered an attacking force of Vikings. The year after the forces of Umall, along with the king of Eoganacht, Locha Lein, dispatched another group of raiders. By 823 the Vikings had been over the entire region and in 824 the island's religious community at Sceilg was attacked off the coast of Kerry and the religious city of Armagh was invaded three times in 832.

From that point onwards there were regular battles. Even though the locals stood their ground, Scandinavian kingdoms were eventually set up at Dublin, Limerick, and Waterford. The kings of Dublin felt that they were sufficiently protected and in the mid-10th century a few of them even controlled both Dublin and Northumberland; however, the probability that Ireland would be bound together under Scandinavian rule was lost during the Battle of Clontarf in 1014. During this battle the Irish Scandinavians, bolstered by the Earl of Orkney and some local Irish, witnessed a tragic downfall. However, in the 12th century, the English invaders of Ireland found the Scandinavians still prevailing (however Christianized) in places such as Dublin, Waterford, Wexford, Cork, and Limerick.

Arts, crafts, and ornaments in Ireland and Britain mirrored those of Scandinavian culture, probably because the Vikings carried out business at Irish markets in Dublin. Some excavations discovered imported objects from England, Byzantium, Persia, and central Asia. By the 11th century Dublin had become so densely populated that the people began to build houses outside of the walls.

Aed Oirdnide from the Cenel nEogain in the Northern Ui Neill worked towards becoming King of Tara in 797, after the demise of his forerunner, father-in-law, and political opponent, Donnchad Midi. This method of kingship was very similar to the usual Ui Neill political development, where power rotated consistently between Cenel nEogain and Clann Cholmain of the Southern Ui Neill. During his reign he campaigned in Mide, Leinster, and Ulaid in order to declare his power; however, he did not fight in Munster, unlike Donnchad (Duncan).

Thomas Charles-Edwards credits Aed for the lack of any significant Viking interest in Ireland during his rule after 798 as the archives do not provide any reference to Aed fighting against the Viking raiders. Aed was associated with the religious group at Armagh, and a supporter of the family of Patrick; however, the Clann Cholmain and the Cenel Conaill, who both struggled for power against Aed in Ui Neill, became supporters of the family of Columba. During Aed's rule the Columban familia set up another convent at Kells, an imperial site under the ownership of Armagh. Since the assembly of Columba tried to suspend Aed in 817, it is very possible that not all contentions were settled after all.

Fedelmid mac Crimthainn of the Eoganacht Chaisil consented to the majesty of Munster in 820, initiating a 130-year control by this administrative office of Eoganachta. Combining military ventures – with the control of religious authorities – he set forth a strategy to obtain land forcefully so that he could oppose the Ui Neill's increase in power. Conchobar mac Donnchada (Duncan) became the successor of Aed Oirdnide, when he became the High King of Ui Neill in 819. Not too long after his ascension to the throne Feidlimid challenged Conchobar and even carried out some attacks upon Mide and Connacht. He also interfered with the affairs of the high king, especially in regards to the issue of Armagh. In 827 Conchobar and Feidlimid arranged to meet at Birr in order to come up with a peace agreement. The fact that the king of Munster could make the high king agree to broker peace was a confirmation of Feidlimid's increasing power.

Niall Caille succeeded Conchobar in 833 and here we observe a reference in the archives of a Ui Neill, who led an army against the Vikings. Niall was able to defeat the Viking raiders in Derry that the same year. He also tried to increase Ui Neill's influence in the south because in 835 he took an army to Leinster, introduced Bran mac Faelain as king of Leinster, and even attacked Mide. This resulted in a conflict between him and Feidlimid, which necessitated a creation of a truce that was agreed upon in 838. However, this great royal meeting – referred to as rigdal mor – did not bring about any long-term peace because Feidlimid soon drove an army into Mide and settled at Tara in 840. With this move he boldly challenged the Ui Neill in the north. In 841 Feidlimid was defeated by Niall in Leinster and forced to retreat. His successors in the south would not have the capacity to challenge the north again for the next 150 years.

During the 830's and 840's the major focus of the Vikings came to bear on the Irish religious groups. Because of the regular civil conflicts and battles in Ireland, the Irish used the religious communities as asylums for high positioned individuals, possessions, domesticated animals, and even clerical resources and adornments. The sacred nature of the religious communities was highly valued by the warring Irish groups, unlike the Vikings, who simply considered the communities as places to be plundered. The typical Viking attack followed the pattern of a hit-and-run strike that was intended to maximize their profits; after that, they usually left the region, long before the Irish could assemble a powerful enough army to defend themselves.

The Vikings plundered religious communities on Ireland's west coast in 795, and afterward spread out to cover whatever remained of the coastline. The raids continued in 821 and became more frequent in the following decades. The Vikings started to set up fortified camps and longphorts along the Irish shore and began to winter in Ireland as opposed to withdrawing to Scandinavian or British bases. The first longphorts, according to records, were at Annagassan (Linn Dúachaill) and Dublin, where they were located on the River Liffey. They were likewise moving further inland to strike, frequently making use of waterways such as the Shannon, then afterwards withdrawing to their coastal bases; eventually these sporadic attacking groups coming together to form a full-fledged army. In 837 the annals mention a fleet of sixty longships on the Liffey that carried 1500 men.

The Viking's raids had a greater effect on the north and east of the island. For the first forty years the raids were solely the doing of scattered Viking groups. From 830 onward the groups were made up of expansive fleets of Viking ships. From about 830, the attacks became much more serious in Ireland. In 832, for example, there was massive plundering in the vicinity of Cianachta while the attackers stayed close to the waterways in Louth and Norsemen hit the regions under the control of Connacht and Ui Neill of southern Brega in 836. A group of sixty boats showed up over the Boyne while an equivalent force appeared over the Liffey in 837 and before long the Vikings had advanced up the Erne and the Shannon and put a fleet on the Lough Neagh.

Between 840 and 841 the Scandinavians – surprisingly – spent the winter on the Lough Neagh and in 841 a longphort was set up at Dublin and at Annagassan in Louth. They used these locations to raid the west and the south. In 841 – 842 they spent the winter at Dublin and with another substantial fleet arriving in 842. In the same year came the first mention of cooperation amongst Scandinavians and the Irish; however, this might have occurred prior to this time. From the shores of Lough Ree the Vikings pillaged a large area of Irish territory in 844. Mael Seachnaill, high king of the Ui Neill struck the Vikings, caught one of the leaders named Turgesius, and drowned him in Lough Owel in Westmeath. From 840 the Vikings started building up regular long-lasting bases on the coasts with Dublin becoming one of the most important settlements for the Vikings in the long term. The Irish eventually became used to the Vikings' presence and culture and at times they even became allies, formed Norse-Irish alliances and intermarried, it was also at this point that the Vikings began to participate actively in the internal political affairs of Ireland.

For a brief period of time around 900 A.D. the Vikings were harried out of Ireland; however, they came back to Waterford in 914 to establish what they thought might turn into Ireland's first city. Alternate longphorts were soon recaptured and formed into their own urban communities and towns. They ravaged convents, places of worship, the fortifications of Irish Lords, and even homesteads. In 840 the Vikings also invaded Lough Neagh and the religious community of Armagh where they pillaged and caused havoc for a whole year. A significant number of researchers and ministers of the Louth religious community were caught and sold into slavery. After this, the Vikings set up their stronghold bases at Annagassan and Dublin in 841. They further plundered Birr, Clonmacnoise, and Clonfert, and the bishop of Armagh was caught and taken away in 845.

This was the most extraordinary time of Viking movement, as the Irish Kings appeared to have little ability to lessen the continuous destruction of large areas of their Provinces. The southern Ui Neill were defeated by the Vikings, even as they made an impressive effort to drive them out. Before the end of the Viking age, a significant number of the ministers themselves had taken to battling the Vikings, but just as it looked as though Ireland was going to be overcome by the Vikings completely, the raids slowly withered away and it was at this point that the Irish kings battled back against the Vikings with ferocity. Since they now had stable settlements and stronger forces, they were in a position to attack. Mael Seachnaill defeated a Viking force close to Skreen in County Meath and murdered 700 of them in cold blood. At Castledermot in Kildare, the joint forces of the kings of Munster and Leinster defeated a substantial number of Viking raiders. The recently established Viking settlement at Cork was destroyed and, in 849, Mael Seachnaill brought the Norse-controlled area of Dublin back under Irish control.

Between the years 849 and 852, new Vikings, presumably from Denmark, landed along the Irish Sea coast where they got into multiple clashes with the more settled Vikings. In 853 Olaf the White landed in Dublin, and with Ivar, he expected to take control of the Viking settlement there. The Vikings at Waterford defeated the King of Osraige, but were butchered in

860, this destruction went even further as a longphort settlement at Youghal was annihilated in 866. In 887 Connachtmen defeated the Limerick Vikings and in 892 the Vikings of Waterford, Wexford, and St. Mullins were conquered.

Thorgest (Turgesius in Latin) is one of the first Viking leaders to be named in history. The Annals of the Four Masters link him to the raids on Mide, Connacht, and the congregation at Clonmacnoise in 844 A.D. He was captured and killed in Lough Owel by the King of Mide, Mael Sechnaill mac Mail Ruanaid.

Olchobar mac Cinaeda of Munster, alongside Lorcan mac Cellaig of Leinster, destroyed a Norse army in 848 at Sciath Nechtain. Surprisingly, the leader of the Vikings is shown in history as having sovereignty from Lochlann. Mael Sechnaill, who was the current High King, disposed of another army at Forrach that same year. These victories shaped the foundation of a consulate that was sent to the Frankish King Charles the Bald, as is described in the Annales Bertiniani.

In 853, Olaf, known as a "son of the king of Lochlann," journeyed to Ireland. Lochlann is part of modern-day Norway and is currently viewed as more of a Scandinavian state in the Western Isles of Scotland. Olaf controlled the governance of the Vikings in Ireland, and most likely shared this rule with Ivar, who was referenced in the Irish Annals in 857. For the next twenty years Olaf and Ivar significantly influenced Ireland and its waterways. Furthermore, for the next two hundred years the descendants of Ivar the Uilmair were involved in political issues.

The Norse, interestingly enough, entered into agreements with different Irish rulers at that time. This happened in the mid-

9th century. In 842 Cerball mac Dunlainge, who had fought off Viking raiders in 846, became the king of Osraige. After 858, however, he allied himself with Olaf and Ivar against Mael Sechnaill while battling in Munster and Leinster. In 859 they attacked Mael Sechnaill's main heartland in Mide but were not successful and as a result Cerball was forced to surrender to Mael Sechnaill later that year. These alliances were in no way lasting. Cerball was allied with Mael Sechnaill in 860 in a campaign against Aed Findliath of Northern UiNeill. Similarly, Olaf and Ivar allied themselves with Aed, but despite these alliances Cerball and Aed still appeared to be allies in Leinster in 870.

Mael Sechnaill had more accomplishments as High King than Niall Caille and Conchobar Donnchada when it came to managing the south. He was able to force Munster to surrender in 858 and also managed to get Osraige to surrender in 859. Since he was successful in controlling Ulaid, Connacht, and Leinster he was portrayed as the king of all Ireland by the Annals of Ulster (ri h-Erennuile). During the last years of his rule he experienced resistance from his UiNeill family of Ailech and Brega, whose interests were aligned with those of the Norse of Dublin. Mael Sechnaill's phenomenal achievement in becoming the high authority over all of Ireland was overshadowed by the constant protests relating to Irish administrative issues. After Mael Sechnaill joined with several regions including that of Ulaid, Connacht, Osraige, Leinster and Munster, a group of UiNeill kings attacked him at the end of his rule.

Aed Findliath, the king of Ailech, was the most prominent king in Northern UiNeill and after the death of Mael Sechnaill he made a royal list of those qualified enough to be High King. This list was based on a planned political system where this position rotated between Ceneln Eogain of the northern region and Clann Cholmain of Mide. His suitability was debated and he never became the High King of Ireland, nonetheless, he had achieved a few victories against the Norse; one such victory was the destruction of all the Norse longphorts in 866. Aed had taken the opportunity while Olaf was fighting in Pictland; he brought a substantial amount of Norse warriors into Ireland with him. Even then the Vikings never figured out how to build long-lasting settlements in the north. Aed Findliath's achievement may have impeded the economic development of the north and eventually triggered the expansion of port-towns like those on the eastern and southern sides, on which the kings of Leinster and Munster relied for their income.

The last report of Olaf mentions that he and Ivar came back to Dublin in 871 A.D. It is important to note that Ivar is eulogized as the great leader of the Norsemen by The Annals of Ulster and after his death there were regular shifts in rule among the Norse in Ireland which caused internal power struggles to occur. Mael Finnia mac Flannacain from Brega, alongside Cerball mac Muirecain from Leinster, joined forces against the Vikings of Dublin in 902, after which the Vikings were forced to leave Ireland.

A group of Vikings, under the control of Hingamund, were forcibly removed from Ireland and given permission from the Saxons to settle in Wirral, located in Northwest England. "The Three Fragments" describes the presence of some Irishmen amongst the Vikings and it is said that while the king was ill the queen sent an appeal to the Irishmen living in Wirral. Further evidence of an Irish population in Wirral originates from the name of the town of Irby, which means "farmstead of the Irishmen," and St Bridget's Church in West Kirby, which was established by the Christian Vikings of Ireland.

Historians often throw themselves into discourse about the possible influence that the Viking settlements had on literature and academia. Scholarly movements, which the Irish were well known for in the early medieval period, comprised of works of poetry, the production of religious Christian writings, the advancement of science and the organization of a great number of legal articles. Sponsorship for academics and research usually came from the Irish kings, who respected the availability of court researchers. They treated them as a vital part of governance because they could be used to strengthen the royal image through the poetry or panegyrics that such academics created.

Since the appearance of the Norsemen, however, it seems that any academics gradually began to lose their sponsorships, what's more, a few kings would have turned their focus to more pressing matters such as the fight against the Vikings and Irish kings – or the settling of treaties with them – while also tapping into the financial advantages that Viking trade would have brought. While this was going on in Ireland, there was a larger presence of Irish academics in Frankish Europe, particularly within the circles of the Carolingian court. Irish researchers (generally known as peregrini), such as Sedulius Scottus and John Scottus Eriugena, were some of the most significant people of mainland Europe at the time, as they were learning and tutoring a number of subjects including theology and political philosophy.

There were several Irish scholars who lived alongside the Norsemen for a short period of time but were forced out, and so it is that the Vikings are often assumed to be the primary cause for impeding the spread of Irish culture.

In 857 A.D. Ivar the Boneless, the son of Ragnar Lothbrok, became the co-official of Dublin and offered control to Olaf, a combined rulership that continued until 873 A.D. when Ivar died. In the meantime the children and grandsons of Ivar set themselves up in Britain as the leaders of Viking Jorvik (present day York in England). After Ivar's demise, and for the following two decades, there were battles and uprisings in Dublin. The rulers of Leinster and Brega consolidated against the Norsemen of Dublin, ambushed their encampment, and expelled them from Ireland in 902.

Later a broad integration between the Irish and the Norse took place. Olaf was the ruler of Dublin around 900 A.D and was married to Aed Finnliath's daughter. Aed Finnliath reigned over the northern UiNeill. Furthermore, the Hiberno-Norse had taken steps toward converting to Christianity. The chronicles documenting Ivar's passing in 872 stated that he went to rest in heaven. In 902, after being forced to flee from Dublin, Ivar's descendants – portrayed in the records as the UiImair – played a significant role around the Irish Sea and other sources mention their movements in Strathclyde, Northumbria, Pictland, and the Isle of Man.

Another Viking fleet arrived in Waterford Harbor in 914 and the UiImair was soon in power again, taking control over the Viking exercises in Ireland. Ragnall communicated with a force in Waterford, while Sitric arrived at CennFuait (thought to be close to Leixlip) in Leinster. After Flann Sinna, Niall Glúndub took over as the UiNeill High King in 916 and moved into Munster to wage war against Ragnall, yet no definitive battle ever took place. The soldiers of Leinster were under the command of Augaire mac Ailella and took a heavy loss in the Battle of Confey while fighting Sithric's forces whereupon Sithric was able to regain power over Dublin through this triumph against Leinster's men. Ragnall sailed out to Ireland again in 918 and made another attempt to become the ruler of York. A Dublin-York alliance was created, with Sithric in Dublin, and Ragnall in York; this would have a tremendous impact on England and Ireland for the next fifty years.

Another and more serious time of Viking establishment in Ireland started in 914. A period of raiding began in 914, with the entry of a vast armada of Viking ships in Waterford harbor. They quickly recaptured their settlement of Vadrefjord (Waterford) from which the Irish had ousted the previous Vikings fifty years earlier. Fortified by a fleet that arrived the next year the Vikings launched a progression of offensive attacks into the region of Munster, and later Leinster, where they met minimal Irish resistance as they looted both ministerial and gradFhene (ordinary citizen) settlements. They ravaged the convents such as the ones in Cork, Aghaboe, and Lismore, then in 915 Munster was attacked, with the ruler of Tara being defeated while attempting to assist the Munstermen. Led by Sitric at Leixlip the Norsemen also killed the ruler of Leinster. The Scandinavian kings of Dublin tried to increase their power in York during the two decades that followed. Their interest in Ireland turned out to be limited to Dublin itself and its surroundings. The Irish had by now started to run counter raids with some level of success. In 936 the ruler of Tara set Dublin ablaze and ransacked it in 944. At the onset of the second half of the 10th century there was a great decrease in power in Dublin.

The Vikings kept on attacking inland from their towns of Dublin, Cork, and Waterford. In 921 they established another town on the south-east tip of Ireland called Wexford, and after a year settled the town of Limerick close to a passage at the mouth of the River Shannon on the west bank. The Vikings in Ireland spent a considerable amount of effort assimilating the Nordic Kingdom that their Viking generations had cut out of Anglo-Saxon England by overcoming and absorbing Northumbria, East Anglia, and parts of Mercia of England, this kingdom would eventually become known as the Danelaw. Back in Ireland, as the impact of the Vikings declined, they focused more on establishing Dublin as a trade city; and by 934 they had control over the other Viking towns in Ireland. In its day Dublin was one of the most important urban communities in the Nordic world as a popular economic center, especially for the slave trade. Dublin separated itself from the Danelaw in 952 and henceforth, after the separation, had its own line of Viking Kings.

In the end the Vikings settled down in the areas they had won and by 950 they had stopped raiding in Ireland and become traders instead. Over time they became farmers and fishermen. In France the Vikings shaped the Kingdom of Normandy on the north coast, which would assume a noteworthy part in history a century later when William of Normandy would conquer England in 1066. The Vikings left numerous place-names in Ireland such as Dublin, Waterford, Limerick, Cork, Strangford, Wexford, Carlingford, Leixlip, Howth, Fingall, and Dalkey. These places were settled mostly between 914 and 922, and even some of their vocabulary was incorporated into the Irish language. In the 20th century substantial excavations in Waterford and Dublin uncovered a great part of the Scandinavian legacy in those urban areas. A lot of entombment stones – referred to as the Rathdown Slabs – have been discovered in various sites throughout South Dublin.

After a few generations of cohabitation and intermarriage various people with Norse-Irish ethnic roots emerged that were regularly referred to as Hiberno-Norse or Norse-Gaels. Norse impact can be found in the Norse-determined names of many contemporary Irish rulers such as Citric, Lochlann, or Magnus. In 2006 Dr. Brian McEvoy carried out a genetic study and according to the results it was found that quite a number of people that had Norse-Irish surnames also had Irish genes. This implies that Norse settlements might have had a Viking elite; however, most of the occupants were from the native Irish population.

In September of 919 Niall Glundub stormed Dublin only to be confronted by Sitric who faced Niall's forces at the battle of Islandbridge (also called the battle of Ath Cliath). Sitric defeated Niall during this battle and made it clear to all that his rule was not to be challenged, so thus did Dublin become safe and secure for the Norse. Sitric visited York in 920 and set his plans into motion so that he could assume control of the region after Ragnall's death. After Sitric came to power in York he helped his relative Gofraid become the ruler in Dublin. Gofraid played a significant role in pillaging and selling people into slavery. In 921, during a raid on Armagh, Gofraid decided not to destroy the religious centers and or to kill the sick; this was a decision that had never been made by the raiders of the earlier century. He is also known for creating conflicts in eastern Ulster, which he supposedly attacked from 921 to 927 in the hope of creating a Viking kingdom similar to the one that existed on the east side of the Irish Sea.

The Norsemen's desire in Ulster was put to an end by a progression of attacks at the hands of Muirchertach mac Neill, the son of Niall Glundub. As indicated by Benjamin Hudson, Muirchertach was referred to as the Hector of the Irish because he was one of the best commanders at that time and in the chronicles it is Donnchad Donn (Duncan) from Clann Cholmain who received the title of High King, as Niall Muirchertach was not able to reign as king of Ailech after his father until 938. Aside from his triumphs over the Vikings, Muirchertach drove crusades that caused other kingdoms to surrender. He is mostly remembered for capturing Cellachan Caisil (the king of Munster) in 941. That year he moved towards the Hebrides with a massive fleet and collected his tribute from those who had surrendered.

When Sihtric passed away in 927 Gofraid traveled to York and tried to become king there. Although he was sent by Athelstan, he came back to Dublin after a year and found that the Norsemen of Limerick had taken over Dublin while he was away. Gofraid was able to recover the city but created a new conflict in doing so. In 934 his son Amlaib succeeded him after he died, which led to Amlaib bringing an unequivocal defeat upon the people of Limerick in 937. Moreover, he reached Northumbria that year and allied himself with Owen I of Strathclyde and Constantine II of Scotland. Athelstan defeated this union at Brunanburh but his control was short-lived. After his death in 939 Amlaib tried to become the king of York and was supported by a relative also named Amlaib (the son of Sihtric), but he was called Amlaib Cuaran in order to avoid confusion.

Congalach mac Mael Mithig (also called Cnogba) took over from Donnchad Donn as the High King of the Ui Neill in 944. This was primarily because Muirchertag, who was to have been the successor, had been murdered in 943. Therefore, Congalach, who was the king of Brega and part of Sil naedo

Slaine, was the first of his line to be called "High King." He ransacked Dublin in 944, which was governed by Blacaire mac Gofrith. When Amlaib Cuaran came back to Ireland the following year he became the leader of Dublin and an ally of Congalach and together they fought against Ruaidri ua Canannain, a rival who was also aiming to secure the High King position from Cenel Conaill. In 950 this alliance came to an end after Ruaidri died and Congalach was murdered in a fight against a partnership of Leinster and Dublin in 956, a result that saw Domnall ua Neill became Congalach's successor.

In the next few decades alliances continued to sway between the diverse divisions of Ui Neill, Dublin, and Leinster. Mael Sechnaill mac Domnaill took over from Domnall in 980 and that same year, during the Battle of Tara, he defeated the forces of the Norsemen in Dublin. After this triumph Mael Sechnaill forced the Norsemen to surrender and his half-brother Amlaib (the son of Gluniairn) became Dublin's king.

In the meantime a significant number of regions began to develop and form into towns from the simple Norse settlements. By the latter part of the mid-9th century the town of Dublin had a flourishing Norse people and had become an essential provider of slaves within the British Isles. Until it was ransacked by an invasion – that was carried out by warriors from Ireland in 902 – the town of Dublin was known as an extraordinary trading center. From that point onward the Norsemen shifted their power to the Isle of Man and the emerging domain of Anglo-Saxon England. As the years went by more Viking settlements, such as Cork (848), Waterford (864), and Youghal (866), were eventually conquered.

The last significant Irish skirmish occurred at the Battle of Clontarf in 1014, in which a substantial number of Norse warriors and their Irish allies challenged Brian Boru, the High King of Ireland. The battle took place in what is now the Dublin suburb of Clontarf, on a Good Friday. Boru gave Sigtrygg Silkbeard (the Viking King of Dublin) one year to prepare for the upcoming attack. Silkbeard reacted by offering the bed of his mother, which was an insult among the Norse. The savage melee that occurred between the vigorous Norse and the unarmored – yet steadfast Gaels – finished in a defeat of the Vikings and their Irish allies. Some of the records were orally transmitted by both sides during the fight, and numerous renowned warriors were able to spread their individual stories of battle in this way. High King Boru, who was about eighty, did not actually take part in the fight but rather resigned himself to his tent where he spent the day in meditation. The Viking Brodir of Man stumbled upon Brian's tent as he was fleeing the battle so, along with a few allies, he took the chance and murdered the High King in cold blood. He was eventually caught but with Boru dead Ireland once again became the divided kingdom it had been before. Nonetheless, there was still something good for Ireland to take home from the battle because the kingdom would be free of any further Viking raids.

Boru's foster son, Wolf the Quarrelsome, later found and murdered Brodir by gutting him. Wolf watched as Brodir walked and encircled his own innards around the trunk of a big tree. The battle was fought for most of the day and each side had extraordinary regard for the ability of the other; however, in the end, the Irish forced the Norse to retreat toward the ocean. A considerable number of the escaping Vikings drowned in the water because of their heavy mail coats; they struggled to reach the safety of their longships while others were caught and killed. After this battle the Viking forces dwindled and their presence in Ireland weakened; however, many of the settled Norse remained in the urban communities and worked with the Irish in business and trade. Following Boru's death in 1014 A.D. the political situation became heated as many individuals from various groups tried to become the new High King. Boru's successors were not able to secure a unified royal position and territorial quarreling eventually led to an indirect Norman invasion in 1169, headed by Richard de Clare.

In the ensuing traditions of both Irish and Norse, Clontarf was mentioned in stories of bravery and courage, in which the children would listen and dream about heroism. The stories became exaggerated and included things that did not actually happen. Mysterious signs and dreams were said to have been seen by the both sides on the eve of battle. A pixie lady supposedly appeared to Boru's supporters and predicted what would happen. Saint Senan is said to have been seen by Boru's supporters the night prior to the skirmish, requesting recompense for an attack Boru had directed on a convent years earlier. In the Isle of Man there were "scary" ambushes on Brodar's boats and ravens with press snouts and paws supposedly defeated his supporters. Strange signs were seen all throughout Norse domains, including Iceland. As a result of these stories, the people wished that their descendants had participated in this major battle.

While the battle of Clontarf was not exactly a conflict between the Irish and the Norse, it signaled the end of Norse control over Dublin and the Viking age in Ireland. After this altercation, there was peace between the Viking and Celtic peoples until they incorporated elements of each other's thoughts and traditions.

Notwithstanding the Vikings, life proceeded as usual in Ireland's territories. During the year 700 A.D. – and even to the year 800 A.D – the Ui Neill's power increased tremendously. Within the period between 750 and 850 A.D. the Northern Ui Neill conquered Airgialla, which was essentially central Ulster. Afterward the Northern Ui Neill began to focus on the eastern area of Ulaid. After considering the might of the Ui Neill, the Ulaid did not try to oppose him; and by the middle of the year 800, most regions and royalties were under the control of Ui Neill. The family of Cenel nEogain controlled the administrative affairs of the Northern Ui Neill. The Ulaid in the east and the Cenel Conaill of western Ulster greatly despised the family of Cenel nEogain. Meanwhile, the southern Ui Neill had gained control over northern Laigin. Although they were divided by the continuing of Connacht into Breifne in the year 700, the two parts of the Ui Neill were amalgamated once more in the east by the end of the year 800.

Subsequent to the year 940 there was a strong political friction between the noble families of the Ui Neill. An assembled Ui Neill kingdom was definitely taking shape and the nobles knew there was a battle coming that would decide the new king. Domnall ua Neill, the ruler of the Northern Ui Neill, became king for a few years before being replaced by Mael Sechnaill II of the Southern Ui Neill. The Ui Neill, who used to be an unknown people in the western region of Ireland, became the rulers of a large portion of the eastern and northern territories of Ireland; however, they never truly controlled Munster or Connacht.

For the past few hundred years, life had been very miserable for the Irish as the people were utterly afraid due to the constant Viking raids. A 9th century friar scribbled the following passage on the edge of an old manuscript: "The wind is fierce tonight. It tosses the sea's white hair. I fear no wild Vikings, sailing the quiet main." The Vikings set aflame a large number of the manuscripts they found because they considered them to have no monetary value and that's why today there are only a handful of manuscripts remaining from the original writings. The Viking raids were incredibly devastating for a number of religious groups; in fact, a few convents in Ireland were never able to fully recover. Unlike France and Britain, where entire devout groups were destroyed, the Irish appear to have been saved from the destruction of such attacks. Actually, the Cork religious community was very close to the Viking settlement, but nevertheless survived the Viking age and continued for years after.

Over time the ordinary people (grad Fhene) realized that their ringforts, which used to be a safeguard, had become outdated when the Scandinavian attacks began. At one time the earthen walls and ditches situated around their homes used to provide effective protection against the occasional Irish attacks; however, the number of the Vikings was so large that the raiders were easily able to pillage the area and take many slaves. So it was that the use of ringforts and crannogs became old-fashioned and irrelevant by the year 900 A.D. Instead of the previously used ringforts and crannogs the Irish people began using a very protective underground hollow known as a souterrain, which was constructed by first creating a deep ditch and then fixing stone walls around it while placing a rooftop over it. Since they were primarily used for shelter – instead of storing valuables – the souterrains' passages could be more than one hundred meters (three hundred and thirty feet) long. Although they are hard to find because of their shrouded nature, more than 3500 souterrains were discovered in Ireland.

Toward the beginning of the Norse era, the Irish convents were comprised of earthen walls in areas that had different storehouses and the friars' living quarters. The Norsemen realized that it was anything but difficult to strip these generally helpless settlements of any and all valuables. Soon enough, the clerics figured out how to thwart the Norsemen – they built high stone towers, generally referred to as round towers. Reachable only with the use of a ladder as the entryway was placed one story up. Each floor in the tower could be reached with the use of extra ladders that were pulled up or down within the tower. On the off chance that Norsemen were nearby the Clerics would secure as many supplies as they could, move into the round tower, and draw up the step ladder. The Norsemen would then raid the vacant convent while the clerics watched from the security of their tower. If the Norsemen ever got in – they hardly ever made any attempt to do such a thing – the Clerics only had to retreat higher, using the ladders before pulling them up so that the Norsemen could not use them. Such a technique did not spare the religious community itself, but rather saved the Clerics and also a few of their possessions from being taken. These towers were built all over Ireland, a huge number of which still exist today.

One of the communities that really felt the heat of the Vikings is that of Iona, which became desolate in the 830's and 840's. Other communities included Skellig Michael and even bigger communities like Kildare (Cill Dara, "church of the oak") also suffered. Kildare, despite the fact that it was the capital of Leinster, was pillaged no less than fifteen times by the Vikings between 836 and 1000 A.D. Armagh was the prime religious center of Ireland and it was pillaged at least eleven times. Settlements close to the Viking camps were more likely than not blackmailed for "insurance money" since they were easy targets for intimidation.

In the first quarter-century of the raids, only twenty-six expeditions of the Vikings are recorded in the Irish Annals. During a similar time period eighty-seven attacks by the Irish themselves are recorded; it should be noted that attacks on Irish religious communities were a normal occurrence prior to the Viking Age as the destruction of places of worship was a part of inter-Irish fighting. It is well know that wars between religious communities took place in Ireland before the coming of the Vikings. The Vikings looted the religious communities since they were rich in land, stock, and provisions. Even though they took valuable objects, this was not their main concern as they needed the necessities of daily life.

The history of the Vikings in Ireland is told by various sources, such as the Annals of Ulster and The War of the Gaedhil with the Gaill. Other sources include the Annals of Clonmacnoise, The Annals of the Kingdom of Ireland by the Four Masters, the records of Ibn Ghazal in Arabic, and stories from the Vikings themselves. In most of these sources the Vikings are portrayed in a very negative light and such a sentiment impacts the tone of the records. It is only recently that archeological studies have attempted to give a less negative, biased perspective of the Vikings' kingdoms in Ireland. The fact of the matter is, the Vikings struck the Irish twenty-six times in the first quarter of a century after initial contact. Yet, a similar Irish Annal that recorded this information says attacks against the Irish people happened eighty-seven times within a similar time frame.

Irish archeologists, working under Dublin's South Great George's Street, unearthed the remaining parts of four individuals that were covered with parts of Viking shields and knives. No less than seventy-seven Viking entombments have been found in and around Dublin since the late 1700s, some unintentionally – by trench miners – and some by archeologists. All have been dated to the 9th or 10th centuries based on extracted evidence. The South Great George's Street entombments only added four more pieces of proof to an already massive collection of evidence that had already been collected over the years.

However, when Linzi Simpson, the excavation coordinator from Dublin's Trinity College, transferred the remaining parts for carbon dating to determine a time frame, she was amazed at the results. At Beta Analytic in Miami, as well as at Queen's University in Belfast, the investigations showed that the men had been covered in Irish soil quite a number of years before the first recognised date of permanent settlement of Vikings in Dublin (and maybe even before the first known Viking attack on the island occurred).

For a long time it was believed that the Vikings were simply thugs, who gave little or nothing to Ireland and took whatever they could. This view is not by any stretch of the imagination endorsed by historians because the reality is much more complex. It is without question that their original entry into the region was dreadful and violent; however, within a brief timeframe, they had made agreements with the Irish to settle, form groups, and develop trading centers. Intermarriage with the Irish followed soon after, which was vital for the flourishing of business in Ireland.

There is even evidence that some started to accept Christian propensities, regardless of the fact that they would have to give up Paganism; for instance actual Viking burial grounds have been found, despite the fact that they would have used memorial service fires, as was their custom, to see the dead on their way to such realms as Valhalla. As seafarers and distinguished merchants, they did much to educate the Irish. The system of coinage can be traced to this period in Ireland. In fact, "pingin" – the Irish word for penny – is derived from the Viking language. This demonstrates that an unmistakable class of tradesmen had begun to develop in Ireland.

They were less intrigued by the acquisition of lands than past occupiers of Ireland, and did not try to control large regions; rather they stayed close to the coastline, taking control of land near harbors where they set up trading centers. A few of Ireland's significant towns and urban areas began as Viking trading settlements. Some still exist today with references in their names that originated from the Vikings, such as Waterford and Wexford. Dublin specifically owes a lot of its subsequent advancement to its Viking founders. One of the Viking leaders in Dublin, named Sitric, is said to have developed the urban areas and the geographical layout of the city.

During archeological excavations in 2002, before the construction of a bypass around Waterford city, an interesting discovery was made near the little town of Woodstown. As the excavations advanced various articles including Viking coins, weapons, and silver nuggets were discovered, the metals being dated to the mid-9th century. Valid signs of human settlement were discovered including encompassing trenches, house ravines, postholes, and hearths. It quickly became obvious that these things were not the scattered remnants of a raiding party, but rather the remaining parts of a densely populated Viking settlement, and a rich one at that.

Additional Reading

Almqvist, Bo. "Scandinavian and Celtic Folklore Contacts in the Earldom of Orkney." *Saga-Book of the Viking Society* 20 (1978-79), pp. 80-105.

Bronsted, Johannes. (1965) *The Vikings*. New York: Penguin.

Byrne, Francis John. (1973) *Irish Kings and High Kings*. London: Batsford.

Chesnutt, Michael. (1968) "An Unsolved Problem in Old Norse-Icelandic Literary History." *Mediaeval Scandinavia* 1, pp. 122-37.

Christiansen, Reider Thoralf. (1959) *Studies in Irish and Scandinavian Folktales*. Copenhagen: Rosenkilde & Bagger.

Clarke, Howard B. (1995) "The Vikings in Ireland: A historian's perspective". *Archaeology Ireland*, Vol 9 No 3, Autumn (The Viking Issue).

Curtis, Edmund. (1908) "The English and the Ostmen in Ireland." *English Historical Review* 23, pp. 209-19.

Doheny, Charles. (1980) "Exchange and Trade in Early Medieval Ireland." *Journal of the Royal Society of Antiquaries of Ireland* 110, pp. 67-89.

Dolley, Michael. (1966) "The Hiberno-Norse Coins in the British Museum." *Sylloge of Coins of the British Isles*, 1. London: British Museum.

Duffy, Sean. (1992) "Irishmen and Islemen in the Kingdoms of Dublin and Man, 1052-1171", *Eriu* 43, pp. 93-133.

Duffy, Sean. (2000) *Atlas of Irish History*. Gill and Macmillan.

Foote, Peter and David M. Wilson. (1970) *The Viking Achievement*. London: Sidgewick & Jackson.

Foster, RF. (1989) *The Oxford History of Ireland Oxford*. University Press.

Goedheer, A. J. (1938) *Irish and Norse Traditions About the Battle of Clontarf*. Haarlem: Willink.

Greene, David. (1978) "The Evidence of Language and Place-Names in Ireland." In *The Vikings: Proceedings of the Symposium of the Faculty of Arts of Uppsala University*, June 6-9, 1977. Uppsala: Almqvist & Wiksell. pp. 119-24.

Gwynn, Aubrey. (1947) "Medieval Bristol and Dublin." Irish Historical Studies 5.20, pp. 275-86.

Henry, Francoise. (1970) *Irish Art During the Romanesque Period (1020-1170 A.D.)*. London: Methuen.

Hudson, Benjamin. (1991) "The Viking and the Irishman", *Medium Aevum* 60, pp. 257-67.

Hughes, Kathleen. (1972) *Early Christian Ireland: Introduction to the Sources*. London: Hodder & Stoughton.

Hughes, Kathleen. (1966) *The Church in Early Irish Society*. London: Methuen.

Jones, Gwyn. (1984) *A History of the Vikings*. Oxford: Oxford Univ. Press.

O Corrain, Donnchadh. (1979) "High-Kings, Vikings and Other Kings." *Irish Historical Studies* 21, pp. 283-323.

Roesdahl, Else. (1987) *The Vikings*. New York: Allen Lane/Penguin.

Schama, Simon. (2000). *A History of Britain: At the Edge of the World? 3000BC-AD1603*. BBC.

Smyth, Alfred P. (1977) *Scandinavian Kings in the British Isles, 850-880*. Oxford: Oxford Univ. Press.

Various authors. (1998) *The Oxford Companion to Irish History*. Oxford University Press

Chapter Eight: Vikings in Wales

"In this year the army went about Devonshire into the mouth of the Severn and there harried as well in Cornwall as in North Wales and in Devonshire; and then landed at Watchet and there wrought great evil in burnings and man-slayings. ...Thence they rounded Land's End and entered the mouth of the Tamar."

(Source: Viking Answer Lady)

In the last decade of the 8th century some historical documents record a series of alarming attacks by Viking raiders on the shores of France, Britain, and Ireland. Despite the fact that Wales did not experience any noteworthy Viking settlement, unlike Ireland, England, and France, it still had to deal with the raids of the Norsemen.

Historical records show that Wales was raided repeatedly, with these attacks being mainly carried out by those Vikings who lived in Hiberno-Norse parts of Limerick and Dublin. The Vikings from Ireland raided the coast of Wales from the mid-8th to the late 10th centuries. St. David's was sacked no less than seven times during this period.

At the time Wales was partitioned into several autonomous kingdoms that were always dealing with interior conflicts and wars, conflicts that ultimately rendered the Welsh unable to unite to successfully avert the new risks coming from abroad.

It is important to note that there were kings such as Rhodri Mawr the Great (844 - 878 A.D.), whose real name was Rhodri ap Merfyn, as well as Hywel Dda the Good (900 - 950 A.D.), who rallied large numbers of Welsh to guard their territories. Together, they took a strong stance against the raids and often disregarded their own conflicts to achieve a common goal. Ultimately, Wales became a site of religious sojourn for the Christian descendants of the raiders.

The absence of Viking settlements in Wales has been a mystery since early medieval studies, especially a study that was conducted on Anglesey. It is surprising because the Vikings were only a day's sail – or march – away from Dublin, the Isle of Man, Chester, and the Wirral.

Physical confirmation of the presence of Vikings in Wales has been somewhat of a challenging for researchers. It is only an assertion that the Vikings knew about Anglesey on account of the Scandinavian place-names that have been given to prominent coastal features as navigational guides. These include Onguls-ey itself (thought to consolidate an individual name of a Viking leader), the Skerries, Priestholm (prestaholmr), Piscar, and Osmond's Air close to Beaumaris. Various other place-names along the coastline demonstrate that there was some Scandinavian settlement there; however, it was most likely close to the coastal "camps" or minor trading stations. There was very limited impact on the way of life, dialect, or hereditary nature of the Welsh.

The first mention of a Norse attack upon Wales can be traced to the Welsh Chronicles such as Annales Cambriae, Brut y Saeson, and Brut y Tywysogion in the archives from 850 A.D.

The raid is said to have occurred after the death of a certain Cyngen, who was killed by the Vikings. During this period the Anglo-Saxon kingdoms of Wessex and Mercia troubled the Kingdoms in Wales in their attempts to expand their territories. Through courageous action and a progression of alliances with both the Vikings and the Anglo-Saxons, the Welsh kingdoms were able to maintain their independence and were not colonized, unlike parts of eastern England and Ireland.

Nonetheless, a few researchers claim that the Viking attacks on Wales started much earlier, and those who pillaged the Church on Lombay Island had come from Wales in 795 A.D. The people of Cornwall, referred to as the West Welsh, had begun to experience attacks from the raiders by 835 A.D. as they had formed an alliance with the Norse to battle against King Ecgberht of the Anglo-Saxons, who is said to have oppressed the Cornish in 823 A.D. This union of Norsemen and Welsh would form again during times of conflict with the English.

The southern Welsh regions of Gwent, Glamorgan, and Dyfedd experienced the ill effects of war from 850 to 870 A.D. In 854 A.D. the Vikings (referred to as Y Llu Du) struck Mon. There were attacks on Anglesey and Gwynedd from 854 onwards.

In 903 A.D. they came to Anglesey after being driven out of Dublin and that same year a gathering of Danes – known as Dub Gint or black pagans – led by Ingimundr confronted the Welsh in a grand battle at Osmeliavn or Ros Meilon. Based on both Irish and Welsh records the Vikings were not able to secure a strong enough foothold to settle in Wales; instead they moved on to Chester; however, they sacked Anglesey again in 918 as soon as the opportunity presented itself.

Be that as it may, for no known reason, the Norse stopped attacks on Anglesey and Wales sometime between 918 and 952 A.D. Some researchers suggest that this may be due to the joint military action that was carried out by Hywel. He combined a significant part of the southern and northern divisions of Wales and created political agreements with the English that enabled the two kingdoms to help each other against the raiders from Scandinavia. Furthermore, yearly Viking attacks upon the Welsh coast continued from 952 to 1000 A.D. This happened so frequently that regular confrontations were seen on the island in the second half of the 10th century.

At first, the king of Gwynedd, Rhodri Mawr the Great, was instrumental in repulsing Viking attacks and at keeping them from making settlements or camps in Wales. In fact, he was part of a notable triumph in 856 because during a raid that year he successfully killed the Danish King Gorm, and also repulsed two other attacks in 872.

In 878 after the death of Rhodri Mawr the Great, Alfred the Great became the King of Wessex. He took bold steps to bring back the government of Anglo-Saxon England from the hands of the Vikings under his control. In addition, forces from Gwent, Gwynedd, and Glynwysing battled alongside those from Wessex and Mercia to overcome a Danish army at the Battle of Buttington in 893. In any case, the Danish group wintered in the Severn valley in 895, using it as a base from where they initiated attacks on Gwent, Buellt, Brycheiniog, Morgannwg, and Gwynllwg. After the death of Alfred the Great the Norse who had been removed from Dublin raided

Anglesey in 899. Merfyn ap Rhodri was the King of Powys and he was killed in one such battle that occurred around 900 AD.

Some time around 909 Rhodri's grandson Hywel Dda became the King of Seisyllwg (which is present-day Ceredigion and some areas of Carmarthenshire). He eventually became the king of the greater part of Wales and maintained strong relations with the ensuing Wessex and English kings, such as Edward the Elder, Athelstan, Edmund the Elder, and Eadred. They all attempted to free parts of England from the hands of the Vikings. Hywel's diplomacy also stopped the Vikings from planning any further attacks on Wales because he ruled in an efficient and wise manner.

Following Hywel's demise in 950 the Viking attacks increased as they returned to their old ways. Places such as Penmon on Anglesey and St David's were attacked quite a number of times. Other places that were attacked include St Dogmaels (Pembrokeshire), Clynnog Fawr (Caernarfonshire), Llanbadarn Fawr (Cardiganshire), Tywyn (Merionethshire), Llantwit Major, and Llancarfan in Glamorgan. With the help of the Norsemen, Hywel ap Ieuaf became the leader of Gwynedd in 979. The Vikings seized 2,000 men from Anglesey and sold them as slaves in 987; and the grandson of Hywel Dda, Maredudd ab Owain of Deheubarth, was forced to pay tribute to the Vikings in 989.

In 982 A.D., Godfridr Haraldsson led a battle into Southern Wales and harried Dyved with the force of a large army; he also invaded the Church of St. David in Menevia. At the Battle of Llanwannawc, Godfridr faced the Welsh in a long conflict and after five years, Godfridr Haraldsson took Anglesey again with a group of men called kenhedloedd duon. Around this time Wales was encountering a period of internal conflicts and civil wars as the rulers of the south and north tried to extend their domains to the disadvantage of neighboring regions. King Cadwallon of Gwynedd was killed by King Maredudd ab Owain of South Wales, who ended up adding Gwynedd to his lands. During this time of the conflict, Godfridr visited the Gwynedd royal family to seek some advice. At the Battle of Mannan Godfridr was victorious against Maredudd ab Owain. About one thousand of Maredudd's men were killed while two thousand were caught. The remaining men had no choice but to withdraw to Dyfed and Ceredigion. Later on, Maredudd recovered his fellow Welshmen at high cost. The Vikings attacked the Church of St. David in Menevia in 988 A.D. and also the religious places of Llanbadarn Fawr (close to Aberystwyrth), Llancarfan, Llanilltrud (close to Glamorgan), and Llandudoch (present day St. Dogmaels, which is close to Cardigan). For the third time the Norse plunderers pillaged the Church of St. David in Menevia in 992 A.D. Maredudd ab Owain hired Norse mercenaries for his vengeful battle against the king of Glamorgan, Edwin ab Einion.

In 1066 the Normans attacked England and this brought new difficulties to Wales. The King of Gwynedd, Gruffudd ap Cynan (1081 - 1137), was a significant figure in the resistance to Norman expansion in Wales. He himself was of Norse ancestry, as his mother Ragnhilda was the daughter of Olaf Sigtryggsson, who was king of the Norsemen in Dublin, in fact Gruffudd had spent his childhood in Dublin. In 1073 Gruffudd tried to become the ruler of Gwynedd with help from the Norse of Dublin but failed, but, on making another attempt in 1081, he was successful – with the help of the Norse from Waterford.

Gruffydd ap Cynan journeyed down to the domain of the Orkneys to gather an army of Norsemen around 1087 A.D. He did this as he wanted to capture the land of Venedotia, located in the northern part of Wales. The king of Dublin, the Isle of Man, and the Hebrides was King Godred Mac Sytric, who was ready to help Gruffydd. Godred Mac Sytric gave Gruffydd sixty ships, each containing many warriors. Gruffydd first traveled to Anglesey with his men and challenged the Norman forces there. Gruffydd, according to ancient records, fought using the Danish double-edged axe and *The Life of St. Gwynllyw* reveals that Gruffydd's forces sailed further along the Severn bay to the Church of St. Gwynllyw (present day St. Woollo's Church), which they raided.

In South Wales, King Rhys ap Tewdwr of Deheubarth was banished from his nation by Bleddyn's sons in 1088 A.D. Rhys ran away to look for shelter in Ireland. It was in Ireland that Rhys used a fleet of Irish-Norse men to reestablish himself as a leader and authority, promising the men that he would pay them with numerous prisoners that could be sold as slaves. He eventually came back to Wales with his Norse allies. At Llych crei or Penlecheru, Rhys crushed those who had usurped him. King Rhys ap Tewdwr was slaughtered by Norman intruders of Brycheiniog in 1093 AD. Gruffydd, his young son, was protected by his people and kept hidden among the Irish-Norse, so neither Cadwgan ap Bleddyn – or the Normans – could do him harm.

Gruffydd ap Cynan led another charge with his Norsemen against Wales, plundering the Norman regions of Tegeingl and Rhos, stealing cattle, and making men into slaves. Wales also had to confront Gruffydd later that year, when he arrived with three ships under Great Orme's Head. The ships were brimming with Norsemen. Robert of Rhuddlan, who was asleep in his manor at Deganwy, was stirred awake and informed about the invasion of the Norse plunderers, who were capturing the cows, women, and children, who would be enslaved afterward. Robert made a rash decision and raced to meet the Vikings in the company of a single knight, his unwise haste to defend his people cost him his life. He was caught and killed by Gruffydd's men, spiking his head on the lead ship to declare their triumph.

Gruffydd ap Cynan, along with his Norse army and with the support of Cadwgan of Ceredigion from the Welsh region, awakened the Welsh to stand against the Norman intruders in 1094 A.D. and at last they drove the Normans away from Wales and Gruffydd became the tribal king.

Norman earls attacked Gruffydd's territories four years later. Under the command of the Earls of Montgomery and Chester, the Normans were joined with the disloyal Welshmen from Tegeingl who helped them over the Welsh border. Gruffydd withdrew to the secure terrain of Anglesey and then allied himself with the Hiberno-Norse so that he could shield his lands from the Normans, who were marching from North Wales. Gruffydd was given sixteen longships that were brimming with Norsemen. Under the control of the Earl of Chester the Normans persuaded the Norsemen to betray Gruffydd and support them (the Normans) with the promise that they would get lots of slaves. They lied to the Norsemen knowing full well that they would not be able to provide as many slaves as they had promised.

Cadwgan of Ceredigion, Gruffydd ap Cynan, and Owain ap Cadwgan had no choice but to escape to Ireland. Coincidentally, Magnus Barefoot, who was the son of Harald Hardrada, landed in Wales and fought against the Normans in

Anglesey. The Battle of Anglesey Sound led to the death of Hugh (the Earl of Shrewsbury) and the retreat of the Normans. After his death, the route was left clear for Gruffydd to return.

Cadwgan and Gruffydd came back to Wales in 1099 A.D. when they heard of the triumph of Magnus Barefoot against the Normans, whereupon Gruffydd established rule that was characterized by peace, success, and steady development. He and the Earl of Chester made a peace treaty that allowed him to regain Anglesey and even though Gruffydd always had an emergency guard that consisted of Norse fighters throughout his reign, the Welsh eventually acknowledged his authority, since they preferred a man of Welsh lineage as opposed to someone from the hated Normans. The Norse-Irish foundation of Gruffydd influenced Welsh culture during this time in crafts, music, and writing with Gruffydd himself becoming an outstanding supporter of the arts. Since Gruffydd was of Norse heritage and brought up in the Norse court at Dublin, he contributed to bringing Scandinavian influence into Welsh craftsmanship, music, and writing. Gruffydd conveyed Norse-Irish skalds to court and also supported the Welsh bards.

Literary parallels between the Welsh Mabinogion and the Irish Sagas are readily apparent, with Welsh stories borrowing form the Irish. Scandinavian impact can be seen, particularly in the story of Branwen ferch Llyr, the Mabinogi of Branwen, the Gudrun cycles, Volsunga adventure, and Pidrek's adventure. Scandinavian themes similarly have a place in the records of Gruffydd ap Cynan, in which Gruffydd's family is said to be linked to King Haraldr Harfagra, the acclaimed Viking Rollo, and Saint Olaf the King.

The tradition of music in Wales was also affected by Gruffydd's preference for the Irish pipes and harps in accordance with the Hiberno-Norse tradition. Gruffydd kept an imperial harper known as Gellan or Crellan until the musician was killed in an attack. Gruffydd's court also scheduled contests for minstrels and musicians where all could demonstrate their skills. Both Norse and Norse-Irish entertainers partook in these contests, as there was no discrimination based on ancestry.

The legitimate king of Deheubarth, named Gruffydd ap Rhys, came back to Wales in 1115 A.D. with a mercenary band of Norsemen and tried to recover his throne. Despite his best efforts he was forced to flee to Ireland and later found some allies there in 1126 A.D. Other displaced Welsh people were invited by King Murchath's court including Madog ap Rhiryd, Owain ap Cadwgan, and Howel ab Ithel.

Gruffydd ap Cynan died in 1137 A.D., leaving behind two sons named Owain and Cadwalladr, their sibling rivalry eventually giving rise to them fighting each other in 1144 A.D. Cadwalladr perfidiously slaughtered Anarawd of Deheubarth, Owain's nephew, an act that saw Owain become enraged, so much so that he ordered his son Hywel to attack Cadwalladr. Cadwalladr asked for help from Ireland and was able to secure a Norse fleet sailing to Abermenai, under the control of Porkell, who was a brother to King Ragnall of Dublin. In any case, Welshmen from the southern area of Bregh finally triumphed over the attacking Dublin Norsemen in 1146 A.D, but during this fight, notable leaders died including King Ragnall, Ottarr Ottarrsson (a war leader), and Herulfr Yscherwlf.

Established Welsh poetry describes the presence of the Vikings in Wales, for instance the "Arymes Prydein Vawr" was composed at some point between 835 and 1066, and was well preserved in the 13th century composition called *The Book of Taliesin*. The sonnet predicted that someday Cynan and Cadwalladr would come back to save the Welsh from their despised Saxon persecutors and harmony would prevail over the lands. To realize this, a coalition of the Vikings in Dublin, the Irish, the general population in Anglesey, Scotland, Strathclyde, and Cornwall would help to save the Welsh from the hands of the Saxon adversaries.

The primary evidence of Norse engagement in Wales originates from the Norse adventures the Jomsvikinga, which recounts the narrative of a Norseman wedding a Welsh Princess in which a large portion of the Welsh kingdom is acquired. Different adventures, such as the Njala and Orkneyinga Sagas, demonstrate the commonality between the Norsemen and the Welsh people who lived along the coast. Remarkably, the chronicles of Loch Ce clearly mention that traders journeyed to Dublin Bay from Wales in 1013 to participate in the battle of Clontarf. It is practically confirmed that these were Norsemen who had established a base in Wales, instead of the local Welsh, as they were not traders of any great significance during this time.

In the Irish archives Welsh stallions are mentioned in different events; they seem to have been the most prized horses of the Viking Age. Clearer indications suggesting Norse contact with Wales originate from the Historic and Municipal Documents of Ireland. These documents contain lists of the people of Dublin toward the late 12th century. The names recorded range from Swansea, Bristol, Haverfordwest, Cardiff, and different villages near the Bristol Channel, of which most had Viking names. This indicates that Scandinavian merchants existed there, living in the villages at that time.

There is no immediate written confirmation to demonstrate that Viking establishments were built in Wales, so we should not give excessive weight to this. A few unpredicted Norse settlements have been found lately including Woodstown, Co. Waterford, and Llanbedrgoch, Anglesey. These places are thought to be where the Vikings engaged in trade; however, what the sources do mention are some examples of Norse attacks along the coast of Wales.

One part of their way of life, which the Norse carried with them to every coast upon which they landed, was their language. This they forced with fluctuating degrees of success upon all regions in which they remained for any significant period of time. In the British Isles, the etymological inheritance of Old Norse comprises primarily of loanwords and in English they are many and very much recorded. Welsh vocabulary is hardly influenced; there are no changes in syntax or morphology that can be ascribed to the Vikings. A few scholars have stated that the expressions of South Pembrokeshire contain signs of influence that must have come from Old Norse, but since significant evidence does not support this assertion it is not used to justify Norse colonization.

It has been observed by researchers that Wales has a different name in quite a number of Icelandic Sagas. It was called Bretland in Old Norse. In the Prologue of Landnamabok, the Icelandic Book of Settlements, it is said that Iceland ("Thule") is a six days voyage on a boat toward the north of Wales.

According to *Heimskringla*, Haraldr gave ships and men to his sons – Erik Bloodaxe, Porgisl, and Frodi. The sons engaged in expeditions toward the West, creating problems in Bretland, Ireland, and Scotland. Eric Bloodaxe succeeded to the Norwegian throne, taking it after his father Haraldr, around 930 A.D. However, around 935, he was forced to escape to the safety of England when his stepbrother Hakon attacked him. When Erik converted to Christianity King Aepelstan of England offered him the territory of York. Heimskringla describes Erik's actions as the king of York in the Hakonar Saga called *Adalsteinsfostra*. Erik was said to have had little land, so he went raiding each mid-year and pillaged Scotland, the Hebrides, Ireland, and Bretland and in this way he was able to collect resources and become rich. Eadmund, Aepelstan's brother, became the English King after the death of his brother. Erik Bloodaxe found that Eadmund (Jatmundr, as he was referred to by the Scandinavians) did not like the presence of the Norsemen as he showed no sign of friendliness toward them. Erik Bloodaxe also did not receive any support from him.

Soon word began to spread that King Jatmundr was planning to find and crown another person as king over Northumberland. When this news reached King Erik Bloodaxe, he set off on a westbound voyage, bringing with him the sons of Torf-Einar (Erlendr and Arnkell) from the Orkneys and sailed to the Hebrides. Once at the Hebrides he met with numerous Vikings and warriors who permitted their men to join his force and with this group of men he led the way to Ireland with every man he could find. After that, he headed towards Bretland, where he pillaged for resources before sailing southward to England.

Egils Saga, Skallagrimssonar also makes reference to Bretland when describing the Battle of Vinheidr. According to researchers, the Battle of Vinheidr might be similar to the 937

A.D. Battle of Brunanburh that is depicted in the *Anglo-Saxon Chronicle*. Based on the saga Hringr and Adils were brothers and reigned over the lands of Bretland, paying homage under the vassalage of King Aepelstan. Their tributary service to King Aepelstan mandated that they participate in the king's army and always occupy the front lines in battle. The brothers, who were great fighters, were presumably from the Kingdom of Strathclyde in Scotland. The brothers' saga may be an indication of Viking settlement and rule in some areas of Wales. Historical records show that the Vikings traveled through Strathclyde on different occasions, whenever they marched from York on the Roman road to Carlisle. A Scandinavian settlement was also situated in Cumberland. In 944 A.D. King Eadmund took over Strathclyde and offered it to the King of Scots (Malcolm) in order to prevent the Scandinavian settlers in Wales from supporting the invading Vikings undermined the Saxon rule. In return Malcolm vowed to keep the Welsh and Scandinavian people in check.

The Saga of the Jomsvikings also describes Scandinavian settlements in Wales. Bretland was under the control of an earl named Stefnir who had a daughter named Alof. Alof was astute and much adored not only by her father but by others as well. Palnatoki arrived in Bretland with his army with plans to ravage the territory. When Alof and her advisor Bjorn became aware of Palnatoki's plans, she made an arrangement to request Palnatoki's presence at a dinner that was meant to honor him. He was asked to view their place as a home and them as companions that could be trusted. Palnatoki agreed to dinner and went to feast in the company of his men whereupon he proposed to Alof and was accepted as a good match by the people. They quickly arranged the marriage and at the wedding Earl Stefnir presented the title of earl to Palnatoki as well as a large portion of his territory. In addition, after Stefnir's demise, Palnatoki would reign over the entire land; he remained there for the summer as well as the following winter.

Sveinn tjuguskegg, who was eventually crowned the King of Denmark, was the foster son of Palnatoki. According to *Olafs Saga, Tryggvassonar*, Sveinn tjuguskegg went to see Palnatoki later in Bretland before he proceeded to run raids into Wales. Sveinn first succeeded in ravaging Bretland but as he moved deeper into the region, and farther away from his ships, he faced a large army on horseback. He was unable to defeat them and – now a prisoner – was thrown into a dungeon along with Porvaldr Kodranson and numerous other leaders. The following day an influential Duke came to the dungeon with a great army to set Porvaldr free, returning a favor Porvaldr had once done him. There was a time when the Duke's sons were caught stealing but Porvaldr had freed them and told them to return to their father, thus the Duke requested Porvaldr's freedom; but Porvaldr refused to leave the dungeon unless King Sveinn and his men were also released. Eventually all of the prisoners were freed because of Porvaldr's actions.

The *Brennu-Njals Saga* also mentions the Viking raids that were led by Helgi and Grimr, the sons of Njall, into Wales. Helgi and Grimr were attacked by Earl Hakon on their way to Iceland and made prisoners but Kari Solmundarson, who acted on behalf of Earl Sigurdr Hlodvisson, saved them. Afterward Kari requested that they join him on a raid of Wales. Earl Sigurdr welcomed Kari and the Njalssons, who both traveled to Orkney and wintered in the company of Earl Sigurdr. When spring arrived Kari suggested that the Njalssons should attack Wales; however, Grimr agreed to go only if Kari would agree to come to Iceland as well. Kari gave his word, so they journeyed together on the raid to Iceland where they attacked the Hebrides and some parts of south Anglesey. They then went to Kintyre, where they battled the occupants and accumulated a wealth of plunder before leaving for their ships; Bretland was their next destination.

Earl Porfinnr Sigurdarson of Orkney, according to the Orkneyinga Saga, assembled an immense army with the assistance of King Magnus Barefoot. With his army he fought against the Welsh in a battle popularly known as the Battle of Menai Straight, which is said to have been so fierce battle that nobody could tell which side would win. While holding a hand-bow beside another archer, Halogaland, King Magnus attacked the Welsh. Hugh the Proud, who was so well shielded that one could only see his eyes, put up a courageous fight. To successfully defeat Hugh the Proud, King Magnus told the archer that they should launch two arrows simultaneously and this is exactly what they did. One arrow crashed into Hugh's nose guard, while the other went into his eye and punctured his head, causing Hugh the Proud to fall. The Welsh, after losing a large number of troops, retreated at last in fear of being killed and as a result King Magnus became famous for his victory over the Welsh.

The Irish referred to the first raiders – who were Norwegians – as Finn Gaill. Interestingly, according to historical records, there was another sort of Norseman who showed up on the Welsh shores in 854. The Welsh (just like the Irish, who referred to the Danes as Dubh Gaill, meaning black foreigners) called the new arrivals on their shores different names to indicate the color "black". Such names include y Normanyeit duon (black Normans), gentiles nigri (the black heathen) and y llu du (the black host). Some Welsh words associated with the Vikings describe them as pagans with a focus on the non-Christian culture of the Norse Intruders: "gentiles" and Paganaid "pagans". Other Welsh names for the Vikings included Gwyddyl (Irish but to the Hiberno-Norse), Nordmani (Northmen), Lochlannaigh or Llychynwyr (men of "Lochlann," which means Norway), gwyr Dulyn (men from Dublin), Daenysseit (Danes), gwyr Denmarc (men of Denmark) and Llychlynwys (Scandinavians).

Wales was located in a central area within the Viking colonies of Ireland and the Danelaw, which is why it could have easily attracted the Vikings. The Welsh coast, and especially Anglesey, experienced a great deal of Hiberno-Norse animosity; this is because of its location, which was conveniently near the Scandinavian settlement of Dublin. The raiders also found Anglesey appealing because it was the center of the spiritual institutions of Penmon, Caer Gybi and Ynys Seirol. As indicated by Giraldus Cambrensis in his *Descripto Kambriae*, Mount Snowdon could yield enough pasture for all the cattle in Wales. Consequently, the Isle of Mona was so rich in meadows and wheat that it had the capacity to supply produce for all of Wales.

The claim that the Scandinavians settled on the isle is not totally confirmed among scholars, but there is the possibility that Scandinavian settlement occurred if we consider that the first Welsh name of the island was Mona. The Old Norse Ongulsey, or Anglesey, replaced this Welsh name, nevertheless, Welsh literature continues to use "Mona" to this very day.

The chaotic history of the Vikings – threatening lives, property and entire kingdoms – has been changed by archaeology, of course first contact with the Vikings was undoubtedly fierce and frightening, but they quickly colonized regions and became farmers, traders, and gifted craftsmen according to various historical studies.

For a more reasonable picture of the Vikings in Wales we must also consider historical studies. Most of the Norse silver that has been found in Wales was located close to coastal regions. The St. Deiniol's religious community in Bangor has delivered two hordes of such silver; one is dated to around 925 A.D. while the other comes from around 970 A.D. The Bryn Maelgwyn accumulation of coins was hidden close to Llandudno in the mid-1020s and is thought to be from Viking' plunder, in addition, a surprising horde of five full Viking silver arm rings was discovered in the 1800s at Red Wharf Bay in Anglesey.

One of the most interesting archeological sites that witnessed Viking activity can be found at Llanbedrgoch in Anglesey. Research conducted by Amgueddfa Cymru uncovered life in the Viking Age, which has puzzled researchers for quite some time, also archeological evidence of the Vikings' presence was found in south Wales, albeit no physical settlement that still remains. Different Viking settlements, hoards, and coins have all been found in Wales, primarily along the shore.

Other intriguing evidence indicating a Viking presence in Wales originates from sculptures. Stone slabs and crosses were common during this period and those found in Wales indicate Viking origin. Take for example the pillar-cross at Nevern, Pembrokeshire, the construction of these crosses is easily explained if contact between the Vikings and the Welsh was direct and continuous, such as through a settlement. Another piece of archeological evidence for Viking presence is the discovery of a likely Viking merchant ship found at

Alexandra Dock in Newport, where a remaining side of the ship was found in 1878 and dated to 900 A.D.

There is much evidence in regards to Viking activity in Wales, which is of great interest among historians and researchers alike. For example, there are some interesting Scandinavian names in Carmarthenshire's family ancestries. Research has also shown the presence of rare blood types among the local population, for example, the regular occurrence of A genes among the indigenous peoples of Pembrokeshire shows up at levels of up to 33.6 percent, which is much higher than any other local population in Wales and is similar to populations from parts of Scandinavia.

Viking activity was more dominant along the coasts, specifically along the south and north regions of Wales. Similarly the movement within Anglesey, North Wales, and the recently discovered site named Llanbedrgoch was of higher significance. Llanbedrgoch lies in the center of Viking activity. The large amount of evidence along the southern coast shows how important the trade route was for the Vikings between Dublin and Bristol.

Despite the fact that archeological data for Wales is limited, a few researchers suggest that there were different regions of Viking settlements along the south coastline of Wales. Additional evidence to support this can be found by taking a look at Viking movement in Wales as a progression of settlements along the coast may have been required by the Viking merchants in order to move freely around the Irish Sea.

The idea of a progression of settlements along the shoreline of southern and eastern Ireland started due to a reinterpretation of an archeological site on Beginish Island, Co. Kerry. The houses uncovered at the site were similar to those of Viking

Dublin and they were as refined as those discovered in the townships of around 1000 A.D. Based on the Beginish site, with regards to its location between the Viking-occupied Limerick and Cork, it is highly unlikely that the island – with a paradise of provisions, timber, and safe houses – could have been overlooked by the Vikings.

Way stations (for example, Beginish) were fundamental during the Viking Age. From various sources, beyond what many would consider possible, we realize that the Vikings would sail during the day to capture the coast and as such they required some place to stay overnight. It has been theorized that the usual Viking longships must have been sailed thirty-six nautical miles per day in such terrible weather conditions. As a result, a series of way stations would have been needed so that they could rest, sleep, and repair their ships before continuing on.

Due to the way the Welsh exhibited a stubborn imperviousness to attack, the Scandinavians never settled the vast and prosperous areas in Wales, as they had in England and Ireland. It is broadly acknowledged that a group of Scandinavians settled on either side of the immense fjord of Milford Haven in South Pembrokeshire. There may, likewise, have been a Norse settlement in Gower, the peninsula that stretches out around eighteen miles west of Swansea. Another Scandinavian settlement in Wales was located in the low-lying coastal plain between Neath, Newport, and Cardiff. Cardiff specifically was a part of the kingdoms of Gwent and Morgannwg. The use of contracts in Glamorgan points to a considerable number of Norse names, indicating that a Scandinavian settlement must have existed there as well at some point.

A significant portion of the Scandinavians that lived in Wales consisted of tradesmen. The supplies they managed often changed with demand and supply; however, the largest and most lucrative business was that of the slave trade. Similarly, wheat was also very profitable for trading. This was likely because Ireland imported a lot of wheat, which originated mainly from Wales. Another prized Welsh commodity was the fine Welsh stallion, as there was a constant need for horses by both merchants and warriors. Different items that were bought and sold by the Scandinavians included honey, malt, wine, hides, shrouds, whale oil, margarine, and woolen fabric.

An island in the Bristol Channel, called Tusker Rock, took its name from Tuska, which was the name of a Danish Viking who ruled the rich Vale of Glamorgan along with his kindred warriors. In Pembrokeshire, the names of Skokholm (Norse meaning "wooded island"), Grassholm, Ramsey, and Skomer islands all have Viking origins. Names of Nordic origins allude to trade zones and small settlements. For example, Swansea is thought to have been set up by Sweyne Forkbeard when he was shipwrecked there. Sweyn's Ey, which means Sweyn's Island in Norse, alludes to the Tawe region.

Alternatively, in England, Ireland, and Scotland, the Vikings had established settlements and even kingdoms. From the 7th century until 1100, they would have a large influence on the administrative decisions of each of the four nations. The Viking invasions destroyed the state arrangement of the English; however, Wessex survived and a battle brought England under the reign of the Wessex dynasty, which was ruled by King Alfred.

Generally, very little research has been conducted on Wales' Viking past when compared with the research that has been done on other parts of the British Isles. Historians and archaeologists, especially from the Welsh regions, have concentrated solely upon their Celtic past and there has been little enthusiasm for the history of Welsh contact with the Vikings, part of the reason behind this is due to the absence of written sources. Wales lacks first hand sources, not at all like Ireland and England, where the Irish records and Anglo-Saxon accounts reveal much about the actions of the Vikings. This has led many to believe that the Vikings had little or no impact on Wales; nonetheless, it is important to mention that a lack of written records should not automatically translate to an absence of Viking activity in Wales.

Additional Reading

Charles, B. G. (1934) *Old Norse Relations with Wales*. Cardiff: University of Wales Press Board.

Jones, Thomas, trans. (1971) *Brenhinedd y Saesson or the Kings of the Saxons*. Cardiff: University of Wales Press.

Sephton, John, trans. (1895) *The Saga of King Olav Tryggwason who Reigned Over Norway A.D. 995 to A.D. 1000*. London: Nutt.

•Sturluson, Snorri. (1990) *Heimskringla: Or the Lives of the Norse Kings*. New York: Dover.

Sturluson, Snorri. (1964) *Heimskringla: History of the Kings of Norway*. Lee M. Hollander, trans. Austin: University of Texas Press.

Chapter Nine: Vikings in Scotland

"The wind is fierce tonight. It tosses the sea's white hair. I fear no wild Vikings, sailing the quiet main."

(Source: Wesley Johnston)

From the 8th to the 15th centuries there was a strong Norse presence in Scotland. It was during this period that the Vikings, a group of Norwegians, a few Scandinavians, and their descendants, colonized parts of what are the borders of present-day Scotland. The particular ethnic group of Vikings that pillaged and started settlements in Scotland and some areas of Ireland were the Norse Vikings (the Norwegians). Around 800 A.D. they settled in Jarlshof on the Shetland Islands and they also settled in Lewis, situated in the Hebrides, where more than one hundred towns still possess Norse names. The Norse-Scots (Gael-Galls), from the Scottish Western Isles, settled throughout a vast area of Ireland. Some of the places they settled in included Iceland, The Isle of Skye, The Isles of Lewis and Harris, and numerous different islands in and around Scotland, Ireland, and England. The entire upper east of England and York consists of Viking-settled territories. Their Longships gave them dominion over the oceans and their bold style of battle, agnostic faith in glory from death in battle, and substantial physical size for their day made them almost unbeatable adversaries.

Scandinavian influence in Scotland started towards the end of the 8th century. During this period, there existed intense enmity between the developing thalattocracy of the Kingdom of the Isles and the Norse Earls of Orkney. Names of the leaders of Ireland such as Dal Riata, and Alba were well known and there were also attempts by the king of Norway to maintain stability in his land. While they undoubtedly struck dread into the locals wherever and whenever they landed, the Vikings settled in Scotland for around 300 years. They were farmers who cultivated crops, such as barley and oats, and reared an assortment of domestic animals such as sheep, cattle, and pigs. They also cultivated and collected plants for medicinal use. The Norse Viking age reached its peak between the 9th and 12th centuries, when Scandinavian seafarers won new territories, creating settlements in Iceland, Orkney, Greenland, and Shetland, and building up states in North America, Scotland, Ireland, England, Russia, and France.

Composed in the 13th century based on prior oral stories, the Icelandic Sagas were frequently utilized as guides for marauders, merchants, campaigners, explorers, and pilgrims. The sagas are surprisingly precise and even helped archeologists to pinpoint the remaining parts of a Norse town in Newfoundland.

In the 8th century the plunderers from Norway were first attracted to Scotland's shores and her outlying islands by the abundance of monasteries and the easy fortune to be found inside. The religious community at Iona – on the west coast – was first struck in 794, whereupon it became desolate for approximately fifty years after several obliterating invasions. The Vikings acquired a near limitless booty of gold, silver, and valuable manuscripts thus, islands like Iona, were regular targets. In 806 all of the people in Iona were killed and the building pillaged, the Monks of St. Ninian's Island in Shetland were likewise struck and the priests – who were pre-warned – immediately hid the most important valuables. The Monks concealed valuables of 8th century gold and silver that were not found until 1958. It is an astonishing collection that is in strikingly good condition, and they are as significant today as they were then, and just as precious now as they were to the pillagers who sought them from the 8th to the 10th centuries. Although there appear to be just a few records from the earliest period there is evidence that a Scandinavian presence in Scotland grew from the 830s.

The isles toward the north and west of Scotland were intensely colonized by Norwegian Vikings. The Hebrides, Shetland, and Orkney came under Norse control now and then as fiefs under the King of Norway. These regions were also under the different Kings of the Isles, the Earldom of Orkney, and the subsequent Kings of Man and the Isles in different circumstances as independent territories. Not until the late year of 1468 were Shetland and Orkney finally brought into Scotland, becoming the last regions to be incorporated. Before the end of the 9th century the Vikings came to Scotland to attack and settle, and interestingly it seems that the Vikings settled more rapidly in Scotland and northern and east Ireland than they did in England. Resistance was similarly as savage in Scotland and Ireland as it was in England but as a rule, none of the local British or English people were capable of stopping the Norsemen. They appeared to be unconquerable, even when they were outnumbered.

The Scots shared some things with the Scandinavians and before long intermarriages occurred in northern parts of Scotland, particularly in Sutherland and Caithness. Intermarriages also occurred widely throughout the Western Isles of Scotland, which were known as the Inner and Outer Hebrides. Even now one can discover Scottish clans with Norse backgrounds, including Clan MacDonald of the Isles and Clan MacLeod in the western area, as well as Clan Gunn in the northern area. They communicated using both Gaelic and Norwegian for several centuries and were further known as talented warriors in battle. The use of lengthy swords and even archery are attributed very early to these Clans.

Norse-occupied regions incorporated the Northern Isles of Shetland and Orkney, the Firth of Clyde, the Isle of Man, the Hebrides, and related regions such as Sutherland and Caithness. The historical documents found in Scotland are neither substantial nor reliable and what is more the Irish chronicles and the other Scandinavian Sagas – including the *Orkneyinga Saga* as a primary source of information – occasionally have conflicting stories. However, present-day historic studies are starting to give a clearer image of life in the Viking period of Scotland.

Different contending speculations exist on the early colonization activities, despite the fact that the Northern Isles were the initial regions to be ransacked by Norsemen and were only surrendered by the Norwegian king at the very end. In the early 1100s, the reign of Thorfinn Sigurdsson allowed growth and expansion into the northern territory of Scotland and this might have been the pinnacle of Scandinavian influence. The eradication of pre-Viking names in the Northern Isles and the Hebrides, and their supplanting with Norse names was not uncommon. All of this occurred in spite of the fact that the rise of partnerships with the local Gaelic speakers created an effective Norse-Gael tradition that had a huge impact on places like Argyll and Galloway.

From the 13th century onward, the Scottish influence increased. In 1231, for example, a sustained lineage of Viking earls of Orkney was brought to an end, and it was then Scottish nobles who secured the position of earl. A disastrous endeavor by Haakon Haakonarson caused the western islands to be given to the Scottish royals. Shetland and Orkney were likewise moved under the rule of the Scottish royals in the 1450's. Despite the negative perspectives of the Viking movement, Norse extension might have made an impact on the development of Alba (the Gaelic kingdom) and the initiating of modern-day Scotland. In fact, the business, political, social, and religious accomplishments of the later Norse administration were very significant in the creation of Scotland.

It has been observed by researchers that there appears to be poor documentation of the Viking age in Scotland, in fact, the available documents are a product of the availability of convents on Iona, which covers the periods from the 550s to the 850s. In any case, from 849 onward, when Columba's relics were taken away during the Viking invasions, historical documents from indigenous sources were nowhere to be found for about 300 years. The sources for information on a large area of northern Scotland, as well as on the Hebrides, within a period of time from the 700s to the 1000s, were mainly Norse, English, or Irish. The fundamental Norse content can be found in the *Orkneyinga Saga*, which was composed in the early 1200s, the author of which is said to be an obscure Icelander. The Irish and English sources are more relevant, yet may have a southern predisposition in the narrative, particularly as a great part of the Hebridean archipelago ended up assuming the Norse language in this period, but the dates can be viewed as fairly accurate throughout this source.

The archeological document for this time frame is generally limited but does help researchers move forward. Toponymy gives large amounts of data on the presence of the Norsemen while Norse runestones are used as valuable evidence. There is a significant collection of material from the Gaelic oral stories that was based on this period; however, its authenticity is questionable.

The territories of the Northern Isles are the nearest areas of the United Kingdom to Norway. The first and most lasting Viking influence on any area of Scotland was directed toward the Northern Isles. Shetland is somewhere in the range of 300 kilometers westward of Norway, and in favorable conditions, one could sail to Shetland from Hordaland within 24 hours on a Scandinavian longship. Orkney is 80 kilometers further toward the southwest.

The Scottish mainland is situated about 16 kilometers south of Orkney, whilst Sutherland and Caithness, the two most northerly areas of Scotland, fell under the control of the Norsemen very early. Moving south the entire western coastline of Scotland – from Wester Ross to Kintyre – experienced a great deal of Norse influence.

The Southern Isles had a wide extent of lands, with the Hebrides or Western Isles, which included the Outer Hebrides and the Inner Hebrides. The Outer Hebrides (otherwise known as the "Long Island") was situated in the west, isolated from the northern Inner Hebrides by the Minch, a strait that ran between the islands. The Outer Hebrides were somewhere in the range of 180 kilometers west of Orkney. The Inner Hebrides included places such as Jura, Skye, Mull, Iona, and Islay. In addition there were the islands of the Firth of Clyde that was nearly 140 kilometers toward the south; Arran and Bute were the largest of these islands. There was also the Isle of Man, situated in the Irish Sea between present-day Scotland, England, Wales, and Ireland.

The aggregate distance between the southern point of the Isle of Man and the Butt of Lewis (the farthest point northward of the Outer Hebrides) was around 515 kilometers. This whole area experienced numerous changes because of the influence of Scandinavian culture over a long period of time, for instance it is very probable that the language of the Scandinavians became widespread throughout the territories of the Inner Hebrides as it did on Lewis in the 10th and 11th centuries.

There was also considerable, direct Scandinavian control in Galloway in the southwestern region of Scotland. For a long duration of that time, until the 1266 Treaty of Perth, Danish and Norwegian foreign policy massively increased. The actions of autonomous Scandinavian leaders of Norse-invaded Scotland affected the governance of Scotland significantly.

Scholarly observations about the Viking period in Scotland have caused some to adopt a unique understanding of Scandinavian Scotland, particularly from the early period. Historians have accepted four contending hypotheses regarding this period.

The traditional clarification is based on the earldom hypothesis. According to this hypothesis there was a period of Viking movement into the territories of the Northern Isles and the making of a distinguished tradition and noble line. The line continued into the Medieval period, which had a significant impact in western Scotland and the Isle of Man up until the 11th century. This variant of events is narrated mainly by the Scandinavian Sagas and is supported by some archeological evidence, in spite of the fact that it was previously scrutinized for misrepresenting Orcadian impact in the Southern Isles.

The genocide hypothesis is the second, which states that the native people of the Western and Northern Isles were destroyed and replaced completely with Norse settlers. The basis of this contention is the almost complete substitution of prior names of places by those of Norse origin all throughout the region. Critics, however, point out this theory's shortcomings because the names originate from a moderately late date and the idea of this change remains controversial. Genetic studies demonstrate that Shetlanders have practically indistinguishable levels of Scandinavian matrilineal and patrilineal heritage, meaning that both men and women in equal number settled the islands.

The pagan reaction hypothesis of Bjorn Mhyre makes reference to a long tradition of mobility among the different people that dwelt along the coastlines of the North Atlantic. This hypothesis adds that the expansion of Christian missions brought about ethnic strains that prompted or exacerbated Viking growth. There are some indications of such mobility, including Irish missionary movements in Iceland and the Faroe Islands during the 8th century; however, very little of this evidence leads to anything conclusive.

The Laithlind or Lochlann hypothesis is the last of the four. The term "Laithlind or Lochlann" shows up in different forms in early Irish writing and is typically thought to allude to Norway itself, albeit some prefer to relate it to within the Norse-dominated parts of Scotland. Donnchadh O Corrain is an advocate of this view and claims that a considerable area of Scotland – the Northern and Western Isles and vast areas of the coastal terrain – was infiltrated by the Vikings in the first quarter of the 9th century and that a Viking kingdom was set up there earlier than the middle of the century. Essentially a variation of the earldom theory, there is minimal archeological evidence to back its claims. Although various Viking attacks on the Irish coasts were occurring around the same time as in the Hebrides, the latter date is a long way from certain. As O Corrain himself concedes, when and how the Vikings overcame the Isles is obscure and maybe even unknowable. The archaeological evidence for the presence of the Scandinavians in Scotland is predominantly localized because – just as they did in the other regions they invaded – the Vikings invaded Scotland to build settlements and to cultivate crops.

The Vikings engaged in a major raid of Scotland that led to the destruction of the Pictish upper class in 893 A.D. but as a result of this attack Scottish Dalriada King Kenneth mac Alpin was able to bring together the remaining Pictish and Scottish groups of people. From that point, Halfdan confronted eastern Scotland after he had separated himself from the Mighty Danish Army. The Danish men struck Moray Firth all the way from the Orkneys. After pillaging as much as possible, they secured the fortification of Dunottar in the southern area of Aberdeen around the year 900. In addition, the amalgamated Celto-Norse warriors executed their own ambush in the west. According to contemporary recorders, the Celto-Norse raids were extremely savage and dreadful.

Augisl and Olaf from Ireland crushed Southwestern Scotland and then effectively blockaded Dumbarton in 870; after the attack they left with a substantial amount of slaves and plundered goods. A record of this invasion can be found in both the Welsh and Irish archives, and – according to a few researchers – the raid was likely an unsuccessful attempt to create a larger trading platform than Viking Dublin.

King Constantine mac Aed (900 - 943 AD) was eventually selected to deal with the miserable state of the Scots. With his men he could challenge the Anglo-Scandinavians and the Vikings from the Danelaw and Northumbria equally and also lessen the frequency of their raids. He was very discrete during the war in that he permitted intermarriages; it was through such compromising war techniques that he was able to keep his lands and territories from the grasp of the Vikings. It even allowed him to extend his domain southward after the Vikings attacked his southern Anglo-Saxon neighbors. It was around this period that the ethnically different Scottish clans began to create a national identity.

The Viking triumphs gradually became few-and-far-between around the mid-10th century and in actual fact the Scots defeated the summer raiders and thereafter the popularization of the name "Sorley" or "Somerled" became known as referring to the Scottish triumph.

Until Jarl Sigurdr digr ("the Stout") Hlodvisson – the Earl of Orkney – was slaughtered in 1014 at the Battle of Clontarf, Moray warriors in the north continued to fight relentlessly against the plunderers that had invaded all the way from the Orkneys. The end of the Scandinavian period in the Celtic region was preceded by the death of Jarl Sigurdr digr the Stout. Despite the fact that the Viking Age is generally considered to have finished in 1066 with the Battle of Stamford Bridge, a few researchers consider that it lasted as much as a century more in the Orkneys. The Neolithic internment hill of Maes Howe gives a clear indication of Norsemen in the Orkneys in the 1100's. The tomb had been torn open by a gathering of Crusaders, who searched unsuccessfully for treasure. Although it is thought that they may have found some valuables, they left behind the runic drawings, which are very important to current researchers.

Norse contact with Scotland is confirmed before the first composed records in the 8th century, despite the fact that their nature and recurrence are unknown. Excavations done at Norwick, situated on the island of Unst in Shetland, demonstrate that Scandinavian travelers had come there as early as the mid-7th century. This information is reliable, just like the dates that are related to the Viking presence at Old Scatness.

From 793 onwards there are records that mention repeated attacks on the British Isles, with every single one of the islands of Britain being raided in 794, with Iona being sacked in 802 and 806. It is important to note that these attacks on Christian settlements on the islands of the west were not new. In the 6th century Pictish forces struck Tiree and Tory Island was hit in the mid-7th century by a foreign army. Donnan of Eigg – along with his fifty-two companions – was killed by the Picts on Eigg in 617. Various named Viking pioneers, who were presumably based in Scotland, show up in the Irish archives: Soxulfr in 837, Turges in 845, and Hakon in 847. Within the words of a record of kings that died during a famous Viking attack in 839, there are various names including Eogan mac Oengusa, the king of Fortriu, as well as aed mac Boanta, the king of Dal Riata. Another early reference to the Norse presence in the Irish records is that of a ruler of "Viking Scotland", whose beneficiary was named Thorir. He directed an army into Ireland in 848 and was followed by Caittil Find, who was a leader of the Gallgaedil fighting in Ireland in 857.

The conquest of the Inner Hebrides by Norsemen in 847 can be traced to the Frankish Annales Bertiniani. *In the*

Fragmentary Annals of Ireland, Amlaib Conung, who was said to have died in 874, is mentioned as the son of the king of Lochlainn. The Annals also state an early date for a unified Scandinavian Scotland kingdom. In a similar source, Amlaib is likewise documented to have gone to the assistance of his father Gofraid, because in around 872 the Norsemen in Lochlainn were attacking him. Gofraid died in 873 and it is most likely that his son, Imar, succeeded him; however, his rule did not last long because he was also killed in the same year as his father. Kintyre also likely lost his territory around that time as the Vikings took over the Isle of Man in 877.

The Northern Isles used to be Pictish in language and culture before the Norse attacks. In spite of the fact that it was documented that King Bridei crushed Orkney in 682, the possibility that the Pictish lords had any real level of continuous control over island activities is low. The Orkneyinga Saga recounts that Harald Fairhair was made King of a unified Norway around 872, a fact that saw a considerable number of his rivals flee to different parts of Scotland. Harald actively sought his adversaries and added the Northern Isles to the lands he was controlling in 875. After that, maybe barely a decade later, he added the Hebrides to his kingdom as well; but the following year the nearby Hebridean Scandinavian leaders revolted. Harald at that point asked Ketill Flatnose to curb the revolt and Ketill accomplished this task rapidly. He then pronounced himself an independent "King of the Isles" and held this title throughout the remainder of his lifetime. Ketill eventually became a leader of an area that had previously been occupied by quite a number of Norsemen. Some researchers suggest that this whole story is a fabrication but as of yet they do not have the evidence to disprove it.

Regardless, the Viking oral tradition expresses that Rognvald Eysteinsson obtained Shetland and Orkney from Harald as an earldom. It is mentioned that Harald gave it to him as compensation for his son, who died in a battle in Scotland. After that, Rognvald left the earldom to Sigurd the Mighty, his brother. Sigurd's lineage experienced a lot of political problems and did not live long after him. Therefore, Torf-Einarr, who happened to be Rognvald's son, but whose mother was a slave, was the one who established a dynasty that ran the affairs of the Northern Isles for a considerable length of time after the death of his father. After Torf-Einarr's death, his son Thorfinn Turf-Einarsson became king. During this period King Eric Bloodaxe from Norway frequently attacked several other regions from his base in Orkney before he was killed in 954. The death of Thorfinn and the presumed control of South Ronaldsay precisely at the broch of Hoxa incited a long stretch of dynastic dispute, but irrespective of the historical information it appears quite possible that Shetland and Orkney quickly became consumed by Scandinavian culture around this period.

The proof of language and toponymy is obvious, for one Orkney's place-names with a Celtic inference are very few since Norn (a native adaptation of Old Norse) was the language of the day – it was also spoken in Shetland. There is no evidence of Pictish influence on place-names except for the three islands of Unst, Yell, and Fetlar.

Jarlshof in Shetland is said to possess the largest remains of a Scandinavian site ever discovered anywhere other than mainland Britain, where the Scandinavians occupied the site constantly from around the 9th to the 14th centuries. Brough of Birsay in Orkney is also a crucial archeological site because it seems to have experienced regular Scandinavian settlements during the Pictish and Norse eras. In Maeshowe, a significant accumulation of 12th-century runic engravings can be found.

Shetland, according to early Irish writing, is called Inse Catt (meaning the Isles of Cats). This might have been the name given to the islands by the pre-Norse occupants. The Cat tribe surely resided in some areas of northern Scotland as their name can be found in names such as Cataibh (the Gaelic name for Sutherland, which means "among the Cats") and Caithness, which might have experienced a transitional period between the Pictish time and the Norse takeover, during which the Gaelic language was spoken.

Thorstein the Red and Sigurd Eysteinsson proceeded onward to the northern territories of Scotland where they conquered considerable ranges of land. The lands are depicted in the Norse sagas as including all of Sutherland and Caithness, as well as conceivably incorporating some places in Moray and Ross during the concluding decade of the 9th century. In the Orkneyinga Saga, there is the story of how Sigurd Eysteinsson crushed the Pict Mael Brigte Tusk before he died from an unusual case of post-war trauma.

Thorfinn Torf-Einarsson is said to have wed into the local gentry and Skuli Thorfinnsson, his son, is documented to have asked for the help of the King of Scots so as to assert himself as the Mormaer of Caithness in around the 10th century. According to the Njals Saga, Sigurd the Stout was the king of Moray and Ross; he was also in charge of the Dales of Caithness and Sutherland. There is the possibility that the Scottish rulers fought against the Mormaer of Moray with the Earl of Orkney as their ally in the late 10th century.

Thorfinn Sigurdsson extended his father's domain south past Sutherland and by the 11th century the Norwegian king had acknowledged that Caithness was controlled by the Earls of Orkney as a territory under the vassalage of the Scottish Kings despite the fact that its Scandinavian character was held all through the 13th century. Raghnall mac Gofraidh was conceded to Caithness subsequent to helping the Scottish lord in a fight against an earl of Orkney (named Harald Maddadson) in the mid-13th century. After 1375 the united earldom ceased and the Pentland Firth became the border between Norway and Scotland.

So far, on the north Scottish side of south Beauly, no Scandinavian place-names have been discovered and no archaeological evidence is available that indicates Scandinavian movement in the northwest. Furthermore, in the mid-9th century, the northern Inner Hebrides, Outer Hebrides, and the Northern Isles were all overwhelmingly Pictish.

In the Outer Hebrides, as well as the Inner Hebrides (for instance Islay, Tiree, and Coll), there was almost a complete loss of pre-Norse names, what is more there was little progression in design, particularly between the clayware of the Viking age and the Pictish clayware in the north. The visible similarities show that the Pictish pots might have been the works of Scandinavians who dwelled in Ireland; however, in early Icelandic historical documents the pots are said to be the works of slaves from Ireland and the Hebrides. Gaelic unquestionably continued to exist as a language that was spoken throughout the southern Hebrides when the Vikings settled there. Yet, place-names show that the language was not highly used and the Norse tongue might have been the main language that was spoken in the Outer Hebrides until the 16th century.

The existence of immediate Norwegian rule in the region has not been confirmed, apart from several brief occupations of land, plus, any collected records are scarce and there are no records from that time of the Norse period from the Outer Hebrides. Nevertheless, it is confirmed that the Ounceland framework was used to tax the Hebrides. Also, based on evidence from Bornais, it can be argued that settlers were more affluent than their counterparts in the Northern Isles. The reason for this comes from a looser political regime. Afterward, the Hebrides sent eight delegates from the Southern Hebrides and eight more from Skye, Harris, and Lewis to the Tynwald parliament on the Isle of Man.

An important Norse graveyard was established by Oronsay and Colonsay and a cross piece from the 11th century (embellished with Ringerike-Viking and Irish design) was found on Islay in 1838. Today, Rubha a Dunain is an uninhabited land stretching toward the south of the Cuillin slopes on Skye, here the little Loch na h-Airde is located, connected to the ocean by a short, man-made waterway. For a long time – during the rule of the Vikings and the Scottish clans – this site was essential for oceanic movement as a lock was made from stone to sustain steady water levels; ship timbers from the 12th century were also found at this location. On the west coast of Scotland, three rune stones in Christian commemorations were found on Iona, Inchmarnock, and Barra.

Norse entombments were on Arran in the Firth of Clyde, although Bute and other toponyms suggest that in comparison to the Hebrides, this settlement design was much simpler. Different Norse toponyms are preserved on the coastal territory that is around Largs. Moreover, a resplendent silver clasp of Irish origin from the 7th century – but with a runic inscription from the 10th century – was found on a slope near Hunterston. In addition, five Hogback landmarks in Govan are likely evidence of inland Scandinavian enclaves.

The limited number of records about Scandinavian settlements on the Isle of Man is found before the end of the Viking period, and is probably a consequence of the belligerent nature of the Norse in Man. However, a record was held in Chronica regum Manniae et insularum, starting from the late 11th century until 1265 when the power of Viking leaders was diminished. The first data was arguably gathered in the 13th century – the evidence it contains shows the recurring impact of the Vikings – and was discovered through runestones and archeological excavations on the Isle of Man.

Before the entry of the Norsemen, the Celtic Manx were the main occupants of the Isle of Man; nevertheless, pre-Norse Celtic place-names seemed to be absent, a fact that has made some researchers claim that the Celtic people were totally destroyed. The Vikings seemed to have brought back the Gaelic dialect in the 13th century around the time the Isle of Man became a vassal of Scotland. In any case, others debate this claim, citing the archaeological findings that appear to demonstrate the possibility that a considerable number of the local Celtic population survived under the leadership of the Norsemen. An investigation that was carried out on twenty-five Norse graveyards showed that the first Viking migrants decided to marry local Celtic women. Other proof demonstrates that the children or grandchildren from these intermarriages likely grew up as Christians and, aside from that, quite a number of such descendants frequently had Celtic language names. In addition, a number of the peasants spoke Brythonic Manx (a Celtic language) despite the fact that the Norse tongue had become the main language of the Manx.

There existed some pagan Norse graves around the 9th century and these graves – of which there were two types – were comprised of grave-merchandise from the Isle of Man. The two types are the mound entombments, in which the deceased person was buried alongside an animal, a slave, or a family member. The design of this type of grave is the typical Christian flat grave that was found in previous Christian burial grounds. At Ballateare, an agnostic entombment hill was discovered that is said to date from the late 9th century. The discovery of this grave indicates the possibility of human sacrifice during the period of the Norsemen.

The presence of the Norsemen in Scotland also led to the introduction of Scandinavian styles of house construction. On Braaid situated on the Isle of Man, it has been discovered that the Norse period houses are constructed like the typical Scandinavian style of long buildings, with curved walls, somewhat like an upside-down boat with squared-off ends. The buildings in the Isle of Man utilized turf to make wide walls, as well as timber for constructing the gabled edges, with two lines of posts typically bolstering the roof of this kind of house the posts were usually placed on a huge stone seated on the foundation as opposed to being covered. The houses at Braaid, not at all like Viking houses found in different regions, show no indication at all of inner walls. In a few areas in the Isle of Man, Scandinavian settlements were set on precipice-top peninsulas, inside semi-round banks, and were thus shielded on all sides from attack.

The Vikings also introduced the Scandinavian system of farming into the Isle of Man. At Cronk Moar, some plowing signs with plogr (a large Norse plow) have been discovered underneath the Scandinavian graveyard. The burial site is among the few that still remain that demonstrates this plowing technique from the Viking era. The kind of plow discovered would have utilized a substantial metallic plowshare that had a part for shredding the grass. The turf would most likely be hauled up and cut under using the share, with the mould-board then turning the turf, it's also probable that these plows incorporated a wheel.

Scandinavian women from the Isle of Man, Iceland, and the Western Isles came up with a weaving method to create warm, shaggy cloaks called roggr. This clothing was very useful because it protected the people against the strong cold that accompanied the North Atlantic winters. The women used the usual straight wrap-weighted loom to weave them; however, as the women wove the fabric, they might simply have knotted the combed tassels of wool into the twisted threads; they might also have placed the combed tassels inside the shed. The end product was a substantial, shaggy fur ensemble.

The center of the Manx government controlled by the Scandinavians was located in Tynwald. The Tynwald Hill was situated at the site of the administrative congress and was a four-meter high, layered, round hill. This was the meeting place for the ping (that is, the Norse congressmen) where they met every Midsummer on the 5th of July. The Isle of Man was ruled and laws made while hearings of judgment were carried out openly in Tynwald. The Manx Parliament is the oldest legislative body on the planet, with unbroken conventions held every year since its initiation during the 10th century.

In 1014 A.D. The Isle of Man partook in the fight at Clontarf. During this fight, Ospak and Brodir of the Isle of Man lead an allied group in the Norse partnership under the control of King Siggtryggr Silkbeard. Ospak had his own ill feelings and deserted the Norsemen to battle in favor of Ard Ri Brian Boru, the Irish High King. However, Brodir remained faithful to Sigtryggr; despite the fact that the Norsemen were defeated at Clontarf, the Irish High King was slain by Brodir.

A significant number of place-names of Scandinavian settlement – near the South of Sutherland – can be found along the whole western coast, yet the Scandinavian settlement in the south appears to have been short-lived. A greater part of the Gaelic names currently found on the seaboard in Wester Ross are of possible medieval origin, as opposed to a pre-Norse source. Based on a convention that is no longer available, it was found that the land of Glenelg was under the control of the king of the Isle of Man. Just as it was in Shetland and Orkney, the Norse seemed to have dominated the Pictish where ever possible.

Amlaib Cuaran was running the administrative affairs of The Rhinns in the mid-10th century. The present-day name of Galloway was derived from a blend of Norse and Irish-Gaelic settlement that created the Gall-Gaidel. The general population of Galloway was greatly oppressed by Magnus Barefoot in the 11th century. Before the end of the first millennium, Whithorn had become a focal point for Hiberno-Norse merchants who engaged in various trades around the Irish Sea; nevertheless, the documented place-name, as well as the archaeological findings of a broad Norse (instead of Norse-Gael) settlement in the region, is doubtful.

The ounceland – a traditional Scottish land measurement – framework appears to have been established down the west shoreline, around a great part of Argyll. This framework was also used in the vast southwest area – with the exception of the territory next to the interior, Solway Firth. The place-name evidence in Galloway and Dumfries is unpredictable and of blended Danish, Norse, and Gaelic influence. One feature of the region is the number of names that have a "kirk" prefix before a saint's name, an example being Kirkoswald.

So far, no proof of a consistent Scandinavian settlement along the east coast of south Moray Firth exists, and neither is there any on the Viking entombments, in spite of the fact that attacks surely occurred here. It was during the rule of Domnall mac Causantin that Dunnottar was captured. According to the Orkneyinga Saga, Margad Grimsson and Sweyn Asleifsson led an invasion of the Isle of May.

The Vikings traveled south of Scotland until they reached Maeyar, where a religious community was situated with the head of the convent being an abbot named Baldwin. The people in this community kept Swein and the men with him as hostages for seven days. Swein claimed he and the men with him were commanded by Earl Rognvald to go to the Scottish King. The friars, however, suspected their claim and further sent a message to other parts of the territory for men to come and defend them because they thought that Swein and his men were liars. As soon as Swein realized this, he pillaged as much as he could from the convent and quickly fled to his ship.

The Scandinavian expansion began with raiding parties who were looking for loot and an opportunity to create new settlements, afterwards the Scandinavians began to integrate themselves into the existing political system, and the most noticeable political system practiced in the early period was that of the Ui Imair in the south, and the Earls of Orkney in the north.

Regardless of the fact that the initiation of an official earldom of Orkney involved some debate, there is little uncertainty that the establishment experienced continuity from that point on. At first, the Kings of the Western Isles and the Earls of Orkney were likely independent rulers; however, the weight of full Norwegian control toward the end of this century caused an end to this in the north. Interestingly, from around 1100 and thereafter, the Norse Earls of the Northern Isles paid tribute to the Scottish king as the Earl of Caithness as well as to the Norwegian king for Orkney. In 1231 the sustained line of Scandinavian earls that had existed since Rognvald Eysteinsson came to an end after the murder of Jon Haraldsson in Thurso. Magnus, the second son of the Earl of Angus, was given the position of the Earl of Caithness. In 1236 Haakon IV of Norway declared Magnus the Earl of Orkney, with the earldom going to the Sinclair family in 1379. This was a noble family of Roslin, close to Edinburgh, despite the fact that Shetland and Orkney were still a part of Norway for about a hundred years more.

The situation in the Southern Isles was more intricate. Diverse rulers might have administered control over different territories and only a few could have been viewed as having any sort of real control over this vast kingdom. The Ui Imair was most likely a strong entity from around the end of the 9th century to the beginning of the 11th century, with rulers such as Gofraid mac Arailt and Amlaib Cuaran, who ruled the Isles with authority. Norse sources list different rulers; for example, Earls Gilli, Sigurd the Stout, Hakon Eiriksson, and Thorfinn the Mighty. These leaders ruled over the Hebrides and were vassals of the Kings of Norway or Denmark. The dates from the Irish and Norse sources do not fundamentally cover everything and it is not clear if these are records of contending domains or records that reflect Ui Imar's influence in the south, and direct Norse control in the north. Besides, two records in the Annals of Innisfallen state that the Western

Isles were not yet organized into a kingdom or earldom, but instead were governed by congregations of freeholders who routinely chose "lawmen" to direct their affairs. The 962 and 974 passages from the Annals of the Four Masters allude to a similar arrangement.

Godred Crovan became the leader of Dublin and the Isle of Man in 1079 and from the early years of the 12th century, the Crovan administration asserted themselves and administered as "Rulers of Man and the Isles" for the following fifty years. The kingdom was then broken because of the activities of Somerled, whose sons acquired the southern Hebrides while the Manx rulers ruled the north isles for another century. The starting points of both Godred Crovan and Somerled are unknown – the former might have originated from Ui Imair's lineage in Islay and the latter might have wedded a Crovan heiress.

In this manner, despite the fact that there were contending groups at play, the Hebrides and Islands of the Clyde were under the control of leaders of the Scandinavians. This control began in the late 10th century and continued until the development of the kingdom of Scotland and its 13th-century venture into the west.

The early Viking raids may have speeded a procedure of Gaelicisation of the Pictish kingdoms who learned Gaelic dialect and traditions. There was a fusion of the Pictish and Gaelic crowns and, despite the fact that historians still debate as to whether it was a Pictish takeover of Dal Riata or the other way around, this ended with the ascent of Cinaed mac Ailpin in the 840s, who gave power to the House of Alpin. The next leaders from this House were of a consolidated Gaelic-Pictish kingdom that lasted for about two hundred years.

In 870, Amlaib Conung and Imar, the two lords of the Norsemen who came back to Dublin from Britain with various captives, attacked Dumbarton, the capital of the Kingdom of Strathclyde. This was obviously a significant attack that may have brought the entire land of Scotland under temporary Ui Imair control. The Vikings had seized Northumbria three years earlier and created the Kingdom of York, thus conquering a lot of England, notwithstanding the diminished Kingdom of Wessex. This left the newly joined Pictish and Gaelic nearly encircled. Amlaib and his brother Auisle demolished all of Pictland, took their prisoners, and continued to trouble the region for a long time. Furthermore, the Battle of Dollar in 875 was another significant misfortune for the Picts and Scots.

In 902 the Norse experienced change in Ireland and lost control of Dublin as a result. This appears to have increased the number of incursions that the rising kingdom of Alba suffered. After a year, Dunkeld was struck and Imar, along with his grandson, was killed in combat with the men of Constantine II on Scottish soil. In the late 10th century the Albans overpowered the Vikings and won the battle of "Innisibsolian." Yet these occasions were mishaps for the Norse instead of decisive moments in history. Their battles, such as the Battle of Brunanburh in 937 and the Battle of Tara in 980, are more historically significant.

In 962 Ildulb mac Causantin, the King of Scots, was slain (as indicated by the Chronicle of the Kings of Alba) while battling the Norse that were close to Cullen at the Battle of Bauds. However, the line of the House of Alpin held firm and the danger posed by the Scandinavian presence to the eminent Kingdom of Scotland eventually diminished. By 1098, Magnus Barefoot – maybe to counter the developing Irish impact in the Western Isles – restored direct Norwegian sovereignty. He initially took Orkney, the northern Scottish territory, and the Hebrides, where in Uists he colored his sword red in blood. In that year, Edgar of Scotland made an arrangement with Magnus, which settled a large part of the dispute between the Scots and Norwegians on the islands. Edgar formally recognized the state of affairs by surrendering his right to the Hebrides and the Kintyre.

In respect to the Scottish state, following the mediation of Somerled and his death at the Battle of Renfrew, the Kings of the Isles were weakened. Yet, over a hundred and fifty years after the fact, Norway intervened once more but was unsuccessful.

In 1468 Orkney was promised the title of a lord of Norway by Christian I due to the political rivalry he had with James II. This is probably because Christian I had promised his daughter Margaret to James III of Scotland.

Despite the fact that there is proof of different burial customs – that were performed by Norse settlers in Scotland – items from graves found on Colonsay and Westray indicate that there is little evidence that suggests Norse gods were revered preceding the reintroduction of Christianity. The Odin Stone has been used as proof of Odinic beliefs and practices, yet the determining factor may well come from swearing upon the stone. A few Scandinavian sources propose that the Orcadian people believed in some aspects of the Norse pantheon, despite the fact that this is not really a definitive verification of a change in beliefs; nonetheless, it is likely that agnostic practices existed in early Scandinavian Scotland.

The greatest source of Scottish influence – after the selection of the Scottish earls in the 13th century – most likely occurred through the priests, even though the Scots affected the lives of people in Orkney and Shetland. However, they were genuinely limited until the end of the 14th century or later. An influx of Scottish tradesmen became vital, creating a wide-range of independent communities, including fishermen, farmers, and traders and they certainly proved themselves progressively, ready to guard their rights against their medieval overlords, be they Norwegian or Scot. This independence of spirit may have been encouraged by the influence of Norwegian rule, which was basically collective and elected in a different way than that of Scotland. It was not until the mid-16th century that a Scottish framework, following expansive scale migration from the south, supplanted the Norse organizations and the islanders, who were presumably bi-lingual until the 17th century.

In any case, the condition of the Hebrides is considerably less clear. Until the late 10th century, there was a Bishop of Iona; then there is a gap of over a century, conceivably filled by the Bishops of Orkney, before the selection of the first Bishop of Sodor and Man in 1079. The changes in Scandinavian Scotland, and the resulting end of servitude, along with the mix of Viking society into standard European culture are confirmed historically. These occurred at an early date, even though the popular view of wild raiding Norse as adversaries of social advancement remains. Although there is ample evidence to show that the Norse advanced society through business, the standard image of bloodthirsty raiders still comes to mind. Pings were outdoor legislative gatherings that were organized within view of the jarl; these gatherings were held to decide matters regarding all free men in a place where laws were passed and any complaints were resolved.

Women experienced a moderately high status in the Viking Age, perhaps because of the high level of mobility in society. There is little information about their role in the Scandinavian provinces of Scotland – though there is some evidence to suggest their presence among graves. Amongst the best-known female figures were Aud the Deep-Minded, Gunnhild Gormsdottir, Gormflaith ingen Murchada, and Ingibjorg (Earl Hakon Paulsson's daughter and King Olaf Godredsson's wife).

The Norse tradition of art and architecture is discussed very little. The first seat of the Bishops of Orkney was at the church near Brough of Birsay (which is no longer available for observation as it was before). St. Magnus Cathedral in Kirkwall is unique when compared to the construction design from the Norse period in Scotland. In the Church of St. Magnus on Egilsay there is a round tower that is specific only to this building. In addition, the famous Lewis chessmen are one of the best-known findings from the Viking Age.

There are clues that hint at the magnitude of trade and commerce, for example, information from the Outer Hebrides shows that pigs were a more vital part of Viking farming than earlier times. The number of red deer may have been controlled since they were not left to be hunted and killed. Fishing became an essential industry and its trade was focused towards the south (e.g. Dublin and Bristol). The coins that were discovered in Cille Pheadair and Bornais were created in England, Norway, and Westphalia, despite the fact that none were linked to Scotland. Other discoveries include ivory and manufactured materials from Greenland.

Norse and Viking colonization, through the establishment of settlements helped to create a connection on the edges of Scotland, the proof of which can be found in place names, dialect, hereditary qualities, and different aspects of social norms.

The influence of the Scandinavians in Scotland was likely at its peak in the mid-11th century during the time of Thorfinn Sigurdsson, who tried to create a uniform political and ministerial region from Shetland to the Isle of Man. The Southern Isles have an aggregate land area of roughly 8,374 square kilometers (3,233 sq miles). Caithness and Sutherland have a consolidated region of 7,051 square kilometers (2,722 sq miles) and the lasting Scandinavian holding in Scotland around then should, in this way, have been at least between a fifth and a fourth of the landmass of present-day Scotland.

A few Scots take pride in their Scandinavian families. For instance, Clan MacLeod of Lewis asserts its origin from Leod, who was a younger son of Olaf the Black. Clan MacNeacail of Skye likewise claims Norse ancestry and makes some references to the joining of Scotland with the Nordic countries as they exist today. It is important to note that there was not one single group of people that controlled Scotland unlike the Danelaw in England; however, this understanding is derived from the lack of records that are available concerning the history of Scotland.

Just as Scotland experienced Roman occupation of its land, the Norse kingdoms experienced something similar. They were, however, bound to areas that were generally remote and far from dense population centers. Moreover, aside from the real effect of Scandinavian culture, the original Scots came from a blend of Pictish and Gaelic ancestry. The Vikings should therefore be portrayed as great contributors to the formation of a multi-cultural society as opposed to just raiders that came and created havoc across Europe.

Additional Reading

Anderson, Alan Orr (1922) *Early Sources of Scottish History: A.D. 500 to 1286*. Edinburgh: Oliver and Boyd.

Armit, Ian (2006) *Scotland's Hidden History*. Stroud: Tempus.

Brink, Stefan (ed.) (2008) *The Viking World*. London: Routledge.

Burns, W. E. (2009) *A Brief History of Great Britain*. Infobase Publishing.

Crawford, Barbara E. (1987) *Scandinavian Scotland*. Leicester University Press.

Dahl, Sverri. "The Norse Settlement of the Faroe Islands". Medieval Scandinavia 14 (1970) pp. 60-73.

Downham, Clare (2007) *Viking Kings of Britain and Ireland: The Dynasty of Ivarr to A.D. 1014*. Edinburgh: Dunedin Academic Press.

Duffy, Sean (1992). "Irishmen and Islesmen in the Kingdom of Dublin and Man 1052–1171". *Eriu*. 43 (43): 93–133.

Etchingham, Colman (2001) "North Wales, Ireland and the Isles: the Insular Viking Zone". Peritia. 15 pp. 145–87

Fitzhugh, William W. and Elisabeth I. Ward, eds. (2000) *Vikings: The North Atlantic Saga*. Washington DC: Smithsonian Institution Press.

Foote, Peter and David M. Wilson. (1970) *The Viking Achievement*. London: Sidgewick and Jackson.

Gammeltoft, Peder (2010) "Shetland and Orkney Island-Names – A Dynamic Group". *Northern Lights, Northern Words.* Selected Papers from the FRLSU Conference, Kirkwall 2009, edited by Robert McColl Millar.

Graham-Campbell, James and Batey, Colleen E. (1998) *Vikings in Scotland: An Archaeological Survey.* Edinburgh University Press.

Gregory, Donald (1881) *The History of the Western Highlands and Isles of Scotland 1493–1625.* Edinburgh: Birlinn.

Haswell-Smith, Hamish (2004). *The Scottish Islands.* Edinburgh: Canongate.

Hearn, J. (2000) *Claiming Scotland: National Identity and Liberal Culture.* Edinburgh: Edinburgh University Press.

Hunter, James (2000) *Last of the Free: A History of the Highlands and Islands of Scotland.* Edinburgh: Mainstream.

Jesch, Judith. (1991) *Women in the Viking Age.* Woodbridge: Boydell

Keay, J. & Keay, J. (1994) *Collins Encyclopaedia of Scotland.* London: HarperCollins.

Logan, F. D. (1992) *The Vikings in History.* London: Routledge.

Marsden, John (2008) *Somerled and the Emergence of Gaelic Scotland.* Edinburgh: Birlinn.

McDonald, R. Andrew (2007) *Manx Kingship in Its Irish Sea Setting, 1187–1229: King Rognvaldr and the Crovan Dynasty*. Dublin. Four Courts Press.

Megaw, B.R.S. (1976) "Norseman and Native in the Kingdom of the Isles: a Reassessment of the Manx Evidence." *Scottish Studies* 20, pp. 1-44.

Murray, W. H. (1966) *The Hebrides*. London: Heinemann.

Murray, W. H. (1973) *The Islands of Western Scotland*. London: Eyre Methuen.

Nicolaisen, William F.H. (1969) "Norse Settlement in the Northern and Western Isles." *Scottish Historical Review* 48 pp. 6-17.

O Corrain, Donnchadh (1998) *Vikings in Ireland and Scotland in the Ninth Century*. CELT.

Sheehan, John and O Corrain, Donnchadh (2010) *The Viking Age: Ireland and the West. Proceedings of the Fifteenth Viking Congress*. Dublin: Four Courts Press.

Simpson, Grant G., ed. (1990) *Scotland and Scandinavia*. The MacKie Monographs, 1. Edinburgh: John Donald.

Thomson, William P. L. (2008) *The New History of Orkney*. Edinburgh: Birlinn.

Wainwright, F.T., ed. (1962) *The Northern Isles*. Edinburgh: Nelson.

Watson, W. J. (1994) *The Celtic Place-Names of Scotland*. Edinburgh: Birlinn.

Woolf, Alex (ed.) (2009) *Scandinavian Scotland – Twenty Years After*. St Andrews: St Andrews University Press.

Chapter Ten: Vikings in Greenland and Iceland

Greenland

Many settlements have been found with ruins made up of hundreds of farms across Greenland by explorers and historians. Proof of their expansive trade regime was found as they moved on from selling ivory to selling walrus tusks. They also moved toward dealing with rope and seals alongside sheep, wool, and cattle. A dependence on Norway and Iceland began to have some repercussions for the expansion in Greenland after a few decades.

Annual trade ships would arrive from Norway and Iceland, bringing everything from supplemental food items, to religious and even social contact to help continue the expansion of culture within this new expansion of the Vikings.

However, the late 13th Century saw a wholesale shift in policy; ships were now required to head from Greenland to Norway directly. As the climate began to worsen in the following decades and centuries, and the Little Ice Age began, life in Greenland became harder to adjust to and prepare for.

By 1261 A.D. the challenges were stark, and after a long period of time following the Archdiocese of Nidaros, which came after the 1126 creation of a diocese at Igaliku – then known as Garðar – Greenland became increasingly more Norwegian. 1261 A.D. was the year that Greenland accepted 'governorship' from the Norwegian King, despite retaining much of their own law. This was followed by the introduction of the Kingdom of Denmark, creating a union with the Kingdom of Norway, which resulted in an interesting boom and bust period for all of the Norse settlements.

This initial boom from the trade unions meant that, for a short period, things were looking up for the future of the Norse in Greenland. Soon though, the 14Th Century witnessed a major decline, and by 1350 A.D. the Western Settlement had been fully abandoned. This major, rapid, and unstoppable decline continued apace.

By 1378 no bishops remained at Garðar, with the last recorded item of Norse Greenlanders dated from the year 1408. A marriage took place at the Hvalsey Church, which is one of the few remaining, relatively well-preserved buildings from the era.

1408 is also roughly the year when mention of settlers arriving en masse begins to stop being recorded – after this written annals of what took place following the year 1408 are also essentially absent. Old maps by Claudius Clavus, as well as old cartography notes, show that they may have traveled to Greenland around 1420. Other than this, there is little knowledge of what happened. By the middle of the 15th Century, life for the Vikings in Greenland was more or less over.

A large number of theories exist as to why long-term prosperity in Greenland could not be achieved; from environmental damage to constant hostility, nothing is confirmed. What we do know is that the Norse settlements here lasted some 450 years. It is likely that a number of different reasons caused the abandonment of Greenland, for example, there was an outbreak of plague that caused mass population reductions in other Norse nations, like Iceland,

and people left because they could not adapt to the harsh and unfriendly environment.

The changing climate and the loss of mass value in the use of walrus ivory played a role in the eventual demise of the Norse in Greenland. While the likes of Kirsten Seaver of *The Frozen Echo* contest that the conditions and quality of life towards the end was better than it has been portrayed, it is still a fact that Greenland faded into obscurity as a Viking center.

Seaver's main belief is that an unrecorded wipeout from Inuit or European attacks, or a mass-evacuation of the colony to Iceland, are the more likely reasons as to why life here ended so abruptly for the Viking people. Others claim that a gradual but unstoppable poverty swept over the land as the environment, the local surroundings, and the general culture of the Norse people began to erode, creating a sequence of events that was nigh impossible to escape.

Iceland

While the Vikings were known for their incredible conquests throughout many parts of the world, all things have a beginning; and for much of Norse history, Iceland plays a crucial role. Discovered by the famous Naddodd, one of the very first settlers of the Faroe Islands, such a discovery could potentially be seen as an accident. Naddodd was on his way from Norway to the Faroe Islands when he got lost and managed to drift further east to the coast of Iceland instead.

Naming it Snowland, it was also discovered – at nearly the same time – by Garðar Svavarsson, a Swedish sailor who also accidentally drifted to the coast. Staying at Húsavík for the winter, he left in the spring; however, he did apparently leave behind a slave named Náttfari, who some claim was the first person to set up permanent residence on Iceland.

The first person to have come to Iceland deliberately, that we know of, was a man known as Hrafna-Flóki Vilgerðarson, or simply Floki. He was also known as Raven-Floki, as he apparently used three ravens to find his way to Iceland in the first place. According to the story, the third raven flew ahead of the ship and they followed it all the way to Iceland where, arriving in the Westfjords, they settled in a bay facing Reykjavik at the behest of one of his men, Flaxi. Sadly, a harsh winter quickly forced them from the area as all of their cattle – a vital source for survival – failed to live through a brutal winter.

Floki settled at Barðaströnd before noticing that drift ice within the winter fjords made a compelling name – henceforth dubbing the nation Iceland. A year passed despite the difficulty to survive, and eventually, they had to turn back and leave for Norway in the summer in order to stay alive. Floki, however, would later return to the location known today as Flókadalur.

The first Norse settlers arrived around 870 A.D. and began the first stages of conquest. The first permanent settler to arrive here was, according to known history, a Norwegian chief known as Ingólfr Arnarson. Arnarson was in the midst of a massive blood feud back home in Norway and had set out along with his foster brother, Hjörleifr Hróðmarsson, to explore Iceland. They stayed in a location that is today known as Álftafjörður, a short time later he left before returning a few years later with his men and some slaves to try and settle in Iceland himself.

As the story tells it he threw two large logs overboard claiming that he would settle wherever the pillars landed. Sending two slaves, Vifill and Karli, to look for the logs, a discovery was made; murderers – who had escaped to the Westman Islands – had killed his brother, and his own men had fled at the same time. Arnarson therefore hunted down his brothers' killers and slaughtered them all. His slaves eventually found the logs and they were able to settle.

Sailing along the coast, he found the pillars near a southwestern peninsula and settled close to there around the year 874. Settling with his family in Reykjavik – in the Bay of Smokes, named as such due to the steam that rose from the Earth – he stayed to help set-up what would become the very beginning of Viking settlements in Iceland.

This first set-up on Iceland soon started a trend, because within sixty years other settlers – who were keen to make this unique new part of the Norse landscape their own – took possession of all the useable land within the region. With a population of over 3,000 and over 1,500 farms and other dwellings recorded in old manuscripts, this was a region that thrived after Arnarson had made it suitable for living.

Academics believe that the number of settlers could have been much closer to 20,000, perhaps even higher. As the 9th Century came to a close the vast majority of what we know as Iceland today was occupied and under control. Various reasons for the expansion here exist, some of which may have been the vast amount of land available and the relatively warm climate compared to other parts of Scandinavia.

Those who were looking to become powerful through trade found that this region offered a very expansive location. Walrus ivory, a major trade item of the time, was in abundant supply, so many established trade in a bid to make good on the massive amounts of options available to them. Also, the centralization of Norway, which was one of the true powerhouse countries of the time, had become problematic due to the policies of Harald Fairhair, who had imposed a large number of taxes on the people forcing farmers to look for new opportunities elsewhere.

However, these are mostly theories; there is no real proof of why this kind of migration took place; all that is known for certain is that it did take place, and that a whole host of personal factors were likely put into the decision to make the move. The rapid expansion, however, came about as it always did at those times: some people took the land through force, others bought land from previous owners, while others were gifted their lands.

One of the main periods of history at this time shows that Iceland was very much a carved up country, new settlers arrived and deemed that any earlier settlers did not 'need' such large amounts of land. Given the total lack of any kind of land rental or centralized management, the land was taken as needed, or wanted, in many cases. The somewhat lawless nature of this time ensured that the age of settlement saw huge changes in Icelandic culture.

People forced their way into regions and took as they pleased, while others tried to be more diplomatic. However, others welcomed such a huge expansion as they saw it as a sort of "extra insurance"; having more people around in times of crisis, *and* helping to ease the burden to maintain the land, livestock, and slaves.

By 930 A.D. it was claimed that Iceland was "fully settled" and thus the age of settlement began to draw to a close. It was at this time that the Althing was first formed, and the age of settlement gave way to the Icelandic Commonwealth, which many believe started in-or-around this particular time.

However, immigration continued well into the 10th Century, albeit not at the original rate that had witnessed Iceland's initial rapid growth in size and population. To help sustain the population, it is argued that migration was never curbed but merely slowed. There was no longer a rush to move everything to Iceland for many, but as is necessary for many nations today, immigration was essential to maintain the populace and to continue to help and grow the culture, military, and economy of the region.

The settlement in Iceland is supposed to have played some rather interesting roles in environmental change as well. Some scholars have previously claimed that soil erosion was essentially allowed to run unchecked, and that extensive deforestation around the region – alongside over-grazing from animals – contributed to the loss of the topsoil.

Deforestation was needed to help clear the way for fields and pastures to create fuel and build equipment. However, the overall settlement and development of the culture of Iceland is recognised as one of the most important parts of Norse culture; the settlement of Iceland became a major reason for an acceleration in the exploration and taking over of other parts of the world – including lands much further afield than Scandinavia.

Chapter Eleven: Vikings in Galicia, Islamic Iberia, and the Levant

Galicia

For many people interested in Viking history the focus is on the battles in areas of Europe such as Britain and France, even though the Vikings had many conquests elsewhere. For example, they had regular battles across the ages in Spain, especially in Galicia. The Viking invasions and attacks within Galicia are a major part of the story of their expansion in Europe.

From the beginning to the middle of the 9th century they spent a lot of time engaging in war with Galicia in a bid to conquer it. Towards the height of Viking dominance they battled and plundered their way through most of the cities and settlements in the area. However, when they started to move to the Black Sea and the Mediterranean, it began to become more difficult to manage their raids and invasions.

This is when they first encountered Galicia. While much of what is known about the Viking times in Galicia comes mainly from written information, some physical items, such as typical Viking anchors, and even small riverside ports, have been found in Galicia.

The first invasion of Galicia, of the many invasions that occurred there, took place in late 844. Using a storm to power their way across the sea the Vikings arrived on the shores of Galicia and began to plunder its many villages. Eventually, the King of Asturias, Ramiro I, led an army to repel the invaders. A close battle took place which forced the Vikings back to sea, but which laid their way for Lisbon of Portugal.

This was to be the end of the first invasion, which played a major role in shaping the future battles that would come. Indeed, Alfonso III, the King of Leon, Galicia, and Asturias in later years, was terrified of the Vikings, so much so that he followed other kingdoms and realms in fortifying his lands and his coastlines, building mighty forts in a bid to prevent the Vikings from getting inland.

By 859 A.D. the second invasion had begun, this time facing off against Ordono I. With a hundred ships from various looting expeditions joining the battle, it was a much larger force than the first invasion. This time they approached from the French coast and arrived at Iria Flavia and then at Santiago de Compostela, there they carried out their customary looting, raiding, and pillaging. Other nearby towns tried to give a generous tribute to the Vikings in a bid to halt their advance, but it did not work; they still tried to force their way in.

This created an immediate situation of war, where Don Pedro led his forces into battle against the Vikings. Here he destroyed over a third of their naval forces, a fact that caused most of the retreating Norse warriors to flee south. However, the Vikings had the last laugh; they had captured the then King of Pamplona, Garcia Íñiguez, and demanded an enormous 60,000 pieces of gold for his return.

Things were getting worse for the Vikings though, and it took nearly ninety years for them to return. On their return in 951, and hoping to make up for the previous centuries mistakes, their reappearance led to a total re-structuring of how the Galician cities defended themselves. The failure of this small invasion saw an increase in the quality of the Galician's naval defense. Needing their sheer brutality to break through each time, the Vikings now faced an uphill struggle to continue laying siege to a land they had been raiding for a long time.

As the forts of Galicia became stronger, the ability to break through and invade became much harder to prepare for. Yet again, over a decade later in 964, the Vikings returned to Galicia in a bid to continue the war. They failed to best Rosendo of Celenova, the Bishop of Mondoñedo, and retreated, not to return for another four years. In 968 they had a breakthrough in an attack against Sisnando Menendez. The Bishop was slain, the Vikings laid siege to the coastline, and the town of Lugo had to put up incredible blockades in a bid to protect themselves. Curtis, a monastery of some repute, was also sacked. This caused great consternation and forced the Galicians to change their thinking and approach in how to quell the Viking threat.

In 1015 the Vikings returned once again to continue the siege, but this time they were led by the legendary Olaf Haraldsson. Olaf would eventually be known as the future King of Norway, Olaf II. In his brutal invasion of the lands of Galicia, the toll taken upon the country was immense. They ransacked major settlements such as Betanzos, Castropol, Tui, and Rivas de Sil. These cities were sacked almost to the point of no return, with Tui lying more or less empty for fifty years!

The Vikings had caused incredible damage via their ransacking of the lands, and it created a huge problem for the Galicians. The unceasing raids were not due to stop anytime soon; history shows that they continued for another two decades. As mentioned before, the Vikings had taken to holding people for ransom whenever they conducted these raids, and more than a few famous examples exist, showcasing the success of this tactic. For example, the Vikings had held the daughters of Amarelo Mestaliz, who was forced to raise money to try and safeguard their return. This forced him to use his own land as the collateral to try and raise the sum of money the Vikings demanded.

The invasions slowly came to an end in Galicia – or at least the frequency and strength of the attacks did – with the creation of the Council of Catoria. This was a group set up by Bishop Crescencio of Compostela. He pushed the Vikings back and then built a major Fortress with the aid of the Council to make sure that Compostela was safe from future attacks.

However, these later raids were the ones that struck the most fear into the Spanish people. Those who chronicled the success of Olaf at the time have noted that he was the most feared Viking across Galicia. He was incredibly successful, being one of the few to sack multiple settlements and make a critical breakthrough. As such, he was given the chilling name: The Galician Wolf.

While the Spanish and the Galicians were never the primary targets for Viking invasions, they happened often enough to have made a notable point in Viking history. Both the Christian and Muslim parts of Iberia bore incredible wounds from the barbarism of the Vikings. In fact, some might argue that their attacks on Galicia and Islamic Iberia caused the Muslims of both North Africa and Spain to take the threat more seriously.

Having grown their military fleets to exceptional power, the Vikings created the incentive for the Islamic world to maintain control of the sea long into the Middle Ages. If not for the Vikings' lust for attacks and power, then the history of Europe – and modern history itself – might be very different indeed.

While the Viking Age would never see the Spanish invasions as a true highlight of their supremacy, they played a crucial role in determining just how much of an impact, perhaps globally, the Vikings had.

Islamic Iberia and the Levant

Many parts of Viking history can be confusing, but one of the clearest and most important parts of their history stems from their battles in Islamic Iberia and the Islamic Levant. These are crucial points in Viking history, but are often underplayed despite, as noted above, the domino effect it had on how much of the subsequent history would play out.

The interesting contrast here is that, for the Norse Lands, there was a regular and simple connection between the Eastern Lands, which were mostly Islamic. They interacted with each other quite regularly and, for the most part, got on as well as could be expected. Indeed, the various Muslim dynasties of the era also sent people out on what could be considered Viking-like expeditions.

They traveled the world, forming trading pacts with other lands and cultures, and this happened a lot in Eastern European cities such as Kiev and Novgorod, which played a key role in their expansion into Europe; and it was during liaisons such as these that they first began to notice the Vikings and make note of their capabilities. However, their reputation with the Western Muslim empires was far more sporadic and subsequently often descended into violence.

One of their most critical challenges in the West came from the Muslims of Iberia and the Levant. These played a key role in how the Vikings shaped many parts of Europe and was a major part of the conflict. As mentioned before, the Viking Age had a profound effect on large parts of the world for centuries.

In 844 A.D. a large Viking fleet swept upon Al-Andalus – the Muslim held territory of the Iberian Peninsula – and with their rapid, ferocious attacks, they destroyed many cities, including Lisbon, Cadiz, and also Medina Sidonia. Ransacked by the Vikings the cities were left in a state of total disarray following the assault. Then, the Vikings launched their most daring attack of all on Seville. They continued to battle back and forth before the Vikings overcame the defenses and held Sevilla for around 42 days. However, they were eventually defeated despite having forces of over 15,000 troops and were forced out of Sevilla.

The capture of Sevilla was a major humiliation and eventually, the forces returned to defeat the Vikings and take back the towns. Ransoming their hostages, the Vikings left in a hurry but had initiated a period of immense conflict.

Following the repossession of Seville in 844 the Islamic Iberians made a major decision. They built the first navy under the Emirate of Cordoba, which was a truly exceptional fleet. There was much embarrassment following the destruction of Seville, so work was done to help ensure that such a thing would never happen again.

After many years of relative tranquility, Danish pirates launched an attack on Nekor, a tiny Moroccan state. This occurred in 859, and it was now that the Vikings captured the King's harem, eventually ransoming them back. So began a period of rapid Viking raids that saw extensive amounts of damage rained upon the region.

It was at this point that a large dockyard commissioned the creation of a large-scale ship. Huge in size and in power, it patrolled the coastline and ensured that the Vikings could no longer so easily subject the coastal regions of Iberia to attack.

From 912-976 A.D., under caliphs Abd-ar-Rahman III and Al-Hakam II, the area was routinely defended from all but the worst invasions.

In fact, at this stage, the Vikings considered the taking of the town of Cordoba and surrounding areas to be more or less impossible. Few tried their luck and over the course of the century a large-scale shift took place. Piracy now ran rife and Vikings began to become less of a threat. The arrival of piracy from North Africa meant that most Vikings had to give up the hope of ever ruling the seas as before.

Indeed, the Viking invasions into Islamic Iberia created major developments in their relations across the wider Islamic world. Following the Sevilla incident, Al-Ghazal, the famous Arab diplomat, was sent to Denmark in 844 to speak with King Harek. It was an attempt to try and make peace, to try and stem the tide of violence.

He returned to Cordoba within twenty months, and this was followed in the long-term by the arrival of the likes of Al-Tartushi, who traveled to trade with the Vikings. Over the course of a long period of time in history, the Vikings used the invasions in this region to gain prominence and to form trade with other parts of the Islamic world.

However, diplomacy did not stop the raids in this part of the world. Far from it, in fact; in 860 a fleet of over sixty ships led by the Viking legends Hastein and Bjorn Ironside launched yet another attack on Galicia. After a brief encounter they moved on to Nekor in Morocco, before continuing their brutal invasion of Iberia.

The last of the great campaigns in Islamic Iberia came in 966 and 968 when they invaded Lisbon and then Galicia once more. The second invasion, led by Gundraed the Norman, saw a hundred ships and over 8,000 men arrive for battle. The attack was a major success and they roamed the lands freely for years. It took three years for Gonzalo Sanchez to eventually round up a force that was strong enough to push the Vikings back and stop the incursions once and for all.

However, another major part of the Viking Age were the invasions of the Islamic Levant. One of the most famous names in Viking history is Harald Hardrada, who was one of the Kings of Norway, reigning from 1046-1066 A.D. He tried to claim the English and Danish thrones in 1064 and 1066, but before this time – at the peak of power – he served for nearly fifteen years as a mercenary and an exile from his homeland.

There, on his travels, he spent time in the command of Kievan Rus and of the Byzantine Empire's Varangian Guard. He also served the Byzantine Emperor in battles in Palestine, as well as in locations as far afield as North Africa and the Middle East. He spent a huge amount of time dealing with Armenia and even Sicily, which is perhaps the location of some of his most famous raids.

These were some of the fiercest battles that he participated in, making up a large part of the history of the Norse invasions and attacks against the Islamic Levant. Many large rune stones can be found across Scandinavia today, dedicated to fallen Viking seafarers who met their end in Serkland or Arabia.

In the Eastern part of the Mediterranean, however, the Vikings carried none of the negative context held against them in other parts of the world. They were seen as people who fought, but who also traded. In fact they were more readily associated with trade than pillaging, murder and violence and seemingly made regular trade in Baghdad, a city of major importance at the time.

While raids took place in the early part of the 900s, particularly in 910, 912, and then much later in 942, raids in the Caspian region were mostly failures, certainly going from what history tells us. Therefore, the Vikings may have dominated many parts of the world, but the Islamic world took them seriously enough to create a fleet that for centuries was the envy of the world.

Chapter Twelve: Viking Weapons, Sports, and Entertainment

Games and Entertainment

Although the Vikings were savage in battle, they were subdued when it came to entertainment. They enjoyed it to the utmost – in their own inimitable way – as it was inherent to their lifestyle and culture. They conquered and partied and were loud in disposition. They enjoyed their beverages, sang loudly, and danced to music that was still in line with their robust and aggressive nature.

Their physical appearance attracted the fairer sex of those they conquered whilst antagonizing the men, which brought about conflicts in most places of entertainment that they attended. They were sometimes a law unto themselves when they were entertained, which left much to be desired in their general behavior even though they saw nothing wrong with it.

They drank intoxicating beverages from large mugs that were as large as a man's head. They kept long unkempt beards and mustaches, to project a tough, manly image. They mastered the art of playing music using harps, lutes, lyres, and fiddles, among other instruments such as large drums and other musical paraphernalia. They gambled and played board games of which there have been several archaeological finds. These discoveries prove that they used wooden and stone boards with dice made of bones, wood, and even materials like ivory.

The games that they played were not specific to any segment in their hierarchy but were spread throughout their society, giving the impression that they did not really have a class-segmented community, but rather a more cohesive relationship across their social structure.

Several board games and respective pieces have been unearthed in areas throughout Europe. Some board games, similar to chess, with black and white boards show that some of their influence exists in the modern world of games as well. However, we do not have substantial evidence to decide if they borrowed these games from elsewhere or invented themselves.

Feasts and festivals were common, some of which included men, women, and children. They had other indoor games that kept them on their toes, such as beer drinking competitions, barrel carrying, and other similar games of an exhausting nature.

Even some of the dances that they indulged in had an element of aggressiveness, and they certainly did not have the very cultured dance moves that we are familiar with in the Western world. Even today, Eastern Europe and Western Europe both have differences in culture, the West seeming more sober, prim, and proper in comparison.

Weapons and Armor

When they built up their armies and gained the expertise to wage war, and developed an array of adequate weaponry to do so, they moved out, unlike any other army, not in a disciplined and organized way but in a savage and violent sweep. They subjected the other armies of the Western European countries to a new strategy of warfare, which became popularly known as "Berserkergang."

It was based on the premise of going "berserk", which did not allow time for their opponents to regroup or reorganize. It was a speedy and savage attack that was meant to annihilate their enemies as quickly as possible. They instilled great fear in their opponents by carrying two-handed axes, long spears, and vicious swords. They wore menacing helmets with two horns, while their body armor was tailored to their large physique.

Many archaeological findings indicate that they carried large shields and were formidable in close combat. They propagated a new brand of strategic warfare specifically designed to instill fear and overwhelm their opponents while creating a sense of instability. It was their savage attitude and the pace of their attacks that prevented counter-attacks from their enemies. It was also believed that they drank alcohol above moderate quantities and probably used narcotics to propel them to such savagery. There were many natural sources of hallucinogenic and psychoactive drugs, and they perhaps used them to aid their savage behavior. There is no evidence recorded to support this argument, but it could be deduced from the fearsome way in which they went into battle and fought on the battlefield.

What brought such a savage trait to the fore is still a puzzle to historians and archaeologists, because other Europeans of the same period never had such qualities. The Europeans eventually even brought a new legal framework to warfare, with many international agreements on how war should be conducted and the way prisoners should be treated. Even World War I and World War II did not see a savagery like what the Vikings practiced.

The "Berserkergang" warfare that they propagated had been never seen before on any battlefield, and it is this mad rushing force – with large weaponry, shields, long swords, huge knifes, and spears – that became their trademark. They did use bows and arrows, and even crossbows, but they had this inherent notion that men had to fight hand-to-hand combat in order to prove their superiority over their opponents.

The Vikings were expected to carry their weapons at all times and it was an integral part of their daily attire. Even though they did not use the normal-sized sword in battle, they carried it as a part of their dress code. The richer and more affluent Vikings wore the iron helmet, which bestowed on them rank, status, and respect in the community. Furthermore, a light steel body armor was worn at functions – especially by those that held higher ranks in the military – while those lower in rank dressed with a different type of body armor made of leather.

Guards who were entrusted with the security of the King and the higher-ranking elite had strong, huge, and heavy axes. They had to be carried into battle with both hands and were menacing to look at as they could split any shield in two or split a man's skull even if he was wearing a helmet.

After the Vikings, many armies tried to emulate them in battle but none could match them, maybe because the Vikings not only practiced "Berserkergang" warfare but also had the brawn to take it to the highest levels. Some people suggest that the Vikings were a different kind of human, while others – with superstitious beliefs – say they were aliens that were reincarnated.

Viking Sports

Viking sports revolved around physical strength, which tested brawn more than brain. In contrast, the English had games that focused more on techniques and the use of cognitive processes. One sport that the Vikings enjoyed, was jumping from oar-to-oar, which generally occurred at the sides of their ships whilst they were sailing and the oarsmen were rowing. Any missed step placed them in mortal danger, or could have caused permanent physical injury, but they continued to play this game even amongst their leaders. The well known, and very popular, King Olaf Tryggvason, played this sport on a regular basis whenever he was at sea.

They swam in the sea and competed over long distances, as there were no meager competitions amongst them. If they competed, they did so to the fullest extent possible, such that the weakest would ultimately be left behind. Others just did not have the stamina to compete. Other sports revolved around testing their fighting skills, something that seems to have been an integral part of their DNA. A signal that would often lead to fighting was the dropping of a helmet, which meant that a challenge had been made.

They would run while carrying huge tree trunks, large cauldrons for cooking, and large buckets of water from one point to another in competition. Their winter sports were not any tamer, as they were designed to test who could withstand the lowest temperatures of cold. They did play a ball game that was similar to hockey and was also popular among Viking children. They tried their skills at skating and skiing during winter, and even that they took to an extreme level – beyond the calling of ordinary men.

Their women swam and even took part in some of the physical sports, as they too were very strong. Hunting skills were tested on a constant basis to determine who was fit to lead. They would hunt deer, hare, rabbit, wild boar, and even birds. Initially, they only used spears, but later developed and adopted a special crossbow. They tested their strength in the fields with horse riding, sword fighting, arm wrestling, wrestling, and mountain climbing on the highest mountains they could find.

As a result, their skills at archery were superlative, swimming was par excellence, fighting was exquisite, their strength was unimaginable, and because of these practices, they were a formidable people of an era that has now gone into the annals of history as one of the most violent periods in the history of Europe. Some of these sports that the Vikings developed are today "played" during certain festivities around Scandinavia. Many people attend these gatherings just to see what it was the Vikings developed and played.

Chapter Thirteen: Viking Art

Lots of Viking history comes in the form of sophisticated art. They worked in ornamental metalwork, horse harnesses, weapon mounts, as well as for personal ornaments. Some organic materials are still preserved in a few towns; such as bones and woodwork, that can be used for research and study. In order to properly assess the history of the Vikings, one must undergo a detailed study of the art pieces that were developed in the early, middle and late Viking age. However, a lot of the essential information about their art is now lost due to the rotting of textiles, painted wood, and wooden sculptures. These art pieces suffered an inevitable decay in quality as time passed, and it is almost impossible to analyze their appearance to any degree of accuracy.

History reveals that Viking Art commonly relies upon a number of durable objects such as textiles, ivory, bone, wood, stone, and metal.

Wood and Organic Materials:

Viking artists considered wood a primary material for their artwork, due to its abundance, cost-effectiveness, and easy carving properties. Most of these works survived from the beginning of the Viking age to the end of that period, which is why Viking woodwork acts as a major resource for information about their creative art forms. Some of the most common wooden art pieces of the Vikings can be seen through the Oseberg Ship Burial carvings, and the attractively carved decorations found in Urnes Stave Church. The Oseberg carvings originate in the 9th century and the Urness Stave Church in the 12th century. These findings provide hints about other missing Viking art as well.

Stone:

History reveals that the stone carvings were commonly made in Scandinavia by the middle of the 10th century. However, exceptions to these masterpieces include the Gotlandic Picture stones of Sweden. Other than this, Viking age stonework can be visualized from the ultimate creation of the Jelling royal mountains in Denmark. Stone art became more prevalent with the influence of Christianity and the stones were converted into permanent memorials.

Metal:

As most of the artwork from the Viking age is missing, the major influence of this art form is seen in the form of ornamental metalwork. Most of these metal objects are well preserved due to their high durability, and they lead to a deeper understanding of the Viking's ability for artistic expression. Both women and men wore decorated jewelry pieces, and other metalwork objects included household goods, tools, and weapons.

Oseberg Style of Viking Art

Norse art is a popular form of Scandinavian culture that was developed during the Viking Age and is recognized for its unique ornamental designs and animal shaped creatures that are somewhat similar to Celtic art. The Viking Artists were more concerned with specific animal shapes like horses, wolves, dragons, and even dogs. This art form was divided into six different styles. Various records of these art forms were found during the Christian and Pagan time periods of Denmark.

Viking Art easily found a market from the 9th to the 11th century namely because of the decorative aspect of the pieces and their unique design inspirations. The Vikings in this era worked on runestones, weapons, jewelry, ship woodwork, and even on several commonly used items. It was developed stage-by-stage – with ornamental style decorations – where the artists used a wide variety of tools to finish their artwork. The very first representation of Viking Art was found in the Oseberg style, which was common from 800 to 875 A.D.

The Oseberg style was popular in the 9th century and touched on the Viking's religious iconography. Some of the major considerations of this art form included sinuous animal forms and the gripping of the beast motif. Apart from these, the focus of artists was on work on the neck, paw grip edgings, and many other essential parts of the creature's body. The gripping beast was popular in that era and it was recognized as an essential part of Viking culture for almost a hundred and fifty years.

The naming of the Oseberg style of Viking art is derived from the Oseberg burial site and it was common between 800 and 875 A.D., whereas Broa was popular from 750 to 825 A.D. Note that the name Bora was derived from the gravesite of a man at the Swedish Isle of Gotland that used to contain bridle mounts. The Broa style of Viking art was often found on several Oseberg-style carved items. History also reveals that the popular woodcarver Oseberg Barque developed his art style by following the basics of Broa. That is why these two art styles are often grouped together.

The major identifying elements of the Oseberg Style are recognized as:

- Use of creative graded relief.
- Lesser usage of Broa style's popular ribbon-shaped animals.
- Several new developments in the form of the gripping beast design and semi-naturalistic animal forms. They were completed with compact and very squat shapes.
- Equal sized Motifs with similar compositional value were also common in this era and they were usually placed on a carpet-like pattern.

The influence of the Oseberg style was also observed in Christianized Scandinavia. One of the common examples of the Oseberg art includes the three state beds present at the Oseberg Burial. Two of these beds are available in fragmentary form whereas the third form is available in the prow. These bed frames were designed with two well-decorated head planks, two-foot posts, two broad type side planks, and base planks. Note that the headboard of these beds was fixed with wedges whereas the sideboards were attached with the help of wooden pegs holding them to the main headboard. It had six bottom planks that were connected to the side planks. Various openwork animal heads were designed on these head planks and these decorated pieces were painted along with partially visible geometrical figures. The artists followed specific measurements for design and the decorations were often completed with simple carvings. Some of the common shapes noticed at the top of the bed were large-erect ears, gaping jaws, and pointed snouts.

Borre Style of Viking Art

After the Oseberg style period ended there were shifts in art forms that led to another type of style, one that would persevere from 875 to 950 A.D. and became known as the Borre Style.

A set of bridle mounts from a burial ship at Borre, Norway, gave the inspiration for the naming of the Viking art style 'Borre'. This particular form is connected to the other two common art styles of the Viking age, namely the Oseberg and Jelling styles. The gripping beast of the Oseberg was followed in a similar way by the Borre style, but the old Oseberg style of sinuous creatures displayed triangular heads. The transitioned face looked like a cat with protruding ears and round eyes. This style was considered to be the purest form of Viking or Norse art, as it did not have any outside influence. It was commonly seen in England, Russia, and Iceland. The popularity of Borre art grew by the end of the 9th century and continued until the middle of the 10th century.

The common identifying elements of the Borre Style include several unique things. The gripping beasts were taken from the old Oseberg, or Broa, art form, and were refined by the artists that followed. Also, the animal structures of the Borre ornaments were a creative mixture of gripping beasts and ribbon-shaped animals. Borre animals were recognized for their four legs, polygon-shaped hips, ribbon body – with a circular design – and a masked type of triangular head with big ears and bulging eyes. These animal bodies were finished with polished legs and heads that had a smooth appearance.

Borre was also known for its knot work, where animals were designed with ribbon-like bodies including plant motifs. The ring chain pattern was another popular knotted motif of the Borre style. It was a unique knotted pattern with a double ribbon plait that resulted in a symmetrical interlace. All the boundaries of every single intersection were formed by circles, followed by hollow sided lozenges. The primary difference between the Oseberg and Borre art forms was defined in terms of a ribbon plait motif that was a special addition to the Borre style. Just as Oseberg art pieces were finished with dragons and ferocious serpents, the Borre style was developed with circular masks, where ribbons were joined to complete the structure.

Borre jewelry designs remained popular for a long time and the materials used for ornaments were durable. These jewelry pieces were used throughout Scandinavia and were also popular in Russia for their creative modifications over the Oseberge style. Following this, the Jelling style became the popular choice among artists.

Jelling Style of Viking Art

The Jelling style of the Viking age dates back to the 10th century where the trend continued for almost seventy-five years. The Borre and Jelling styles overlap each other with the similarity of the objects they portray. This Viking art was focused on stylistic animal shapes with an "S" form, profiled heads, pigtails, and spiral hips. It was classified in terms of motifs alone and gained more attention among the Vikings between the years of 870 to 1000 A.D.

The Jelling stones are recognized from their brightly painted polychromatic palettes. The runestones were painted with unique designs throughout Scandinavia. They were named after the popular Jelling Town in Denmark.

Popular Shapes of the Jelling artwork style:

- Solid bodies with fine shapes.
- Attractive neck tendrils.

- Designer heads in profile.
- Jelling art pieces were popular for their curled lip-lappets.
- The open jaws can be identified as unique art pieces of the Jelling style.
- Artists of the Jelling style used pellets that crossed limbs with joints.
- They were finished with attractive round eyes.

The most common forms had perfect geometric regularity. The commonly used patterns were striated ribbons, contours, double-stranded ribbons, and semi-open loops.

Jelling art motifs were very popular in the Viking Age. It also included a few harness bows that were a part of Mammen art. Another popular motif of the Jelling style was where three ribbon animals – each designed in an S-shape – are attached to each other with pretzel knots. This design was inspired by the Borre style composition. The mirrored S-shaped creative ribbon animals make another motif of Jelling Viking art as they were commonly observed on mounts and brooches.

Mammen Style of Viking Art

After creating several masterpieces in the early Viking age, by following the trend of Oseberg, Borre, and the Jelling styles, the artists shifted their interests towards the Mammen style.

The commonly known Mammen style gained a great deal of attention near the end of the 10th century. It was inspired by Jelling but the creativity was a little more redefined and injected with new scopes of artwork. The most common art patterns of the Mammen style include serpents, birds, lions, and foliate patterns. The point worth noting was that the name Mammen was actually derived from the little ax head situated on gravesites in Denmark. This popular ax head was well carved and finished with a silver pattern. One side of it was decorated with foliate patterns, whereas the other side was covered with attractive ribbon style birds that had tendrils on their tails and wings.

The Mammen style took most of its elements from Anglo-Saxon England and Western Europe where the semi-naturalistic bird and lion motifs were inspired by Europe, and the plant-scroll motifs were a part of English culture. However, instead of simply copying these styles, the Vikings translated them into their own art form. Harold Bluetooth, at Jelling Churchyard in Jutland, developed one of the most popular examples of the Mammen Viking art style.

Commonly used shapes in the Mammen Viking art style:

- It was developed with tendril terminals that were loosely scrolled to create a unique impression.
- Most of the tendrils followed S-Shaped designs with long appearances.
- Spirals were also used as the most common tendril terminals.
- The Mammen style of Viking art was popular for pellets that used to intersect the ribbons.
- This art form was incomplete without concave dents.

The flow of ribbon-like elements was developed using single, double, and even triple loops. It was well known for its multi-loop finish and pretzel knots that gave a creative appearance to all pieces fashioned in this way. Some of the most common patterns of the Mammen style of Viking art were semi-open loops, along with stylish knots that had visible backgrounds.

The counters were well finished and they had double-stranded ribbons as the most common type of symbol. Some of the most popular motifs of the Mammen style were human masks, birds, snakes, great beasts, and vegetal ornaments. The human masks were usually fashioned from durable materials such as wood, bone, and stone.

Ringerike Style of Viking art

Last-but-not-least is the style known as the Ringerike style. It found its origin from somewhere in the Mammen style and got its name from a popular district of Norway where carved slabs were very common.

The Ringerike style was defined in terms of lion-shaped beasts and other prevalent collections including foliate patterns and plant motifs. This art form was popular in the first half of the 11th century as artists in this era focused on runestones to complete their artwork. The animals engraved were highly curvy in nature and had almond shaped eyes along with long, thin tendrils. One of the most common representations of the Ringerike style is found in a great beast fighting with a snake. This image spread like wildfire throughout the region of Scandinavia, as well as southern England, and even in Dublin.

Popular shapes in Ringerike Viking art:

- One of the most popular artworks included tendril terminals with a tightly scrolled design.
- The artists of this era focused more on short and slim tendrils.
- The designs were mostly completed with single lobe-type tendrils that gave a unique impression.
- The style followed alternative rounded sides with the main body of the creature.

- It was inspired by the clusters of tendrils where creatures were centrifugally projected.
- The pallets were developed with intersecting ribbons.
- Hip joints usually followed the common spiral form of the Mammen style.
- The eyes of this art form were almond shaped instead of the old round designs.

Most of the ribbon-like attractive tout loops were designed with simple curves in only one direction. The common structures in the art pieces were completed using multi-loops, pretzel knots, figure of eights loops, and pear-shaped loops. Some of the unique patterns of this style were designed with visible backgrounds of knots and semi-tight loops. It also had several double-stranded ribbons and ornament lines that were creatively crossed to form various panels.

The style was popular for its single motif and attractive tauter compositions. Clusters of tendrils were formed by following the additive principles, and designs were completed with great symmetry. Some of the most popular motifs of this era include the vegetal cross, animal intertwined snake, bird intertwined snake, and pear-shaped loops that had three snakes. All of these motifs were observed in the Brooches of Scandinavia. The animal intertwined snake form was the most popular among all of these motifs and eventually became popular in the British Isles as well. The decorative pieces of the Ringerike style were later discovered in Sweden, Skane, Lund, Norway, Oslo, and Trondheim.

Chapter Fourteen: Norse Mythology

Norse mythology contains various legends and myths. Most of these have to do with ancient gods and heroes, but are also connected to the creation and destruction of the Universe. These legends and myths are believed to be the heritage of original Germanic peoples, and all that is known about Germanic mythology comes from them. History indicates that human awareness of spirituality developed at a more rapid rate after the Noachian era. This brought with it the proliferation of religions and beliefs, which could help to explain why Norse mythology was slow in developing, and why different gods, goddesses, and heroes gained different levels of acceptance by different people.

Much of what was known came from the oral tradition of telling stories from one generation to the next. As expected, there were some alterations and omissions that occurred in the process. It was not until the learned Christian historians of the medieval times developed an active interest in Norse stories that documentation began in earnest. Since the beliefs, practices, and attitudes of the Norsemen were largely viewed as paganistic in nature; the parts of their culture that were written down by the Christian scholars were severely altered.

However, Old Norse literature is still rich with the history of Scandinavian civilization. Even the most cursory look at both Norwegian and Icelandic Literature should show an unbiased researcher that the history of mythology has been carefully preserved, regardless of the aforementioned disadvantages attributed to the Christian scholars' bias. Some of the Norwegian and Icelandic works date back to 1075 A.D. and it these that form the foundation of our current understanding of Scandinavian mythology.

Norse Gods and Beings

The world of the Norse is full of interesting escapades by gods, demigods, spirits, and other beings, apart from humans. In Norse mythology, humans were not the only intelligent beings in the world. Other animate and inanimate things in the world were believed to have consciousness. So, animals, plants, bodies of water, rocks, and other natural elements in the world were referred to as either "beings" or "gods".

If these elements were not treated as deities, they were viewed as having at least a god in charge of their lives. For the most part, these gods – or beings – were not invisible. But Norse mythology thrives on the plight of its gods, and tells fascinating stories of interaction between the gods themselves and between the gods and other beings; some were friends while others were foes. The following sections mention sets of gods in groupings according to their similarities.

Aesir Gods and Goddesses

This is the principal tribe of divine beings. According to Norse cosmology, the deities in this tribe reside in Asgard, above the underworld and in the sky. They are the ones believed to be maintaining the order of the Norse World.

The Aesir gods and goddesses include Odin, Tyr, Thor, Heimdall, Loki, Frigg, Baldur, Idun, and Bragi. These are the most prevalent gods in the tribe of Aesir. There are also other minor gods and goddess contained within the pantheon. These are Vili and Ve, Vali, Forseti, Hodr, Gefjun, Sif, Ullr,

Vidar, Fjorgynn and Fjorgyn, Sol and Mani, Jord, Hoenir, Hermod, and Lodurr.

- o Odin

Odin was a male god who was considered to be the wisest of all Norse gods. He was also regarded as having the strongest magical power and was revered as the god of war. He was the god of death and poetry. He had a strong, deep and age-long connection with ravens, which dated back to the mid-600s, long before the Viking Age. In fact, Odin was called the raven god (Hrafnaguð), the raven tempter (Hrafnfreistuðr), and the priest of raven sacrifice (HrafnblótsGoði). Numerous illustrations of him flanked by ravens can still be seen today.

It's said that he daily sent ravens out to gather knowledge for him, a knowledge he craved to the extent that he sacrificed himself for it, hanging himself on the world tree known as Yggdrasil. He also sacrificed his eye for wisdom and knowledge, so that he would be able to form a well that would give him great knowledge (the Well of Mimir or the Well of Urd). This is why he was described as a one-eyed god, who wore a cloak and grew a long, grey beard. Any picture of Odin usually portrays him as wearing a wide hat that covers his face, so that it wouldn't be obvious that he only had one eye.

He was also said to have a high seat that was called Hlidskialf, from where he could see every part of the world and observe all that was going on. He had a place reserved for some of his slain warriors, who were called Einheriar. This place was called Valhalla. Odin was also said to have a spear and a bow with ten arrows. The spear never missed its mark and was called Grungir. The bow usually shot ten arrows at once, such that no one could escape being hit. He also possessed a magical ring called Drapnir, a horse named Svadilfar and two wolves called Geri and Freki.

Odin's destiny was to die by being swallowed by Fenris-Wolf at Ragnarok. He was not deterred even after learning of how he would die before his time arrived.

- Tyr

This was the god of law and justice in the pantheon of Aesir; which is why he is referred to as the god of war. He would lead the war to redeem justice and enforce laws. He was a brave god; brave enough to give away his right hand, resulting in him being referred to as a left-handed god, even though there is no consensus regarding the cause of his left-handedness. Some traditions say that he put his hand in the mouth of Odin's wolf and the wolf bit off his right hand. Others say that he gave his hand as a pledge of honor.

- Thor

Thor was the defender of the Asgard and the son of Odin and the goddess mother Jord. He was also a brother of Frigg, who was another famous god. He was described in inscriptions as the fiery-tempered god of thunder. As a defender of his community, he would defend everyone from the giants. Recognizing the giants as his nemesis, he would smash their heads with his strong hammer, Mjollnir, which was believed to be one of the inventions of the dwarfs. He would always use a pair of iron gloves and fasten a belt of strength to use his mighty hammer. He lived in a place called the Land of Strength, or Thruthheim, and married a beautiful, golden-haired goddess named Sif.

- Heimdall or Heimdallr

Heimdall, also known as Heimdallr, was the white-skinned god who was the watchman of the Asgard. He was said to have been born of nine mothers, who were sisters. He would watch the rainbow bridge (called Bitfrost) to see if the frost giants were on the horizon. The ever-vigilant god never slept, seeing and hearing everything going on from his heavenly mountain abode, Himinbjorg. He was vigilant enough to see clearly in the dark and to hear the sound of sheep wool growing. He also had three classes of men, including the slave, freeman and noble, all of which are correspondingly referred to in the mythology as Thrall, Carl, and Earl.

- Frigg

This goddess was considered to be a loving sorceress, and a goddess of wedlock and marriage. She was the powerful wife of Odin and lived in a place called the Ocean Halls (Fensalir) – probably because she was believed to have the ability to weave the clouds – she also had the ability to see the future. But she wouldn't reveal whatever she had seen to anyone because she was also secretive. Her husband couldn't see as much as her, so she held a special status. She had a son named Balder (or Baldr) from Odin. She's also referred to as Frigga in many works and some traditions even say that the fifth day of the week is named "Friday" in her honor.

- Loki

Loki was regarded as a cunning god who employed many tricks to accomplish the tasks that were considered to be difficult or impossible. He was considered to be one of the giants by some historians, even though he belonged to the Aesir. He was filled with a series of machinations and mischief, but was still made a member of the Aesir by Odin himself when he declared him to be his blood brother. Eventually, he caused the death of Balder by his crafty actions and that is why he was bound and will remain bound until Ragnarok – the end of the world – when the gods will free him. However, the punishment meted out to him could not undo the damage he had done. He had a trick he usually employed to kill the giants in order to free their captives.

- Balder/Baldr/Baldur

Baldur was the god and a son of the king and queen of gods, Odin and Frig. His name means "The Glorious." Other designations for him are "the god of tears" probably because he died young and "white as" perhaps due to his handsomeness and wisdom. Since he was full of brightness and would radiate light, he was called the god of light. He had a wife named Nanna and a son named Forseti; they dwelt together in their home, which was called The Broad-Gleaming (Breidablik) and was considered to be too holy of a place to accommodate anything unclean. Baldur's home was covered with a silver roof that was placed on golden pillars.

His death was foretold in a dream that indicated that his fraternal twin Hod or Hodur would cause his death. To prevent this, his mother Frigg made everything that lived above and below swear that they wouldn't hurt her son. Everyone except the mistletoe swore. Loki was disguised as an old woman and found out that only the mistletoe would be able to kill Baldur since it had not sworn in front of Frigg. He then tricked Hod into using the mistletoe to kill Baldur. In a bid to bring Baldur back, Hermod went to Hel's realm to facilitate an arrangement that would bring Baldur back to life.

This would have been possible if everything living were to weep for Baldur.

Everyone wept for him except Thokk, a giantess. It was Loki who, disguised as the giantess, refused to weep. After this, no more efforts were made to bring Baldur back to life.

- Bragi

Writers differ on the identity of Bragi with some describing him as a 9th-century god, with the full name Bragi Boddsason. A few others think that he was raised to be a god from a lower level, while others believe he was a fictional character conjured up by Odin himself so that "Bragi" could be used as a pseudonym. But the most popular opinion states that he was a son of Odin from the giantess Gunlod. This skaldic god was the poet of the court of Odin. Myth has it that he was the skald of Valhalla, who was responsible for heralding the dead into the royal hall. He was known as the one to be called upon to come and render poetry with his eloquence and skills. The depictions of him indicate a god with a long beard playing the harp. He was married to the goddess Idun.

- Idun

Idun was a goddess who usually bore apples, which were instrumental in keeping the gods ever young. According to mythology a giant known as Tjasse abducted Idun and this led to the gods suffering the effects of aging. Later, the eevr tricky Loki killed the giant and brought Idun back to court. She was called the goddess of youth but the literal translation of her name means "Rejuvenating One."

Vanir Gods and Goddesses

This realm contains the gods and goddess of the second tribe and they are unlike the Aesir gods as the Vanir deities associate more with the natural world. Gods and goddesses such as Frey, Freya or Freyja, Odr, Njord, Gullvieg, and Nerthus are in this hierarchy of divinity and lived in the Alfheim.

- Frey

Frey was the most popular god in the Alfheim, the home of the Vanir gods. As the ruler of their realm, the meaning of his name is "Lord." He was believed to be in command of the weather and fertility. As Norse mythology has it, his father was Njord and his mother was Njord's sister. He was the brother of Freya and a stepson of Skadhi. He lived among the gods of Aesir as a result of the peace treaty made between Aesir and Vanir. He and Njord, together with Freya, were sent there by the Vanir since there was an exchange of hostages between the two realms.

Frey, also known as Freyr, had a ship called Skidbladnir which could move on land, sea, or through the air. It was the dwarves that manufactured this ship, which was large and spacious enough to contain all of the gods. It was at the same time flexible and small enough such that it was foldable and could fit into a pocket. He also had a chariot, but it was not drawn by horses as any usual chariot, but rather by two boars known as Gullinbursti and Slidrugtanni, such that he would ride through the sky. This chariot was also made by the dwarfs, at the command of Loki.

He married a beautiful giantess named Gerd, their love having developed when Frey espied Gerd from the throne of Odin. In order to woo Gerd, Frey sent his servant Skirnir to seek her hand in marriage. Frey lent his magical sword (that could rotate automatically) and his horse to his servant so that he could successfully accomplish this task.

- Freya/Freyja

This was the most popular goddess among the Vanir and she had no match among the heathen Norse. She was the goddess of war, wealth, love, and fertility. She was the sister of Frey and also a daughter of Njord. She had a beautiful daughter from her husband Od (which some thought was also Odin). Her other name was Hnoss (which means "treasure) and everything that was considered to be valuable was named after her. The Battlefield (Folkvang) was her home where she could choose as many as half of the slain warriors daily as was her want.

She had a chariot that was drawn by cats and a Brisings necklace which she acquired after sleeping with four dwarves; which is why she considered the necklace precious. Later, due to the tradition of exchanging hostages, she went to dwell among the Aesir as a hostage. It was at this time that she allegedly taught them seiðr or magic.

- Njord

This is another god in the tribe of the Vanir who was the father of Frey and Freya and the god of the wind and sea. He lived at Noatun and accidentally married the giantess Skadhi when the gods decided to ask her to demonstrate her sorrow over the death of her father Thjatsi. When the gods asked Skadhi to choose a husband among them, she chose Njord by mistake but the choice, once made, was binding. She wanted to marry Balder and when she was asked to pick a husband by the feet, she picked Njord's feet instead of Balder's because she thought Balder's feet were the most beautiful. In any case, because Njord and Skadhi could not agree upon a place of residence, they ultimately parted.

- Gullveig

Gullveig was another Vanir goddess whose identity is also a matter of debate. She is identified as the Triple Goddess and the ideal that permeates almost all cultures and religions of the modern world. She was called the Heid, which means the witch, even though her name means "Power of Gold." When the Aesir attempted to kill her for an unknown reason, it triggered the first war in the world that took place between the Vanir and the Aesir. Since the Vanir won this war, Gullveig survived. The end of this war brought peace between the two tribes of the gods, to the extent that they exchanged gods and ruled together.

- Nerthus

She was thought to be one of the goddesses of wealth, peace, and prosperity. Some thought her to be an earlier manifestation of Njord or his sister. In Denmark she was held in high esteem among the Norse goddesses in the tribe of Vanir.

The Giants

Another group of beings in Norse mythology is that of the giants. They are also known as fellers or devourers. They were the enemies of the Aesir; the spirits of darkness, night, winter, and death. The famous ones among them are Skadhi, Hel, Aegir, Ran, Ymir, Fenrir, Ragnarok, Jormungand, Nidhogg, Skoll, Hati, and Garm.

- Skadhi

Some historians say Skadhi was one of the Vanir but she was not. As detiled above, she married Njord who was a Vanir, but she was a huntress and the goddess of snowshoes. Her father was Jotun Thajzi. As a giantess she was considered to be among the earliest gods of the Scandinavians.

- Aegir

Also called Hler, Aegir was somehow connected with water and revered as the god of the ocean. Although he could be considered to be one of the Vanir, history favors his inclusion among the Norse giants. Anything that happened in the ocean was credited to him under the name of Snorri, the ruler of the sea. For instance, whenever there was a storm at sea, it would be interpreted to mean that Aegir was agitated; and any ship that was wrecked was believed to have entered Aegir's wide jaws. He always had nixies and mermaids in attendance.

Aegir's father was Mistarblindi, or Mist-Blind, and he also had a brother called Logi, which means Fire. Together with his sister who became his wife, Ran, Aegir lived on an island called Hlesey under the sea. They had nine daughters who were poetically named after the waves. Norse mythology says that he was hospitable to the gods, as they would come to his home to drink beer and ale. This was clearly different from the relationship between the giants and the Aesir or Vanir.

His home was always lit with gold instead of fire and he had cups that magically refilled themselves. His other name was Gymir, which means blinder. Sailors naturally feared this god, so they would make human sacrifices to him, in the hope that he wouldn't come up and destroy their ships.

- Ran

Ran was Aegir's wife and also a sea goddess of storms. She was believed to be the one who would collect the bodies of the drowned and place them in her net.

- Hel

Hel was another giantess and a goddess of the underworld. She was the daughter of Loki and the sister of Fenrir, or Fenris-wolf, and Jormungand, or the Midgard serpent. She was known to be half-black and half-white while she lived in the Niflheim. Her hall meant Elvidnir, which means misery. She was the giant identified as Hella in many literary works.

The Dwarfs

Dwarves are another kind of being found in Norse mythology. They are pitch-black in appearance and their underground abode is called Svartalfheim, which was considered to be a complex of mines and forges. The word "dwarf", in Old Norse mythology, does not really have anything to do with the smallness of their stature. Nevertheless, no one can say for sure where the expression was derived from.

One thing that was agreed upon regarding the dwarves was that they were very skilled in smithing and metalwork crafts. The production of Mjollnir, the hammer of Thor (protector of the Asgard) is credited to them. Other treasures created by the dwarves include Gleipnir, the chain used to bind the wolf Fenrir, when it would otherwise break all and any chains and fetters; Skiobladnir, a ship belonging to Freyr that could move in the wind; the Brisingamen, a precious necklace of Freya; and Gungnir, the spear of Odin.

The dwarves also possessed a lot of magical powers, immense wisdom, and vast knowledge. In fact, they could transform into stone if the need arose. The mythology credits the four strong dwarves with holding aloft the four corners of the earth and sky. This shows the extent of their strength. The four dwarves were Austri, in charge of the East, Vestri, in charge of the West, Nordri, in charge of the North, and Sudri in charge of the South.

Other beings in the Norse mythologies are:

- Elves
- Dead humans
- Land spirits
- Ancestors
- Norns
- Disir
- Kvasir
- Lodur
- Lofn
- Magni
- Mimir

But the descriptions of these are so similar to each other that it may be confusing to identify one from the other. Granted, it would be presumptuous and stereotypical to say, in a blanket way, that these categories of gods and beings are the same. However, the lines separating them are so fine that you may have a hard time placing each of them into the tribe that he or she belonged to.

Norse Cosmology

The structure and nature of the cosmos in the mythology of the Norse is nuanced. Norse cosmology is quite different from what most people learn today, regarding the order of where and when things occur between life and death. The Norse practiced a polytheistic religion. The ideas regarding heaven and earth that come from the modern monotheistic religions find no relevance in Norse cosmology.

Nevertheless, some of the teachings in Christendom about heaven and hell and the condition of the dead are said to come from Old Norse cosmology. In Norse mythology there was a world-tree, Yggdrasil, which was at the center of the cosmos and grew from the well of Urd. In the branches of this tree were the nine worlds, where various gods and beings, visible and invisible, lived. Humans and other elements also found a home somewhere in these Nine Worlds. The worlds are:

1. Asgard
2. Midgard
3. Vanaheim
4. Niflheim
5. Muspelheim
6. Jotunheim
7. Alfheim
8. Svartalfheim
9. Hel

Asgard

Asgard was considered to be the home of the gods and goddesses of the Aesir tribe. It was also their fortress and believed to be located in a spiritual realm in the sky. There was a narrow bridge called Bifrost that connected Asgard to the Midgard. Innangard (inside the fence) – which stands for orderliness, civilization and law-abiding condition – derives its model from Asgard, according to an old Germanic concept. Thus, things were orderly in both Asgard and Midgard.

Midgard

Midgard was the only one of the Nine Worlds of Norse cosmology that was mostly in the realm of the visible. Other worlds were mainly invisible, although they had the ability to intersect with the visible world. This world was understood to be the abode of humankind in mythology and was also understood to be in the middle between Asgard and the underworld. In the era before Christianity arrived – among the Germanic peoples – Midgard occupied an important place because it represented civilization.

The word Midgard, which stands for Middle Enclosure, might mean civilization in the midst of a wild world that was surrounded by wilderness and contained no life. The world tree, Yggdrasil, was believed to hold Midgard toward the base of its trunk. The gods protected Midgard and the humans from the onslaught of the giants by building fences around Midgard from Ymir's eyebrows. Ymir was a god who was slain by both Odin and the other gods while they used his body parts to form sections of the world.

Vanaheim

This was the world of the gods and goddesses that were from the tribe of Vanir and was supposedly constructed around the Yggdrasil. Vanaheim was the home of fertility. This world could be more aptly described as the home of nature in comparison to the Asgard, its exact location could not be ascertained. There are mere fragments of facts gathered here-and-there, that presume Vanaheim was located somewhere toward the west of Asgard. This can be inferred from a poem titled *Lokasenna* – or the Taunting of Loki – where the poet tells of the Vanir god Njord traveling westward on his way to Asgard as a hostage.

There are no detailed descriptions of what Vanaheim looked like, but it's clear that it wasn't a world of orderliness and civilization. It wasn't an innangard world, which means inside the fence, but was instead an utangard world, which means beyond the fence, a connotation that evokes chaos, anarchy, and disorderliness.

Niflheim

This was the world of ice. The name was believed to mean World of Fog. In Norse cosmology, this was the home of cold, mist, ice, and darkness; the climatic conditions were in direct contrast to those of Muspelheim. Norse mythology has it that the giant Ymir was born at a time when ice from Niflheim interacted with fire from Muspelheim in the middle of an abyss, known as Ginnungagap, that had hitherto demarcated the two realms.

Muspelheim

This was the world of fire and heat. It was the world that stood opposite, in both direction and condition, to the Niflheim. It was the home of giants. It was the literary work of Snorri Sturluson, and the Prose of Edda, that gave prominence to Muspelheim as being either a place or a world, rather than a condition or people. But Muspelheim was believed to play a major role in the creation of the world of Norse cosmology and its destruction. According to Snorri's creation account, it was the fire from Muspelheim and the ice from Niflheim that forged the giant called Ymir when the two elements met inside Ginnungagap. It was the fire from Muspelheim that was thought to destroy the gods and their world.

Alfheim

As suggested by its name, Alfheim is considered to be the home of elves, a tribe of gods in Norse mythology – and in the religions of some Germanic peoples. There are enough reasons to conclude that Alfheim was a place of light and beauty, as strongly evidenced by the description of the elves themselves. They're described as gods that are luminous, even surpassing the sun in beauty. Many scholars have tried to solve the puzzle of the relationship between Freyr and Alfheim. If Freyr was a Vanir and lived at Vanaheim, how could he be the ruler of Alfheim? As of yet there is no satisfactory answer to this question.

Jotunheim

This was the world of the hostile giants, as the name means "the Homeland of the Giants". Another name for this world is Utgard, and it is the model for utangard in disorderliness, anarchy, and chaos. This shows that it occupied an extreme place in the Germanic concept of the innangard and utangard. Jotunheim was understood to be a place of vast, wide, and mighty wilderness, which surrounded innangard. The Norse usually visualized Jotunheim as a dark, deep forest, full of mountain peaks. They and other Germanic people held the view that the invisible Jotunheim was inhospitable because of its grim landscape and constant, harsh winter.

Svartalfheim

Svartalfheim is one of the nine worlds of Old Norse that is inhabited by the dwarves or the black elves. Svartalfheim, also known as Nidavellir, which means Low Fields or Dark Fields, was thought to be a labyrinth of mines and forges. It was the home of the craft masters that lived in the underworld.

Hel

This is the world recognized as the world of the dead and goddess Hel and is perhaps the root word of the English word Hell. In Norse cosmology it was the underworld where many of the dead gods lived. Hel was also referred to as Helheim, which meant "the Realm of Hel". It was understood that physical graves were located underground in Hel. Some traditions say Hel is in the North because it is a grave like place: cold and dark.

The concept of Hel in Norse cosmology is similar to that of other religions, but there is no evidence linking it directly to them.

These nine worlds are not the only ones in Norse mythology. Another location that Old Norse refers to is Valhalla, where Odin placed the chosen ones from among the dead elites. There was also Ginnungagap, which was understood to be a chasm that had been in existence before the cosmos was created, and which would remain after its cyclical destruction.

Norse Concept of Death and Afterlife

Norse mythology doesn't have a lot of detail emphasizing what happens to the dead. However, literary sources of Old Norse contain some references here and there which help to understand Norse concepts about death and the afterlife. As it should be expected in cases like this, there are some contradictions in the positions of the historians that have studied them.

The Dead Abodes

In Norse mythology, the dead usually went to a place known as Valhalla, which means the hall of the fallen. It was Odin, together with his Valkyries, that would choose those who would dwell here as fallen heroes, and who would be brought back to participate in the final battle of Ragnarok, which would cause the destruction of the gods and the cosmos.

Another place that the dead went to was Folkvang, which was the hall of the goddess Freya, which means the field of the people (or the field of the warriors). This was where she welcomed some of the dead. Those who died at sea would go to the giantess Ran, who would take them to her underwater abode.

Any who ended up in Hel continued to live a normal life, virtually doing all the things they had enjoyed before their death, so it was that this place was not used to punish the dead.

There is no clear demarcation in the descriptions regarding the abodes of the dead; and the facts are hazy as to who would go to any one particular realm and why, and who determined where each would go after his or her death.

The Rebirth of the Dead

The concept of reincarnation is present in the Old Norse afterlife. The Norse are said to have believed that the dead would be reborn back into the family of a relative. No one can explain the process clearly. However, children were usually named after loved ones who had passed, with the hope that the dead would be reincarnated in the child who was named after him or her.

Norse literature sometimes described dead ancestors as elves. The only logic here would be that the dead would become elves, since Norse mythology already says that every living thing that had a spiritual presence could change its being.

No Punishment and Reward After Death

The Norse did not have any of the beliefs that are common today concerning reward or punishment after death. There were no concepts such as salvation or damnation in the worldview of the Norse.

The Helgafjell

Helgafjell means the holy mountain, one of the places that occupied the Norse concept of the afterlife. After the death of a Norse clansperson, he or she would go up to this mountain, a place so holy that before people could look towards it they would have to wash their face. But the dead who resided in Helgafjell had the ability to lead a normal existence, just like those who lived life on earth.

The Soul

Beliefs concerning the soul deserve consideration when analyzing the Norse concept of the afterlife. The Norse believed the soul to be the last breath taken by a person in the process of dying. This means that life evaporates when a person breathes their last "soul". Another understanding of the soul suggested that it was an immaterial part of the human being that was immortal and would leave the body when a person became unconscious, either momentarily, or when life evaporated and the body began to decay.

Ancestor Worship

Since the Norse believed that those who died could continue to live and exert more power, they worshipped their dead ancestors. This tradition has been adopted and continues today, albeit with many variations depending upon the culture that holds it. But central to the belief of the Norse was the view that if the ancestors were well pleased, they would come back to protect their home and their people.

Norse Concept of Destiny - WYRD/URD

Destiny is one of the major concepts in the mythology of the Norse and other Germanic peoples. Still, it's one of the most difficult concepts to explain and to grasp. The reason is not far-fetched; the Greek tradition of fate and the Hindu belief in karma has simplified the concept of destiny to such a level that any modern scholar can easily understand it. But the pre-Christian Norse worldview of destiny is unique in its own ways and does not readily conform to the modern way of thinking in terms of cause-and-effect and the influence of the past on the present.

Yggdrasil and Urd

It will be difficult to make any sense out of the Norse concept of destiny if one does not understand what Yggdrasil means, and how it influenced the lives of people according to the Old Norse. As we read earlier, Yggdrasil was the tree at the center of the cosmos on which the Nine Worlds of the Norse hung. That means that Yggdrasil was the home of gods, humans, and other beings.

Another thing central to the understanding of this concept of destiny was the Well of Urd. It basically means the Well of

Destiny. It was the water from this well that nourished the Yggdrasil at its root. Logically, the destinies of all beings in the Nine Worlds on the Yggdrasil derived their destinies from Urd. It stands to reason also that the future of everyone in the Norse cosmos had been shaped by the Urd, and the past of everyone was represented by the well, while their future was represented by the tree. According to tradition, if someone wanted to understand whatever was happening to anyone in the World Tree, he or she would have to go back to the Urd.

However, something here might confuse someone's understanding of the concept of destiny. The past, in the Norse mythology, was not viewed as a blueprint that couldn't be altered in the future. It was believed that dewdrops would usually fall from the trunk of the tree back into the well and change its composition. In other words, the present would be able to influence the past in Old Norse understanding. Thus, inhabitants of the Norse cosmos could change their world, even though a series of events had been fed into the tree by the Well of Urd.

Defining destiny through Norse eyes is based on the understanding of the relationship between the Well of Urd/Wyrd and the Yggdrasil, that is, the relationship between the past and the present. That understanding influenced a scholar's definition of Norse concepts of destiny as "governing the working out of the past in the present (or the working in of the present into the past)."

Freewill and Fate

Freewill and fate also had a place in the concept of destiny for the Norse. The Norse had it that there were three wise women, known as Norns, who lived in the Well of Urd. The Norns are generally called the goddesses of destiny and were believed to carve the fortunes of those to be born. Again, through that process, the past influenced the future. The Norns would carve the future of all beings; humans, gods, and even salamanders, into the tree. Whatever they formed anyone into was what they would become in the Yggdrasil, but that was not the only thing they could become. Their destinies could be changed.

That was a major deviation from the ancient Greek concept of fate that confers absolute powers unto the fate. Since it was possible for the dewdrops from Yggdrasil to alter what had been written about a thing, a human, a god, or any other being, it could cause a change to occur from the Tree and change their destiny from the initial form they were carved into. For the most part, however, most of the beings with the power to change their destinies only used the power passively by merely influencing the flow of the Water of Destiny into the Well of Destiny.

Some, however, took their destinies into their own hands, so to speak, shaping it more powerfully and actively. The system of things and interaction between beings also played a role in shaping fortunes. Some beings were able to exert influence on this process and rewrite their destinies, allowing dewdrops from the cosmos to change the composition of the Water of Destiny as it affected them.

From all the available information about the Norse view of destiny, there was no life course that didn't obey the writings or Norns, and there was also no life that was completely and absolutely preordained by the Norns. In summary, it wasn't possible to have absolute free will or be free from fate altogether. At the same time, the Norse concept of destiny wasn't unalterably binding. Thus, their lives resided somewhere in-between.

Norse Concept of Innangard and Utangard

Norse mythology and belief also capture geographical locations and psychological states. Every being living in any of the worlds of the Norse cosmos was believed to be in either innangard or utangard. Some scholars suggest that the suffix, "-gard" likely forms the etymology of the Old English word "guard" and its derivatives. In one analysis, innangard and utangard mean "inside guard" and "outside guard" (or with guard and without guard), respectively. Gods, humans, and other beings lived in these two locations or states.

Innangard

Innangard means "inside the fence" or "within the enclosure." It's used to describe a place, condition, or state of mind characterized by orderliness and civility where everyone is law-abiding. Going by this, there was peace and harmony in the Norse innangard. They lived and acted in the innangard within boundaries; there was no absolute freedom for anyone to do as he or she liked. The expression "innangard" featured prominently among the pre-Christian Germanic people including the Norse to denote responsibility for actions.

Utangard

Utangard is the direct opposite of Innangard. It means "outside the fence" or "beyond the enclosure." The connotation of this description is that the place, the condition or the state of mind is wild, chaotic, anarchic, and uncivilized. So all those who lived in utangard had no respect for law and they knew no boundaries. Everyone was absolutely free to do as he or she pleased. Of course, it would seem as if no one would like to be in utangard and the Germanic peoples of the pre-Christian era had a great preference for innangard over utangard. Yet, they accepted it as one of the realities of life. Some deities are even said to have preferred to live in utangard because not everything about it was negative.

Cosmological View

About three of the Nine Worlds had names ending with " – gard". They were either innangard or utangard. Midgard and Asgard were innangard worlds while Utgard (which is another name for Jotunheim) was quintessentially an utangard world. While the gods and goddesses of the tribe of Aesir lived in Asgard, Midgard was the home of humankind. The lawless and uncivilized giants who lived in Jotunheim or Utgard always dealt ruthlessly with those in Asgard and Midgard if they were not protected.

The Usefulness of Utangard

Utangard was a place considered to have its own use in the world of the Norse. Norse mythology has it that they did not consider utangard as entirely evil and destructive in nature. Some Norse gods even had reasons to go to utangard for positive purposes. At times, when they wanted to initiate others into a military group or a force for war, each member to be initiated would spend some time alone in the wilderness, there they would have to go through situations that exposed him or her to hardships.

It might be that a military group had a totem animal. In that case, the initiate would have to learn from the totem animal during their time in utangard. This totemism would bring the initiates into a state of semi-unification with the totem, and in effect, with the military group as a whole. This usually gave the new member strength and increased their understanding of the nature of the trials they went through. Coming back stronger, they could choose to employ the use of those antisocial and chaotic skills that they had learned for the benefit of the society they would settle into.

Little wonder then that the patron and chief of the elite warrior, Odin himself was half-giant, half Aesir, despite being the head of the Aesir tribe of gods and goddesses. His mother was a giantess. Even though he was revered and venerated by other gods and Norse, even up until the Christian Era, Odin had several serious utangard qualities about him. This included his adoption of the feminine gender in some situations, befriending the giants to gain their knowledge and wisdom, and his skill at being a trickster. He was also seen as having selfish longings for his own personal acquisition of power. In spite of all of this, he was still an object of veneration among the Norse and other Germanic peoples.

Norse Mythology in Modern Literature, Television, and Film

Centuries ago, publications about Norse mythology could be only found in Scandinavia. But since the 19th century literary works about Norse myths and legends have spread across the globe, and at the dawn of the 20th century information and representation of the Norse gods and goddesses could be found in science fiction and fantasy literature. Norse mythology became the subject of passionate discussions on TV and has been featured in epic films and television series as well.

Below are 7 examples of modern literature, television shows, and films that have featured Norse mythology.

Literature

1. *American Gods.* (2001): This novel by Neil Gaiman features Odin, Loki, and other figures in Norse myths. It was complemented in 2008 by *Odd and the Frost Giants,* the book based on the narratives of the Master Builder as found in *Gylfaginning: The Tricking of Gylfi.*
2. *The Sea of Trolls* (2004): This novel by Nancy Farmer was based on the inspiration from Norse myths and was made more conspicuous by the 2007 work entitled *The Land of the Silver Apples.*
3. *The Thrall's Tale* (2006): This book, written by Judith Lindbergh, is an excerpt of the story that was allegedly narrated by an Old Norse priestess known as Thorbjorg the Seeress in the *Vinland* Sagas.
4. *Norse Code* (2009): Written by Greg van Eekhout, the novel regurgitates the Ragnarok story.
5. *Tales from Wyrd Museum:* This trilogy (a set of three works) by Robin Jarvis dwells on Norse mythology. In fact, the third in the set, *The Fatal Strand,* vividly referenced Odin and Yggdrasil.
6. *Ragnarok Conspiracy* (2012): Erec Stebbins, in this publication, highlights a plot by terrorists to cause a world war by instigating Western and Islamic nations against each other. He makes some references to Old Norse and Norse mythology about what happens at Ragnarok. He also mentions Norse runes like *Elder Futhark.*
7. *Magnus Chase and the Gods of Asgard* (2015): This is also a trilogy by Rick Riordan and he bases the book and another one, *Camp Half-Blood Chronicles,* on Norse mythology.

Television

1. *Hercules: The Legendary Journeys:* In a Season Five episode of this TV show, Hercules is depicted as traveling to Asgard and finds himself in the middle of a major conflict of the Norse gods and goddesses.
2. *Xena: Warrior Princess:* The TV series features Odin and the Valkyries several times.
3. *The Almighty Johnsons:* This is a New Zealand TV series that is based on a family whose members are entirely Norse gods reincarnated.
4. *Steins; Gate:* In this TV show, the protagonist in the series of Japanese anime, Rintaro Okabe, names several operations to prevent a dystopia in 2036 after Norse mythology.
5. *Vikings:* This Canadian television series is based on the story of Ragnarr Lodbrok of the Vikings legend. The characters that feature in the show see Odin in visions and pray to Freyr, Loki, and Thor among other gods and goddesses.
6. *Snow White and the Seven Dwarfs:* This is a Walt Disney's animated film that tells the story of how the goddess Freya goes to Svartaheim to beg dwarfs to craft for her the magical necklace called Brisingamen.
7. *Clash of Gods:* Episode 10 of this production centered primarily on Thor.

Film

1. *Erik the Viking:* This movie that features Tim Robbins is loosely based on Norse mythology.
2. *Son of the Mask:* This film is a story of a crafty Loki who is the antagonist and is repeatedly disciplined by the chief god Odin, who is omnipotent in the film.

3. *The Viking:* This 1958 film has active worshippers of Odin as characters. They share some parallels with Norse gods who lost one eye and one hand. Kirk Douglas and Tony Curtis played this role well.
4. *The Virgin Spring:* This 1960 film by Ingmar Bergman deals with how Odin's energy is unleashed by someone who worships Odin secretly among the medieval Christians.
5. *How to Train Your Dragon:* Part 1 (2010) and Part 2 (2014) of this film feature the Vikings that make some references to the Norse gods Odin and Thor.
6. *The Mask:* This film features Jim Carrey as playing a man who accidentally comes across a mask that possesses the powers of Loki and his life changes thereafter.
7. *Thor:* This film, which was directed by Kenneth Branagh, featured Chris Hemsworth and contains intriguing interactions between the gods Loki and Thor. It also refers to Yggdrasil and the Bifrost Bridge among other features of the Norse mythology.

Conclusion

Norse mythology has its own unique features; it was often used to frighten children, just as different myths have frightened people through the ages. Norse beliefs were so prevalent that they were evident in the everyday lives of people, and – even during the establishment of the Christian era – Scandinavian mythology was generally accepted in many places across Europe.

Chapter Fifteen: History of Denmark, Norway, and Sweden (14th to 19th century)

During the Middle Ages (from 1100 to 1600) the aftermath of what the Vikings had left behind came to fruition, a legacy that in turn saw the descendants of the Vikings also leave their mark upon history.

During this period, several unions were created and a reformation took place. The Kalmar Union, a series of personal unions that were formed between 1397 - 1520, united the three kingdoms of Denmark, Sweden, and Norway under a single monarch. These three countries make up what today is known as Scandinavia.

In the 17th century, the Thirty Year War took place; a major conflict that erupted in Central Europe among influential continental powers between the years 1618 and 1648. Although it was a religious conflict between Catholics and Protestants, self-preservation of the Habsburg Dynasty was the underlying motive. The 17th century also marked the rise of Sweden and its empire as its power began to rise under the administration of Charles IX.

Several wars broke out in the 18th century. The Great Northern War started in 1700 and continued until the year 1721, between a coalition of Denmark-Norway, Russia, and Poland on one side, and Sweden on the other. It started with an attack on Sweden in 1700 and ended with the conclusion of the Treaty of Nystad and the Stockholm treaties in 1721. Another important theme of the 18th century was colonialism, which began in the 17th century and lasted until the 20th century.

Moving on, important events that took place in northern Europe in the 19th century include the Napoleonic Wars (which divided Scandinavia), the Finnish War, industrialization, and the formation of the Monetary Union.

The main aim of this chapter is to shed light on the important events in the history of Scandinavia from 1300 to 1800, as this period was closer to the Viking Age and absorbed much of its influence.

Scandinavia during the Middle Ages

The traditional animosity between Denmark and Sweden had given way to feelings of sympathy and the formation of alliances. The Kalmar Union was a point of reference for this new period of friendship, depicting a time when the Nordic countries of Denmark, Norway, and Sweden stood together before a threatening world full of hatred. In June of 1397 a Scandinavian union was formed at Kalmar, bringing together the kingdoms of Denmark, Sweden, and Norway under a single monarch. The union of the three kingdoms was known as the Union of Kalmar and its capital was the city of Copenhagen. In Denmark and Sweden the union was idealized and the countries argued that unity had always been the main dynamic between the Nordic nations.

The Union was created to allow the three Scandinavian states to present a united front against foreign encroachments. Margaret I of Denmark, the driving force behind this union, was crowned monarch of both Norway and Sweden. Margaret, the Queen of Denmark, Sweden, and Norway, was regarded as the mastermind behind the pan-Nordic union of these three kingdoms. She has been considered to be the only ruling female monarch in the history of Norway and is undisputedly one of the most talented and interesting political figures throughout Scandinavian history.

Under the Kalmar Union, the monarchs expanded royal power, which brought them into conflict with the nobles. The nation found the price it paid to form a union with the Danish empire to be costly. On almost all occasions, the Swedes distinguished themselves with a loud tone and complaints that the most honorable and lucrative posts were always given away to the Danes, while they themselves were totally overlooked.

In due course the union fell apart due to the antagonism between the Danish and Swedish nobility. The battle that was fought between Denmark and Sweden took many resources away from Finland, which exposed it to attack by the Muscovites. The 15th century witnessed an expansion in the power of the Muscovites, which was, in due course, to form the basis of the Russian Empire. In 1497 Sweden tried to make amiable relations with Muscovy but the nobility of Finland and Sweden had to safeguard Finland without much help from Denmark.

In 1523 a revolt broke out against the union that resulted in the separation of Sweden and Denmark and as a result Norway sank to the status of being a Danish province. At this time, in 1523, Gustav Vasa was crowned king of Sweden.

The Union was a result of the inability of the three Nordic royal families to raise more than one candidate at a time, along with the rebellious behavior of the Swedish magnets of the 14th century, but during the 1400s it became clear that any rebelliousness was due to various factions striving for power. Due to connections – through inheritance and marriage in various countries – some of the Swedish magnets vested interest in maintaining the Nordic Union, while others could see an advantage in supporting the Danish kings to make their positions stronger. However, it was seen that having a Union without a king offered the best chance for not having to share the power with the king; this was why the Union existed for so long.

Protestant Reformation

The Reformation saw a transition from Roman Catholicism to Lutheranism in the regions ruled by Denmark in the first half of the 16th century. During the early 16th century, Scandinavia was comprised of two kingdoms – Norway and Denmark, and Sweden and Finland. The two kingdoms loosely belonged to the union of Kalmar before they disintegrated during the Reformation. As the result of this disintegration, Lutheranism became the major religion, giving a flavor of the constitution to national churches. Even today the influence of Lutheranism can be felt, although the churches are no longer so full of people.

During the early years of the Reformation – a religious revolution that led to the establishment of Protestantism – King Frederick I found himself on the Danish throne. Frederick had assured his Roman Catholic bishops that he would fight for their rights, but instead he invited in Lutheran supporters. His underlying motive was to expand his power at the cost of the Church's decline. As a result, in Denmark, Lutheranism was introduced and the principles of the Lutheran Reformation were imposed on the population, making Lutheranism the kingdom's main religion. All those who refused to convert to Lutheranism were ejected from their jobs and the possessions of the Catholic Church were given away to the Lutheran church. The University of Copenhagen became Lutheran, and even the Bible was translated into Danish. Like other Scandinavian countries, the Protestantism in Denmark was along the same lines of the German model where a main body of regional states was under the control of its prince.

Norway was under the control of Denmark and hence, Lutheranism was imposed on Norway in 1537. As in Denmark, Danish replaced Latin as the main language and Catholics were banned. But the poor people didn't welcome the changes and they continued to follow the Catholic traditions until the beginning of 17th century. Because of this, Lutheranism made its way into the country at a very slow pace. But later, it was decided that all the Catholic followers who still did not renounce their faith would have their possessions seized.

In Sweden, Gustav Vasa forced the Danish people to flee from Sweden in the year 1523, when he was crowned king of Sweden. His policy was to break off all ties with the Papacy and free the country from the clutches of The Church. In 1527 he declared that the word of God would be preached throughout the kingdom, and this helped the Swedish national church to come into the picture. King Gustav was able to consolidate his financial powers when the possessions of the Church were seized. However, the situation gradually changed, with Denmark and Norway adhering to the Reformation movement on the one hand, and the Catholic priests supporting the peasant's revolt on the other. On the advent of this the king broke off the relations with the Catholic Church in the year 1529 and the Swedish National Church officially became Lutheran.

Scandinavian Countries in the 17th Century

The 17th century marks an important era for the Scandinavian powers. The leading country in the region, Denmark, lost its dominance to Russia and Sweden, which led to a series of wars over ports and lands in and around the Baltic. Although Sweden initially won, it later lost to Russia who gained territories extending from Finland to Lithuania. In the 18th century, Russia didn't miss a chance to expand its western – as well as southern – borders at the expense of some of the weaker powers, namely the Ottoman Empire and the Polish Republic. By 1800 Russia had become one of the greatest powers in the world whereas it had been just a peripheral force before 1600.

Throughout the 17th and 18th centuries warfare and great personalities continued to dominate the region, demonstrating their sovereignty in campaigns and patronage programs. They encouraged the arts and several artists traveled to Scandinavia and Eastern Europe from Italy, Germany, and France. These artists designed and decorated fortresses, weapons, palaces, and gardens and created breathtaking paintings and sculpture. This shift in style and taste is reflected in artistic pieces across Western Europe. In the early 17th century the Dutch and the German Baroque prevailed, but later years show definitive influences of Italian Baroque. However, the beginning of the 18th century saw the French court become the key source of inspiration for monumental development and, by the year 1800, neoclassicism was favored for interiors and architecture, as well as sculptures and paintings.

Some of the key events that took place in Scandinavia in the 17th century are mentioned below.

Rise of Sweden

Despite being scarcely populated, the 17th century marked the rise of Sweden as a great power. After winning wars against the Holy Roman Empire, Denmark-Norway, and Russia, Sweden emerged as a powerful nation under the influence of foreign rulers. Its contribution during the Thirty Years' War helped in understanding the political and religious powers throughout Europe. Charles IX became the king of Sweden in 1604 when Duke John abandoned the throne. That same year the members of parliament declared themselves Protestants at the Riksdag, and excluded Catholics from all rights to succession of the throne, and from the right to hold any office in Sweden. During the reign of Charles IX, Sweden became a Protestant as well as a military monarchy. Charles assumed the title of King of the Lapps of Nordland, which got him involved in yet another conflict with Denmark known as the Kalmar War.

Dominions of Sweden

The dominions of Sweden, also termed as "possessions of the Swedish", were the regions that came under the control of the Swedish crown historically, but were never completely incorporated within Sweden. They were governed by Sweden, while still retaining their own political systems within certain limits. On the other hand, Finland was not a dominion; it was an integral part of Sweden. As predetermined by the Instrument of Government in 1634, the dominions did not have representation in the Riksdag of Sweden. Sweden conquered regions in the Eastern Baltic from 1561 to 1629. These Eastern Baltic dominions were lost in the Treaty of Nystad, with which the Great Northern War was concluded in 1721.

In 1561 Estonia was placed under Swedish rule so that it could be protected from Poland and Russia, at the time it was consisted of the northern region of modern-day Estonia. This part of Estonia was full of Estonian Swedes who continued to inhabit it for centuries even after Sweden relinquished it.

In 1629 Livonia was conquered by Sweden from the Lithuanian-Polish Commonwealth in the Swedish-Polish War. Following the Northern War, according to the Treaty of Olivia signed between Sweden and Commonwealth in 1660, the Lithuanian-Polish King gave up all rights to the Swedish throne as Livonia was given away to Sweden. Swedish Livonia consisted of the southern part of modern-day Estonia and the northern part of modern-day Latvia.

Following the Ingria War, as part of the Treaty of Stolbova signed in 1617 between Russia and Sweden, Russia ceded southern Karelia and Ingria to Sweden. Russia conquered the area again after a year, giving Czar Peter the Great a chance to lay down the strong foundation of his new capital in Saint Petersburg in 1703. Finally, in 1721, the Treaty of Nystad formally ceded it.

Domestic consolidation of Sweden

For some time Sweden held a fragile position in terms of leadership, but with cautious statesmanship, permanent dominion could have been achieved on the Baltic coastline. Unfortunately, the two immediate successors of Gustavus created great difficulties for the newly established empire. Their financial extravagance brought the kingdom to the verge of bankruptcy, financial issues that created unrest among ordinary Swedes. The people feared that this artificial, external greatness might be purchased at the expense of their political and civil rights. The Swedes looked to a new king to handle the issue of too much power being wielded by the nobility.

Charles X Gustav, primarily a soldier, was an unusually sharp politician. He placed great focus on military strength, while focusing on the point that domestic unity was needed for a powerful foreign policy.

The most pressing domestic need was the reduction of alienated crown lands; and the king did his best to recover from the financial extravagance of the previous rulers, but his desire for military glory created several other problems for the country. Eventually, he gained more personal glory than renown for doing something good for his country.

Kalmar War

In order to take control of the northern part of the Norwegian coast and hinterland, Denmark and Sweden began fighting the Kalmar War (1611-1613), which led to Sweden's acceptance of sovereignty of Denmark-Norway. Christian IV, Denmark's king, declared war on Sweden in 1611 after Charles IX, Sweden's king, claimed sovereignty over the Finnmark region; a strategic point along the trade route that had provided furs and fish to the Danish-Norwegian kings. The development of a Swedish port and growing Swedish power in the Baltic were some of the additional reasons for the outbreak of the war, which was named after the Swedish port Kalmar.

The Ingrian War

Fought between Russia and Sweden, the Ingrian War started in 1610 and lasted until 1617. This period – known as the Time of Troubles in Russia – came about due to an attempt by Sweden to put one of her dukes on Russia's throne. By the time it ended Sweden had gained substantial territory through the Treaty of Stolbolvo, which signified an important turning point in Sweden's rise to power. During the Time of Troubles Russia was driven to misery due to an ongoing Polish intervention. Looking to the interests of Sweden in Russia's affair, the king of Poland declared war on Russia and on engaging both the Swedes and Russians destroyed most of the Russian force, with Swedish mercenaries surrendering. The battle had severe consequences for Russia, and Sweden was asked to install either Gustavus Adolphus or Cart Filip as their monarch. In the end Gustavus took the throne.

Although the Riksrad remained the nominal dominant power of the state, gradually all of the real power was transferred to the crown. The Riksdag also changed in set up, and the Privy Council (cabinet of medieval origin that consisted of magnates and those who co-ruled with the king) lost its uniqueness in the form of a grand council that used to represent the semi-feudal landed aristocracy; it instead became an administrative bureaucracy that held the chief offices of the state. While in most other European nations – other than the Polish-Lithuanian Commonwealth and England – the ancient representation of *estate* was disappearing, it grew into an integral part of the Constitution in Sweden under King Gustavus. He held the eleven Riksdag that were always occupied in finding means to support the increasing burden of the German and Polish wars.

The Polish War

While the battles between Denmark and Russia were considered to be exclusively Scandinavian wars, the Polish had an impact on the whole world. This was mainly for two reasons – it was a war for the Baltic littoral, and the Polish

Vasas didn't let the king of Sweden, Gustavas, attain his right to the Sweden throne. For the Swedish King the Polish war was a war of religion. He regarded the Scandinavian kingdoms as the key pillars on which reposed the Evangelical religion. He believed that the disunion would lead to the opening of doors to the Catholic league in the north and hence it would destroy Denmark and Sweden. It was because of this that he joined Denmark to safeguard Stralsund in the year 1628.

However, in reality, the Polish-Lithuanian Commonwealth was not in any way a threat to Protestantism. The obstinate insistence of Polish Vasas to take over the Swedish crown was one obstruction to the conclusion of the war that Poland halted and held back. Apart from this, no one in Poland dreamed of getting involved in any Swedish matters, in fact Poland prevented its martial monarch from getting involved in the Thirty Years' War. The king of Sweden was agitated by the religious ardor and overstated clerical influence in Poland but sensed dangers – real or not – every now and then.

Polish Vasa Sigismund was dethroned, but even then he didn't give up in his attempts to regain the throne of Sweden, and most of his policies revolved around these efforts to conquer the state of Sweden. He signed a pact that stated that the "then-Sweden" territory of Estonia would be part of the Commonwealth, and that the Polish nobility supported this. The Szlachta (the noble class in Poland) assumed the pact would only be confined to the Estonian region, and expected gains in the form of grain and an increase in exports through the Estonian ports on the Baltic Sea. He didn't consider Swedish power and underestimated it. He assumed Poland would be able to ward off any attacks from the Scandinavians easily, Poland having been undefeated for more than a century. They completely forgot that the Commonwealth had a small military to population ratio when compared to the Swedish army, which was both highly motivated and trained.

As expected, Sweden managed to draft a huge army in no time due to its centralized government. On the other hand, the Commonwealth had to fight on two fronts, as they had to deal with the south as well. In 1600 – at the beginning of the war – the Commonwealth army had the ability to deal with the Swedish forces under the command of the Great Lithuanian king "the Thunderbolt", but eventually Sweden took control over – not just the Estonian territory – but also most of Livonia – a territory that belonged to the Commonwealth in Southern Estonia. The Polish-Lithuanian leaders reacted to this dire situation by recalling commanders from the southern front to the threatened northern front. Poland also recalled the powerful leaders from Moldavia in order to fight the Swedish incursion that threatened Estonia and Polish territories located towards the south of it.

Sweden was defeated in the first major war and was only left with control of a few territories. Sweden was repeatedly defeated on the open field by the Commonwealth forces. Another crowning achievement of the Commonwealth forces was the Battle of Kircholm in 1605. On the other hand, Sweden under the command of Charles thought the Lithuanians were retreating – with small support from the Poles – and so they advanced, spreading out their formations. But the Swedes didn't know that the opposing forces were waiting for this specific move. The Commonwealth army fired at the Swedes and charged their formations. The Swedish army broke ranks completely but the victory was meaningless for the Commonwealth, which was wracked with domestic disagreement for next five years.

After signing the Treaty of Stolbovo, which marked an end to the Ingrian War with Russia, Sweden, under King Gustav II, once again returned its focus to the Commonwealth and expanded its control over the part of Livonia that was still in question. The Commonwealth, which was involved in a major battle with the Ottomans, couldn't send significant forces to stop the Swedish king and had to give Livonia away.

Taking full advantage of the opportunity, Sweden quickly occupied the whole of Livonia in 1625; and in 1626, Gustav took all of the coastal towns along with Danzig, which is considered one of his biggest achievements.

The Commonwealth Parliament approved the contribution of monies for war, but the condition of the Polish forces was very poor. The Lithuanians were dealing with a major collapse in Livonia and retreated while Sweden decided to attack from the direction of Vistula and from the Swedish-held Pomernia, but nature was against them; the Vistula was flooded, which wreaked the Swedish plans and let Koniecpolski (from the Commonwealth) seize Swedish forces coming from the Pomernia side. Gustav met the Poles around Danzig, and forced them to retreat. Koniecpolski, in turn, reacted to this by suddenly attacking in order to stop the Swedish army from reaching Danzig. Finally, fighting broke out in the area around the marshlands of Moltawa. Sweden wanted to attack with cavalry, however, they failed to draw the enemy units into range. The following attacks by the Swedish army caused serious damage to the Poles but they still couldn't cripple their army. Finally, the battle came to an end when the Swedish King was hurt decided to retreat.

After the battle Commonwealth forces readily saw the need to restructure the army, and to modernize their artillery and firepower, if they were to compete with the Swedes. In turn Sweden learned the art of charges, cavalry attacks, and several war techniques from Poland. In 1628, with limited funds, the Polish were forced to stop their attacks, while Sweden captured Brodnica and Nowy. Despite all his efforts Koniecpolski wasn't lucky enough to gain victory because a ceasefire brokered by the Truce of Altmark favored Sweden. Sweden now won the right to tax Polish trade, move through the Baltic, and was recognized as the dominant power in the Southern Baltic Sea. The only thing Sweden was upset about was its inability to capture the key port of Danzig, but apart from that, Sweden controlled almost all of the ports she'd set out to take, and it was now Sweden could proudly feel she'd achieved the goal of making the Baltic Sea her 'Inner Lake'.

The Polish War dragged on for eight years (1621-1629). Sweden occupied the fertile delta of the Vistula and treated it as a permanently conquered land, but this marked the limit of advancement for the Swedish king as all of his efforts after this were skewed by superior Polish strategies. Finally, in 1629, the king accepted the Treaty of Altmark, according to which Sweden was to retain the possessions of the Livonian conquests for six years, along with the Vistula delta, and a few other regions.

Thirty Years' War (1618 – 1648)

The Thirty Years War, which started in 1618 and continued until 1648, took place within the borders of the Holy Roman Empire, but it also involved several major continental powers. Although from its outset it seemed to be a religious conflict between Protestants and Catholics, the preservation of the Habsburg dynasty was another important motive behind the war. In order to protect their interests the Danish and Swedes got involved at different points in the conflict. The Danish intervened when Christian IV, the Lutheran king of Denmark-Norway, tried to help German Protestants against the Holy Roman Empire because he feared that the sovereignty of Denmark as a Protestant nation was being challenged. The intervention began in the year 1625 and lasted until 1629. The king benefitted from his policies in Germany and gained a level of stability and wealth for his kingdom that was unmatched anywhere else in Europe.

Sweden decided to intervene in 1630 and her involvement continued until the year 1635. The brief but effective campaigns of Gustavus Adolphus, the king of Sweden during that time, dominated the war. The fight between the Imperial forces and Sweden became predominant. Although Sweden was encouraged more by the political issues than the regional problems, it became the supporter of the Protestant cause. The Imperial forces performed quite well in the war, the original provinces of Habsburg were recovered and Denmark was meticulously defeated. Emperor Ferdinand, upon sensing the victory, restored all the lands to the Catholic Church that had previously been seized by Protestant rulers, but this step alienated important Protestants who would have otherwise remained loyal to him. All this resulted in the uprising of two main forms of Protestantism in Europe – Calvinism and Lutheranism – and these two factions were actually more against each other's teachings than they were against Catholicism.

The war destroyed entire regions by unleashing disease and famine, leading to a huge loss of life and property in the Italian and German states, as well as the Southern Netherlands. It was so severe that it almost bankrupted several combatant powers.

The Dutch Republic concluded its war with Spain in 1648 since it was a time of great prosperity and success; it was a period that became known as the Dutch Golden Age and one that also saw Denmark became one of the world's leading economic powers.

Danish Absolutism

The significant military destruction in the second half of the 17th century indicated that the nobles of Denmark were unable to handle their situation, and their rejection of taxation by the crown angered the monarchy. Considering the situation, the councilors of the king came up with a new law that removed the special privileges the nobility had, and proclaimed the crown to be fully inheritable, giving the king absolute power. This law of inheritance, along with the Law of 1665, led to a state of absolutism in the whole of Europe and thus began the era of absolutism in Denmark.

Absolutist Denmark was controlled by a bureaucracy – that relied on political leaders from the landowning class – and the state was compensated for its losses from former crown lands by raising the taxes on peasant holdings, although nobles continued to pay the taxes for the peasants on their estates. The tax was calculated by an assessment of land based on both the area's size and its productivity. The main aim of the country was to recover its lost provinces from Sweden. Finally, by the 1670s, Denmark-Norway had rebuilt its forces enough to wage war against Sweden in order to recover all that it had lost, yet, in spite of external support – and naval resources given to Denmark – the war ended in a pungent stalemate.

Scandinavian countries in the 18th century

From 1560 to 1658 Sweden created an empire centered on the Gulf of Finland, comprised of Livonia, Estonia, Ingria, and Karelia. The growing nation of Sweden, as part of the Thirty Years' War, also gained control over territories in Germany, which included Wismar, Western Pomerania, Verden, and the Duchy of Bremen. Around the same time, Sweden also conquered Norwegian and Danish provinces lying towards the north of Sound. All this could be attributed to a well-trained army that seemed to be more professional than the armies of several other nations. Although the size of the Swedish army was quite small, it was equipped with some of the modern techniques that had helped the monarchy utilize the resources of the country and its empire in an effective manner, but although the Swedish army may well have been capable of making quick marches on the battlefield, the state was unable to maintain and support its capable army for a prolonged war. Several campaigns were proposed to make the army self-sufficient, but the cost of warfare proved to be much higher than what the countries could fund and therefore resources eventually dried up over the course of any prolonged conflict.

The Great Northern War

The Great Northern War, which started in 1700 and continued until 1721, was fought between Sweden and a coalition comprising of Russia, Saxony-Poland-Lithuania, and Denmark-Norway. It started when the coalition attacked Sweden in 1700 and lasted until 1721, concluding with the Treaty of Nysad and the Treaties of Stockholm. It was a battle in which a coalition led by Russia challenged the supremacy of Swedish power in Central, Eastern, and Northern Europe. Leaders who initially stood against the Swedish included Peter

I of Russia, Augustus II of Saxony-Poland-Lithuania, and Frederick IV of Denmark-Norway. Charles XII led the Swedes. The Great Northern War was divided into several phases: 1700-1706, 1707-1709, 1709-1714, 1714-1718, and 1718-1721. The causes of the war had been brewing since 1690 before it finally broke out in 1700.

During the Thirty Years' War, Sweden had emerged as a great power and occupied territories in Estonia and Livonia along the Baltic coast and Finland. Likewise Russia – at the beginning of the reign of Peter the Great – turned out to be a territorial power, but had no access to the Baltic Sea. To win this untouched region became the goal of Peter's foreign policy. He formed an alliance with Poland (which had joined in a Union with Saxony) and Denmark, which led to the Northern war.

The war broke out when the alliance of Russia, Denmark-Norway, Saxony, and Poland sensed an opportunity with Sweden being ruled by a young King. War was declared on the Swedish Empire and a threefold attack was launched on Swedish Livonia, Swedish Holstein, and Swedish Ingria. The Swedish forces fended off the Russian and Danish attacks at Narva (Peter was defeated by Sweden's king Charles XII on the Baltic coast during the early stages of the war) and Travendal respectively, and pushed the forces of Augustus II to Saxony through the Polish-Lithuanian Commonwealth. This led to the dethroning of Augustus as he was forced to accept defeat. This was a turning point because instead of destroying the Russians, Charles turned against Poland to expel the Saxons out of the country to ensure a Polish King would be crowned.

In the meantime, the forces of Peter the Great recovered from the defeat at Narva and won access to the Baltic provinces of Sweden, where he paved the way for Russia to have access to the Baltic Sea by founding St. Petersburg in the year 1703. Charles XII commenced his Russian Campaign from Poland, where he joined with the Cossacks to free Ukraine, before turning his attention to Moscow. Russian raids on his troops and the onset of winter weakened the Swedish army and Charles XII decided to turn southwards. It was in Southern Ukraine that the Swedish and Russian armies clashed and fought a battle at Poltava in 1709. Czar Peter prepared the battle himself and transformed the shape of the battlefields with the help of his engineers who were asked to create modern weapons. The core of the army had artillery and rifles, which meant better arms and better training. He required individuals with the kind of skills and training that people were getting in the West. He needed shipwrights and artillerymen, as well as those who were experts in navigation. His fort, built on marshland, eventually became St. Petersburg. In the end Peter won the battle and the wounded Swedish king escaped to Turkey.

The Northern Great War, the first battle of modern times in Russia, marked victory for Peter at Poltava. This was followed by multiple attacks on Swedish territory along the Baltic coast; an act that now saw Russia replace Sweden as the major power in the Baltic Sea.

Sweden refused to make peace with Russia, even after the death of Charles XII, so to put pressure on Sweden the Russians sent a large fleet to Sweden's Baltic Sea Coast in 1719. The raids continued for over a month and destroyed several towns and buildings in Stockholm. Since the 18th century, Sweden had not been at war with Denmark, which gave it an opportunity to field more forces against Russia; however, these forces were insufficient to prevent the Russians from continually raiding Swedish towns.

Modernization by Peter the Great

The 17th century marked a turning point in the history of Scandinavia, particularly when Peter the Great's administrative reforms – based on Western European models – started to be implemented in order to modernize the Russian Empire. Up until the 17th century Russia was considered to be a barbaric and backward country in the eyes of most of the European players; however, this view changed after the rule of Peter the Great. Before Peter took over the throne, the country was already modernizing, so he was not the first Russian to begin the process, but he certainly put into action policies that helped bring about changes quickly.

He devised plans to bring his kingdom up to the cultural and technological standards of advanced Western European countries. He traveled to these so-called modern European countries and ordered men to shave their beards, wear western attire, send their sons to other countries for schooling and to free the females of the houses from seclusion so that they could also adapt Western culture. He was mainly influenced by the English and the Dutch, after which he refashioned the army, reorganized the administration, got major works translated, established newspapers, created a navy, secularized the monarchy, and founded the Russian Academy of Science. In the field of fine arts and architecture, the majority of the practitioners working in Russia were French or Italian. He even moved his capital from the ancient city of Moscow to the modern city of St. Petersburg to portray a Europeanized Russia.

Well equipped with both the firepower of a new army and navy, Peter extended his kingdom in each direction and earned respect and status among other European nations. After winning the Great Northern War against Sweden, Peter declared his state to be an empire and the ruler as an emperor. During and after this time, Russia was engaged in several commercial, cultural, and political affairs with the major European powers.

Peace Treaties of the 18th century

The anti-Swedish allies, after the death of King Charles XII, focused on how to fill the gaps left behind by the defeated Swedish army. George and Fredrick IV both dominated the Northern part of Germany while Peter the Great, whose forces had spread across the Baltic Sea, visualized dominance in East Central Europe. Hanover-Great Britain and Brandenburg-Prussia signed peace treaties with Sweden that led to the division of the Northern German dominions of Sweden among the victorious parties. The treaties were negotiated by French diplomats, who wanted to prevent Sweden from completely collapsing from its position along the southern Baltic coast. According to the negotiated treaty, Sweden was to retain northern Sweden Pomerania and Wismar, while Hanover gained control over Swedish Bremen-Verden and Brandenburg-Prussia gained southern Swedish Pomerania.

When Sweden finally came to good terms with Great Britain, Hanover, Brandenburg-Prussia, and Denmark-Norway, the nation hoped that the anti-Russian sentiments of France and Vienna would conclude in an alliance that would restore its Russian occupied eastern regions. But due to internal conflicts in France and Great Britain, this never happened, the Treaty of Nystad finally concluded the war between Russia and

Sweden in 1721. According to the treaty, Finland was given back to Sweden, while Russia was given control over Swedish occupied Livonia, Estonia, Ingria, Karelia, and Kexholm. But Sweden was not happy with the results and continued to make fruitless attempts to recover the lost territories. Some of these battles include the Russo-Swedish War of 1741-1743 and the Russo-Swedish War of 1788-1790.

Thus, it can be seen that in the 18th century, Sweden lost almost all of its foreign holdings and was no longer a major power, whereas Russia gained control over its Baltic territories, turning into one of the most powerful forces in Europe if not the world.

Scandinavian Colonialism

Beginning in the 17th century and continuing until the 20th century, both Denmark-Norway and Sweden maintained numerous colonies outside of Scandinavia. Scandinavian colonialism discusses the role of these nations in terms of the benefits they gained from outside of their cultural circle. While Iceland, Greenland, and the Faroe Islands were Norwegian dependent territories – that were controlled by the united kingdom of Denmark-Norway – Denmark initiated the colony of St. Thomas in 1671, St. John in 1718, and St. Croix in 1733. It also established colonies in India. Sweden created a colony called New Sweden in Delaware (in North America) during the 1630s but it was short-lived. The nation later acquired the islands of Saint Barthelme and Guadeloupe.

Denmark

Denmark and the political union of Denmark-Norway maintained a colonial empire throughout large parts of America that ran from the 17th to the 20th century. Denmark-

Norway also maintained colonies in Greenland. Norway became a part of the Kalmar Union with Denmark and Sweden in 1397 with its overseas territories – including Greenland – controlled by the monarch in Copenhagen (which was the capital of Scandinavia). After the establishment of the independent state of Sweden in 1536, Denmark and Norway were restructured into an entity known as Denmark-Norway. The so-called Norwegian sovereignty over Greenland was controlled by this new kingdom. Even after losing the contract, Denmark-Norway continued to claim its control over Greenland. The intervention of Denmark on behalf of France during the Napoleonic Wars ended with the treaty of Kiel, which gave away mainland Norway to Sweden, while still retaining the former Norwegian colonies under the crown of Denmark.

Merchants, scientists, settlers, and explorers from Denmark-Norway took over the Danish-owned West Indies region in the late 17th and early 18th centuries. In the 18th century the Virgin Islands in the Caribbean Sea were split into two – one being British and the other Danish-Norwegian, which was controlled by the Danish West India Company until 1755. There existed a triangular trade with the manufacturers of Denmark that involved trading African slaves in return for sugar that was meant for Denmark. Slavery existed until 1848 even though the slave trade was abolished in 1803.

Sweden

Sweden maintained several overseas colonies during the 17th century and by the mid-17th century, Sweden had colonized as much land as possible and the inhabitants wanted to have an impact on the world by launching fur trading and agricultural colonies to surpass the British, Dutch, and French merchants.

This included Dutch, German, and Swedish stockholders. Once they landed on the shores of modern-day Delaware, they christened it Fort Christina after Queen Christina of Sweden. Most of the settlers were of Finnish origin.

The Swedes invaded the territory of the New Netherlands to establish their own settlement. The founder and first governor of New Netherlands, Peter Minuit, was appointed the Director General of the region until he was dismissed from his post in 1633, the now displeased Minuit decided to launch a Swedish expedition to a strategic location just out of spite of his former employers. Even though Minuit succumbed to a hurricane near the Caribbean Island of St Kitts, his colony established itself north of present-day Salem (New Jersey) in 1643.

In 1654 New Sweden seized New Castle in Delaware, which was then known as Dutch Fort Casimir. In retaliation for the attack, Peter Stuyvesant, the Dutch governor, dispatched an army that led to the surrender of the Swedish contingents, thus it was that the only Caribbean Island to ever become a Swedish colony was Saint Barthelme. Guadeloupe, on the other hand, was colonized only briefly at the end of the Napoleonic Wars. Sweden provided support to France's enemies during the Napoleonic Wars, an act that earned King Charles XIV John the island of Guadeloupe.

One year later, when the Treaty of Paris was signed, the king had to give his island to France. However, in exchange for the island, Sweden forced Great Britain to pay a settlement of 24 million francs, paid out to them through the Guadeloupe Fund. Interestingly, the last instalment was not paid until 1983!

Apart from other annexation attempts, the Swedes also tried to invade Tobago in 1733 but were ultimately overrun by the

Indigenous People. However, Tobago could not defend themselves against the British and so inevitably became a colony.

Until Denmark's successful colonization in 1650, Sweden controlled many settlements in present-day Ghana, which was also known as the Gold Coast. In 1652 Sweden took over modern-day Ghana, which, until that point, was being controlled by the Portuguese, who in turn were followed by the Dutch.

Towards the mid 17th century the Swedish slave trade began, but it was brought to an end when the Dutch defeated New Sweden. However, the trade picked up again in 1784 when the Swedish monarch, Gustav III, began negotiating a new alliance with France. In his negotiations Gustav offered Gothenburg as a port city to the French, and in return wanted Saint Barthelme – along with other subsidiaries. Sweden was able to acquire the island in the year 1784, but it was scarcely populated and there were no trading ports. Cotton and sugar only offered four shiploads of exports per year.

The islands were close to the French and British trading posts of the Windward and Leeward islands, but then there a new town, Gustavia, was constructed to facilitate trade. The population doubled within a year and the king found it appropriate to form the Swedish West India Company. The Napoleonic Wars, and free trade with Sweden, benefited trade, also the island was noticed for its liberalism, especially in terms of religious toleration. Back home the Swedes followed Lutheranism strictly, and people were forced to attend church services. Following any other religion or domination was considered to be against the law; for instance, conversion to Catholicism resulted in banishment. However, these islands had inhabitants coming from various parts of Europe, which is why French and English were considered to be the official languages.

Agricultural Reforms and the economy

Denmark, poor in natural resources except for soil, made important gains in international trade and agriculture in the 18th century; however, no important industries developed during this period, with the government merely supporting trade to benefit the Copenhagen merchants and, what is more, the nation also seemed to lack the political strength to exploit the strategic position of its capital. Eastern Norway, in the 1730s, created an outlet for Danish grains, but since the quality of the grain was poor, it couldn't compete with the Baltic grain on the international market and apart from grains and meat Denmark didn't have much to export.

At the beginning of the 18th century Danish agriculture was not as productive as other regions in Europe. Just like other European elites, Danish landlords wanted to experience a rise in their standard of living, but they needed to increase their income to do so. In the 1720s a decrease in the price enabled landlords to further pressure the peasants by increasing the obligatory work owed by peasants to an average of three days a week. The landlords started exploiting the peasants to the bone in order to increase their revenues from the estates, but productivity remained low under this system, despite all of these changes.

Over the course of time, influenced by the writings of French physiocrats – who believed that the wealth of the country came from the hard work of the peasants and not from trade – a reform movement began which influenced the whole kingdom. The freedom of the press of 1755 addressed the economic and agricultural issues, leading to a lively debate. It became evident that if agriculture had to be made more productive, both technical (better farming methods, tools, and stock) and social changes were required. Technical changes could easily take place on land that is owned by one person, but it is difficult to put into place with joint tillage. Hence, the changes came first to the estates and then to church farmlands.

In 1759 some of the enclosures were put in place, such that all of the lands of one farm were bounded by a permanent barrier or stonewalls, and the peasant's corvee was replaced by a monetary payment system. After ten years the Royal Danish Agricultural Society was created to encourage technical improvements in several areas connected to farming. Land reform reached its peak between the years 1784 and 1797, when foreign minister Bernstorff was the leader politically.

The Great Agricultural Commission studied the agricultural situation in Denmark and recommended the next steps, which led to various sweeping reforms. The recognition of how crucial peasant ownership of the land was resulted in low interest loans, backed by the government, and various other benefits to the peasants. Towards the end of the 18th century nearly all of the villages were examined for an enclosure and most of the farms became freeholds. Even the landlords were given compensation for the rights they had lost and then, along with the new landowning farmers, they were assured a stable work force.

The land reforms became possible due to the continuous increase in grain prices in the second half of the 18th century. These reforms ultimately resulted in an effective agricultural sector that was capable of delivering high-quality products for both the international and domestic markets.

Scandinavian Literature

Nordic or Scandinavian literature is the body of work (both oral and written) that is available in the language spoken and understood in the Nordic countries of Europe, which are mostly North Germanic languages. The term "Scandinavian" traditionally refers to the countries on the Scandinavian Peninsula, namely Norway, Sweden, and Denmark. Iceland and Finland are called Scandinavian countries on political, cultural, and geographical grounds. The term Nordic is frequently used to collectively refer to all of these countries and their associated autonomous territories. Over the course of history these people produced literature that has been undeniably influential.

Medieval Scandinavian Literature

In medieval times Old Norse and Proto Norse were common languages, with the earliest written records from Scandinavia found on memorial stones and other places. The oldest of Eddic poems tell of the heroic legends and myths, but the advent of Christianity brought Scandinavia in contact with European learning. The 13th century was considered to be a golden era for Icelandic literature.

Danish Literature

The body of writings created by the Latin and Danish languages are termed Danish Literature. Danish, the official language, became the most commonly used medium for literature in the combined kingdoms during the long union of Denmark and Norway (1380 – 1814). It is important to examine some of the work created in Danish and Latin by writers of both Norwegian and Danish birth. Work created by Norwegians after the 16th century would be categorized under Norwegian literature, and the work created by Faroese writers in Danish and Faroese would fall under Faroese literature.

During the Middle Ages the first examples of literature in Denmark appeared in the form of inscriptions, with the help of the runic alphabets, which were carved in metal and scraped on stone. This included the epitaphs of kings, warriors, and priests who occasionally used to inscribe short and unrhymed writings in the spirit of the Vikings. With Christianity coming into the picture Latin took over as the predominant language for literature. The first major input by the Danish into the world of literature occurred with the *GestaDanorum*, which was translated into English as *The History of Danes*. Some of the most important medieval ballads were written in Denmark; there are roughly 539 ballads that are known to exist in more than 3000 versions but most of these were written after the Middle Ages with the first printed edition available in 1591.

The 16th century brought along the Lithuanian Reformation in Denmark and a new period in the advancement of literature. Several pamphlets were printed for and against the Roman Catholic Church. Some of the major authors of that time include Poul Helgesen, one of the most gifted authors who never favored the Reformation, and the humanist Christiern Pedersen, who supported the Reformation and helped translate the New Testament into Danish. He also translated the pamphlets of Martin Luther into Danish. This century also saw some of the earliest plays of Denmark, which include the brilliant work of Justesen Ranch. Danish poetry of the 16th century was mostly polemical and religious, with fine examples of love hymns and poetry.

The Literature Renaissance touched Denmark in the 17th century, giving rise to an adherence to classical patterns in religious, literary, and political matters. The 17th century marked an era of renewed interest by the Danish people in Scandinavian antiquities, with scholars at the forefront. Although religious dogmatism was seen to be increasing, the brilliant hymns of Kingo surpassed the genre with personal expression.

Danish poetry during this time tended to obediently follow the classics, with the sonnet, hexameter, and the alexandrine as some of the more popular forms. With preciosity as the predominant style, easiness was not encouraged. The era demonstrated richness in occasional poetry, and pastoral and didactic poems were also quite common. An expert of Danish elaborate poetry, Anders Bording, was the forefather of the first Danish newspaper *Den danske Mercurius*, which published the news in the form of alexandrines. Some of the works of this century, that gained special interest, include the chronicles of Leonara Christina (a descendant of King Christian IV), which described her captivity in the Blue Tower of Copenhagen.

The external tension with Sweden – and internal struggles among the nobility – resulted in an absolute monarchy being established in Denmark in 1660, and this event is chronicled from the redemptive perspective of a royal prisoner in the prose of Leonara Christina of the Blue Tower. Some of the later authors in Denmark included Karen Blixen and Hans Christian Andersen.

Quite a rich era in the history of Danish literature – one of the most popular names that came up in the first half of the 18th century was that of Ludvig Holberg, who was born in Norway. His most important works – including more than thirty comedies of manners and characters (including some moral stories) – were written for the first Danish theatre in Copenhagen. With the aim of producing modern Danish literature along the lines of European literature, he worked towards creating something to make the readers laugh at their own foolishness. Highly influenced by French and English thinking, Ludvig was a moderate and rationalist professor and the creator of several historical works. He even contributed towards writing satire poems and fiction novels. *Moral Reflections & Epistles* (translated into English) is one of the best examples of Danish essays.

In the second half of the 18th century a significant revival in literature took place in Denmark. One of the finest humorists (originally from Norway) – who used Danish – drafted a parody titled *Love Without Stockings* (in English) in 1772, which involved work similar to the French tragedies and Italian Operas. Emotional poetry was also being looked at for a potential revival, which was influenced by English and German literature. One of the greatest lyric poets of Denmark, Johannes Ewald, discovered the poetic wealth of antique Scandinavia for the first time in the ballads, myths, and sagas, his work also comprised of descriptive poems and verse dramas. He came up with the first serious drama *The Fishermen* in which the commoners were treated as heroes and in 1792 he described his travels across Europe in *The Labyrinth*.

Inspired by the Neoclassicism of Schiller and Goethe as well as by the Jena Romantics, the Romantic Movement came to

Denmark from Germany. Adam Gottlob, a popular name within the Romantic Movement of Denmark, depicted the inspiration of some of the works that were created by Schiller and Goethe. He used elements from German Romance with unmatched versatility in drama, prose, and poetry. Some of this can be seen in *Aladdin* and also in some of his Northern stories. The philosopher Steffens of Denmark, originally from Norway, translated the philosophy of Friedrich Schelling but the classic Romantics in Denmark was translated in a manner that caused it to be very different from the original version.

Swedish Literature

The body of writings created in the Swedish language – within the modern day political boundaries and geography of Sweden – is categorized as Swedish literature, so can it can be seen that Swedish and Finnish literature were closely linked. From the mid 12th century until the year 1809 Finland was under Swedish control, with Swedish being the dominant language – particularly for the upper classes – until the end of the 19th century.

After a long period of linguistic changes, Swedish literature emerged in the late Middle Ages, with old Swedish now considered a separate language. The foundations of native literature were established in the 13th century, and the first representation of chivalry poetry was reflected in The Songs of Euphemia, which were written between 1303 and 1312. A renewed interest in the romance genre can be seen in the anonymous ballads that were scribed in the 14th and 15th centuries, and although these ballads were mostly taken from foreign sources – combining the flavor of courtly love with native historical events and pagan themes – they form the most accessible genre of Swedish medieval literature.

There are two important dates that mark the beginning of modern Swedish history, these being:

- 1523 – the break from Denmark and accession of Gustav I Vasa as the king of Sweden
- 1527 – the break from Rome and the formation of a national Lutheran church

Although Sweden experienced a political revolution that elevated her to a position equivalent to that of a major European power, it had no noticeable impact on the literature of the country until a century later when the Reformation totally dominated the Swedish letters in the 1500s. One of the most important literary events of this era included the translation of the Bible into Swedish, in 1541. This caused literary skills to spread among the Swedes, offering opportunities for poets of later times. The two brothers Olaus Petri and Laurentius Petri, the supporters of the Swedish Reformation, were closely involved in the translation of the Bible.

Driven into exile as a consequence of the Reformation, were two more brothers – Olaus Magnus and Johannes Magnus – who were the two most distinguished scholars of Sweden during that period.

Swedish literature was limited in scope and quantity until the first half of the 17th century. However, a unique contribution, made by Lars Wivallius, reveled in a feeling of nature, which was something new and unique for Swedish poetry.

Sweden had established itself as an important European power with its intervention in the Thirty Years' War and as a result the pride and culture of the nation began to develop, as can be seen in the literature of this era. One of the most outstanding works of this period is reflected by the allegorical epic *Hercules*, which was published in 1658. It reflected several political and social problems that were faced by the people during that time. Stiernhielm, the creator of Hercules, was another great name that was listed among the authors of humor-filled writings. He aimed to integrate the cultural heritage of the nation with the accepted ideals of Classicism. His brilliant work Hercules is full of old Swedish letters that he wanted to revive.

With the death of King Charles XII in 1718, and the collapse of his empire, a practical attitude was developed among the lives of the people, a feeling that came to influence the letters that were written in Sweden. Dalin was one of the most famous people to popularize the novel ideas of the enlightenment period, which he expressed beautifully in his rational work titled *History of the Swedish realms*. It was commissioned by the realm estates and remained the standard piece of history to go to for a long time. This period in Swedish history also saw the creation of significant journalistic works that marked a new beginning, an era in which orthodoxy gave way to enlightenment and skepticism, Baroque to Classicism and Germanism to French and English.

Conclusion

Thank you again for purchasing this book.

I hope it helped you learn more about the History of the Vikings.

The next step, if I may be so bold to suggest, is to share what you have learned with others. To discuss it, and share opinions, ideas and... histories!

Finally, if you enjoyed this book, I'd like to ask you a favor. If you would be so kind as to leave a review on Amazon it would be greatly appreciated!

Thank you and... good luck!

Printed in Great Britain
by Amazon